Songs, Naval and National, of the Late Charles Dibdin; With a Memoir and Addenda

POOR JACK.

SONGS,

NAVAL AND NATIONAL,

OF THE LATE

CHARLES DIBDIN;

WITH A MEMOIR

AND

ADDENDA.

COLLECTED AND ARRANGED BY

THOMAS DIBDIN,

AUTHOR OF " THE ENGLISH FLEET," " CABINET," &c. &c.

WITH CHARACTERISTIC SKETCHES BY

GEORGE CRUIKSHANK.

LONDON:
JOHN MURRAY, ALBEMARLE STREET.
(PUBLISHER TO THE ADMIRALTY.)
1841.

LONDON :
Printed by WILLIAM CLOWES and SONS,
Stamford Street.

TO THE RIGHT HONOURABLE

THE EARL OF MINTO,

FIRST LORD OF THE ADMIRALTY,

&c. &c. &c.

MY LORD,

THE patronage with which you have been pleased to honour the productions of a minstrel who appreciated Melody as the Soul of Music, and whose metrical attempts to portray the rough-hewn natural characters, and stimulate the gallant exertions, of a class to whom their Country is so infinitely indebted, entitles your Lordship, and the patriotic Board who have added their distinguished sanction of the following Selection, to the thanks of all lovers of Old English Ballads, who retain what SHAKSPEARE calls a *smack* of predilection for home-brewed excellence; and, above all, to the heartfelt, proud, and filial sense of obligation conferred on,

My Lord,

Your Lordship's

Most humble

and

Gratefully obedient servant,

THOMAS DIBDIN.

London, January 1st, 1841.

A 2

Patrons.

SUBSCRIBERS.

Arnold, A. W., Esq., 4 *copies.*
Abbott, J., Esq., 2 *copies.*
Atlee, J., Esq.

Byng, Hon. Edmund, 60 *copies.*
Balch, W., Esq.
Barnfield, W., jun., Esq.
Bates, R., Esq., 2 *copies.*
Bates, Mr., Ludgate-street.
Baxter, T. C., Esq.
Behnes, —, Esq., R.A.
Bentley, R., Esq.
Berry, Lady.
Blake, J., Esq.
Bosbery, —, Esq.
Boyd, Benjamin, Esq.
Briggs, T., Esq.
Burford, B., Esq.
Burford, Mr., jun.
Burton, A., Esq.
Burton, W. S., Esq.
Bush, T., Esq.
Byerley, Mrs.

Codrington, Admiral Sir
   Edward, 4 *copies.*
Cattermole, —, Esq.
Cloves, D., Esq.
Cloves, P., Esq.
Clowes, W., Esq.
Cobbett, R., Esq.
Colburn, H., Esq., 4 *copies.*
Cribb, —, Esq.

Digby, Admiral Sir Henry,
   4 *copies.*
Dance, C., Esq.
Davidge, G. B., Esq.
Dixon, T., Esq.
Donne, S. E., Esq.
Dowding, Mrs.
Downe, T. J., Esq.
Durrant, J., Esq.

Edington, J. C., Esq.
Evans, W., Esq.
Evered, W., Esq.

Fane, Admiral, 4 *copies.*
Field, —, Esq
Firmin, —, Esq.
Fish, W. C., Esq.
Fitzgerald, T., Esq.
Foote, —, Esq.
Forrester, C., Esq.
Forrester, A., Esq.
Forster, Rheinold T., Esq.
Fox, C., Esq.

Goding, James, Esq., 10 *copies.*
Grove, —, Esq., Henrietta-
   street, Cavendish-square,
   4 *copies.*
Grove, —, Esq., New Bond-
   street, 2 *copies.*

Harrison, Sir Geo., 20 *copies.*

Harrison, W., Esq., 20 *copies*.

Hall, Captain Basil, R.N., 4 *copies*.

Haddon, Mr.

Hall, W., Esq.

Hall, C., Esq., 2 *copies*.

Hall, W., Esq.

Halsted, J., Esq.

Haes, John, Esq.

Haselwood, E., Esq.

Helsdon, J., Esq.

Hobhouse, W., Esq.

Hoffman, A., Esq.

Houlding, —, Esq.

Hughes, John, Esq.

Hutcheson, J. W., Esq.

Ibbettson, —, Esq., Regent's Park.

Jones, R., Esq., Chapel-street, Grosvenor-place.

Jones, S., Esq., Bartholomew-lane.

Keegan, Mr., Burlington-arcade.

Kenneth, Mr.

Kenny, James, Esq.

Kilpack, Mr.

Kirkaldy, J., Esq.

Leeson, J. E., Esq., Abingdon House.

Lewis, —, Esq.

Lilley, John, Esq.

Limbird, Mr.

Lover, S., Esq.

Lyndhurst, Right Hon. Lord.

Moore, Admiral Sir Graham, 4 *copies*.

Maule, Hon. Fox, M.P.

M'Callan, A., Esq., 4 *copies*.

Martin, —, Esq.

Mathews, C., Esq.

Melton, Mr. Hen., 12 *copies*.

Mitchell, Miss.

Murray, John, Esq.

North, Mrs., East Acton.

Novello, Mr., Dean-street.

Ogle, Admiral Sir Charles, 10 *copies*.

Oswald, John, Esq.

Outram, Dr., Hanover-square.

Outram, Mrs.

Ouvry, Miss.

Parry, John, Esq.

Peake, R. B., Esq.

Peake, —, Esq.

Purday, Mr. Z. T., High Holborn.

Purday, Mr. C.

Purday, Mr., St. Paul's Church-yard.

Radstock, Right Hon. Lord

Ranking, Joseph, Esq.

Rhodes, Mr. John.

Rhodes, Mr. W.

Rhodes, Mr. G.

Rippon, J., Esq.

Roberts, J., Esq., 2 *copies*.

Ross, W., Esq., sen.

Ross, W. C., Esq., A.R.A.

Rogerson, —, Esq., Liverpool.
Rovedino, Signor Tomaso.
Rounding, T., Esq.

Somerset, his Grace the
   Duke of, 20 *copies.*
Somerset, her Grace the
   Duchess of, 20 *copies.*
Sykes, Admiral, 8 *copies.*
Shirreff, Captain, R.N.,
   4 *copies.*
Savory, —, Esq., Regent's
   Park.
Sawyer, John J., Esq., Park-
   street, Grosvenor-square.
Smith, G. T., Esq., Lynn.
Stone, —, Esq.
Sylvester, —, Esq., Strand.

Taylor, W., Esq., Brompton.
Toby, H. E. Esq., R.N.
Tozer, Henry, Esq., 4 *copies.*
Tucker, R., Esq.

Upton, E., Esq.

Walter, —, Esq.
Watson, W., Esq.
Watts, F., Esq., 4 *copies.*
Weeks, Henry, Esq.
Wilkinson, Rev. T.
Wilkinson, J. S., Esq., 2 *co-*
   pies.
Williams, Mr. T., Charing
   Cross.
Woodfall, T., Esq.
Woolmore, Mrs.

MEMOIR

OF

CHARLES DIBDIN.

CHARLES DIBDIN was born at a village called
Dibden, near Southampton, in the year 1745;
and, having very early lost his father, was removed to Winchester; where, from his previous
love for, and proficiency in, Music when quite
a boy, he was placed under the organist of
the cathedral, and officiated in the choir till he
was old enough to become a candidate for the
situation of organist himself. His intuitive com-
prehension of the theory as regarding the " composition and accordance of sweet sounds" was so
aided by a most excellent ear, that at the age of
fifteen he would return from an opera or a concert,
and, from memory, draw out and fill a correct
score of any overture, song, chorus, or concerted
piece that had happened to strike his fancy.
Friends advised him to try the metropolis as a
more expanded field for his improving talent;

and he went to London with the intention of
teaching singing and the harpsichord, when cir-
cumstances threw him in the way of Mr. Garrick,
Mr. Bickerstaff, and the theatres.   Mr. Bickerstaff was so pleased with his dawning genius as a
musical artist, that, after employing him to com-
pose the music of great part of the opera of the
" Maid of the Mill," he prevailed on him to appear in it, and sing his own compositions in the
character of RALPH, the Miller's Son, in which
he most completely established himself as a bur-
letta performer of the first rank.   The amazing
success of his MUSIC, and his MUNGO, in the
" Padlock," secured him a long engagement at
Drury Lane ; and after having furnished music for
" Love in a Village," " Lionel and Clarissa,"
" Love in the City," and other pieces written by
Mr. Bickerstaff, he commenced author as well
as composer on his own account, and produced
the words and music of " The Waterman," " The
Quaker," " The Deserter," " The Wedding Ring,"
and numerous other successful pieces at various
theatres, as " The Shepherd's Artifice," " Damon
and Phillida," " Rose and Colin," " Annette and
Lubin," " The Recruiting Serjeant," " Poor Vulcan," " The Islanders," " The Touchstone," " The
Mirror, or Harlequin Everywhere," " The Mis-
chance," " The Ladle," " The Cobbler," " The
Metamorphoses," " The Gipsies," " Wives Re-

venged," " Chelsea Pensioner," "Shepherdess of
the Alps," " Jupiter and Alcmena," " None so
Blind as those that will not See," " Liberty Hall,"
" Harvest Home," &c. &c. &c., and the much ad-
mired Songs, Dances, Serenades, and Processional
Airs in the " Stratford Jubilee," in honour of
Shakspeare, the words of which were written by
Mr. Garrick. His last dramatic efforts were " A
Divertissement" at Covent Garden, for the intro-
duction of his own most popular songs, and a
ballad farce at Drury Lane, called " Broken
Gold." He also wrote two novels, " The Younger
Brother," and " Hannah Hewit, or the Female
Crusoe ; " his own " Professional Life," " Musical
Tour," "History of the Stage " (in 5 vols.), &c., &c.

In the year 1788, tired of dramatic contin-
gencies, and feeling (as Charles Mathews did
after him) that he possessed resources in his own
mind to entertain an audience in a theatre of his
own, he singly and individually wrote, composed,
recited, sang, and accompanied, a medley mono-
drame, at Fisher's auction-rooms, in King Street,
Covent Garden, under the title of " The Whim of
the Moment, or Nature in Little ;" in which Entertainment the song of " Poor Jack " was alone suffi-
ciently attractive to insure him a profitable season
of some weeks ; and this was the commencement
of a series of similar fashionable and profitable ex-
hibitions of unaided genius, which were the annual

delight of the town for many years, at the before-mentioned rooms, at the Lyceum, at Scott and Idle's premises in the Strand, and at his own theatre, which he built and opened as the SANS SOUCI, in Leicester Place, Leicester Square; and he, latterly, gave some public Musical *Soirées*, assisted by his pupils, in Beaufort Buildings.

His retirement on a gratuity of 200*l*. a-year, awarded him rather late, for having, at the express desire of the *then* ministry, put himself to an expense of more than 600*l*., by quitting highly lucrative provincial engagements, and opening his theatre in a hot July to considerable nightly loss (in town), where he was *instructed* to write, sing, publish, and give away what were termed War Songs, is well known, as he publicly stated the particulars, accompanied by the melancholy fact that before he had enjoyed the said income long enough to repay his actual losses in earning it, it was withdrawn by a succeeding ministry. A *part* of it was restored a short period antecedent to his death, which took place in 1814, in his 69th year, in Arlington Street, Camden Town. He was followed to the grave by his sons Charles and Thomas, his medical attendant, and the celebrated philanthropic oculist and eccentric writer John Taylor, of the Sun newspaper. He was interred in the burial-ground of St. James, Camden Town, where, in the midst of a clump of flowering shrubs, his "frail memorial" quotes, from his own beautiful song, that

> " Though his body 's under hatches
> His soul is gone aloft! "

which lines he had written in memory of a brother, who was many years master of a vessel in the merchant service, and from whom he imbibed that devotedness to members of the nautical profession which characterised his works and life.

He had another brother (an auctioneer) and a sister, long since dead. He had three sons—the youngest died at sea quite a youth, in 1794; the eldest, Charles, many years a proprietor of Sadler's Wells Theatre, and author of the Operas of the " Farmer's Wife," " My Spouse and I," and innumerable Burlettas, Songs, and Pantomimes, died in 1831. He also left a married daughter, and the son who, with perhaps too minute prolixity, has attempted this Memoir. Mr. Dibdin wrote above 1300 Songs, and his sons nearly double that number.

Mr. Garrick, Mr. Sheridan, Mr. Harris (of Covent Garden), and Dr. Arne (of whose music he was enthusiastically fond), were, among many others, warm patrons and admirers of his talent. Charles Bannister, and his exemplary son John, were two of his most intimate friends.

In 1824 a few gentlemen, who considered it a

disgrace that no testimonial had been erected to
the memory of the Ocean Bard, whose Songs were
so many irresistible appeals to the heart—in-
spiring the most illiterate with brave and generous
sentiments, and exciting to acts of loyalty, bravery,
and patriotism, which (in the most arduous of her
struggles) assisted to maintain the honour and glory
of the British Empire, determined to open a sub-
scription for funds to defray the expense of some
public mark of respect to the deceased; and as no
public matter can be well or prosperously arranged
without a *dinner*, a public Festival was held in Free-
masons' Hall, under the special patronage of his late
Majesty William IV., at that time Duke of Clarence.
The lamented Admiral Sir Joseph Yorke, K.C.B.,
was in the Chair. The most eminent vocalists of
the day, to their great credit, aided the attraction
of the entertainment by singing an excellent selection of the Songs of the deceased. Mr. John
Parry directed this department, and Mr. T. Cooke
presided at the piano-forte. Upward of four hundred guests attended, and a sum was collected,
which, though insufficient, induced the Committee
to authorise Mr. R. W. Sievier to prepare the model
of a monument; when, for want of additional funds,
the matter laid dormant for five years. Finally,
in April, 1829, an appropriate Musical Perform-
ance was given at Covent Garden Theatre, under
the title of the " Feast of Neptune," which pro-

duced the gross receipt of £600. 12s.: £200 being deducted for the hire of the theatre, and some other expenses paid, the remainder, in addition to the money subscribed at the dinner, was given to Mr. Sievier, who soon completed the Monument now to be seen in the Veterans' Library at Greenwich Hospital.

But for the friendly perseverance of the deceased John Young, Esq., late Keeper of the British Gallery in Pall Mall, and the unwearied professional zeal and labour of John Parry, Esq., of Cambrian musical celebrity, the above desirable object would have never been accomplished.

Mr. Parry says that out of these festivals sprung the present popular Melodists' Club. So delighted was every one with the beautiful Melodies of Charles Dibdin, that several literary gentlemen, many of them connected with the public press, agreed to establish a Society for the promotion of British Ballad Composition.

ADVERTISEMENT.

Correct Copies of the Music of Mr. DIBDIN's Songs may be had, either singly or in Pocket Numbers, of Novello and Co., in Dean-street, Soho ; as also of Messrs. Purday and Co., 45, High Holborn, and in St. Paul's Churchyard. Of whom may also be had the Music of all the old National Songs in the latter part of this volume, either singly or in volumes, as collected by the late Dr. Kitchiner.

SONGS, &c.

POOR JACK.

Go patter to lubbers and swabs, d'ye see,
   'Bout danger, and fear, and the like;
A tight water-boat and good sea-room give me,
   And t'ent to a little I'll strike:
Though the tempest top-gallant masts smack smooth
      should smite,
   And shiver each splinter of wood,
Clear the wreck, stow the yards, and bouse everything
      tight,
   And under reef'd foresail we'll scud:
Avast! nor don't think me a milksop so soft
   To be taken for trifles aback;
For they say there's a Providence sits up aloft,
   To keep watch for the life of poor Jack.

Why, I heard our good chaplain palaver one day
   'About souls, heaven, mercy, and such;
And, my timbers! what lingo he'd coil and belay,
   Why, 'twas just all as one as High Dutch ·
For he said how a sparrow can't founder d'ye see,
   Without orders that come down below;
And many fine things that proved clearly to me
   That Providence takes us in tow:

B

For, says he, do you mind me, let storms e'er so oft,
    Take the top-sails of sailors aback,
There's a sweet little cherub that sits up aloft,
    To keep watch for the life of poor Jack.

I said to our Poll, for d'ye see she would cry,
    When last we weigh'd anchor for sea,
What argufies sniv'ling and piping your eye,
    Why, what a damn'd fool you must be!
Can't you see the world's wide, and there's room for us
        all,
    Both for seamen and lubbers ashore,
And if to old Davy I should go, friend Poll,
    Why you never will hear of me more:
What then, all's a hazard, come don't be so soft,
    Perhaps I may laughing come back,
For, d'ye see, there's a cherub sits smiling aloft,
    To keep watch for the life of poor Jack.

D'ye mind me, a sailor should be every inch
    All as one as a piece of the ship,
And with her brave the world without offering to flinch,
    From the moment the anchor's a-trip.
As for me, in all weathers, all times, sides, and ends,
    Nought's a trouble from duty that springs,
For my heart is my Poll's, and my rhino's my friend's,
    And as for my life, 'tis the king's:
Even when my time comes, ne'er believe me so soft
    As for grief to be taken aback,
For the same little cherub that sits up aloft
    Will look out a good berth for poor Jack.

BLOW HIGH, BLOW LOW!

Blow high, blow low, let tempests tear
　　The main-mast by the board;
My heart with thoughts of thee, my dear,
　　And love well stored,
Shall brave all danger, scorn all fear,
　　The roaring winds the raging sea,
　　　　In hopes on shore
　　　　To be once more
　　Safe moor'd with thee.

Aloft while mountains high we go,
　　The whistling winds that scud along,
And surges roaring from below,
　　　　Shall my signal be
　　　　To think on thee,·
　　And this shall be my song:
　　　　Blow high, blow low, &c.

And on that night, when all the crew
　　The mem'ry of their former lives
O'er flowing cans of flip renew,
　　And drink their sweethearts and their wives,
　　　　I'll heave a sigh, and think on thee;
　　　　And, as the ship rolls through the sea,
　　　　The burthen of my song shall be—
　　　　　Blow high, blow low, &c.

FAREWELL AND RETURN.

THOUGH hard the valiant soldier's life,
   They some sweet moments know;
Joy ne'er was yet unmix'd with strife,
   Or happiness with woe.
'Tis hard, when friend, when children, wife,
   Reluctant from him part,
And fancy paints the muffled drum,
   And plaintive fife,
And the loud volley o'er the grave,
That sounds sad requiems to the brave;
     All this he hears,
     And calms their fears
   With smiles, though horror's in his heart.
But when the smiling hour shall come,
   To bring him home at last,
How sweet his constant wife to greet,
   His children, friends,
And in their circling arms to find amends
   For all his sufferings past.

'Tis hard when, desolation spread,
   Death whirls the rapid car;
And those invaded hear and dread
   The thunder of the war.
Ah! then, indeed, friend, children, wife,
   Have you true cause to fear;
Too soon, alas! the muffled drum,
   The mournful fife,

And the loud volley o'er the grave,
Shall sound sad requiems to the brave,
  While those alive
  Faint joy revive,
 And blend hope's smile with pity's tear.
But when the smiling hour shall come, .
 To bring him home at last,
How sweet his constant wife to greet,
 His children, friends,
And in their circling arms to find amends
 ·For all his sufferings past!

YE FREE-BORN SONS.

Ye free-born sons, Britannia's boast,
Firm as your rock-surrounded coast;
 Ye sov'reigns of the sea;
On ev'ry shore where salt tides roll,
From east to west, from Pole to Pole,
Fair conquest celebrates your name,
Witness'd aloud by wond'ring Fame,
 The lads who dare be free.

Mistake me not, my hearts of oak,
I scorn with Liberty to joke,
 Ye sov'reigns of the sea;
Assist, uphold your Church and State,
Your great men good, your good men great;
Awe all abroad, at home unite,
And jolly join in faction's spite,
 Then, then, my friends, you're free.

WHILE UP THE SHROUDS.

While up the shrouds the sailor goes,
    Or ventures on the yard,
The landsman, who no better knows,
    Believes his lot is hard;
But Jack with smiles each danger meets,
    Casts anchor, heaves the log,
Trims all the sails, belays the sheets,
    And drinks his can of grog.

When mountains high the waves that swell
    The vessel rudely bear,
Now sinking in a hollow dell,
    Now quiv'ring in the air,
        Bold Jack, &c.

When waves 'gainst rocks and quicksands roar,
    You ne'er hear him repine,
Freezing on Greenland's icy shore,
    Or burning near the Line.
        Bold Jack, &c.

If to engage they give the word,
    To quarters all repair,
While splintered masts go by the board,
    And shot sing through the air.
        Bold Jack, &c.

NOTHING LIKE GROG.

A PLAGUE of those musty old lubbers,
  Who tell us to fast and to think,
And patient fall in with life's rubbers,
  With nothing but water to drink !
, A can of good stuff, had they twigg'd it,
  Would have set them for pleasure agog;
    And spite of the rules
    Of the schools, the old fools
Would have all of 'em swigg'd it
  And swore there was nothing like grog.

My father, when last I from Guinea
  Return'd with abundance of wealth,
Cried, Jack, never be such a ninny
  To drink. Says I, Father, your health ! ·
So I pass'd round the stuff—soon he twigg'd it,
  And it set the old codger agog;
    And he swigg'd, and mother,
    And sister, and brother,
And I swigg'd, and all of us swigg'd it,
  And swore there was nothing like grog.

One day, when the chaplain was preaching,
  Behind him I curiously slunk ;
And, while he our duty was teaching,
  As how we should never get drunk,
I tipp'd him the stuff, and he twigg'd it,
  Which soon set his rev'rence agog;
    And he swigg'd, and Nick swigg'd,
    And Ben swigg'd, and Dick swigg'd,
And I swigg'd, and all of us swigg'd it,
  And swore there was nothing like grog.

Then trust me, there's nothing as drinking
   So pleasant on this side the grave :
It keeps the unhappy from thinking,
   And makes e'en the valiant more brave.
For me, from the moment I twigg'd it,
   The good stuff has so set me agog :
     Sick or well, late or early,
     Wind foully or fairly,
I 've constantly swigg'd it,
   And, damme ! there's nothing like grog.

POOR TOM!

THEN farewell, my trim-built wherry !
   Oars, and coat, and badge, farewell !
Never more at Chelsea-ferry
   Shall your Thomas take a spell.

But to hope and peace a stranger,
   In the battle's heat I'll go,
Where, exposed to every danger,
   Some friendly ball may lay me low.

Then, mayhap, when homeward steering
   With the news, my messmates come,
Even you, the story hearing,
   With a sigh may cry—Poor Tom !

THE BUSY CREW.

THE busy crew, their sails unbending,
   The ship in harbour safe arrived,
Jack Oakum, all his perils ending,
   Had made the port where Kitty lived.

His rigging, no one dare attack it;
   Tight fore and aft, above, below;
Long-quarter'd shoes, check shirt, blue jacket,
   With trousers like the driven snow.

His honest heart, with pleasure glowing,
   He flew like lightning to the side;
Scarce had he been a boat's length rowing
   Before his Kitty he espied.

A flowing pennant gaily flutter'd
   From her neat-made hat of straw;
Red were her cheeks when first she utter'd
   It was her sailor that she saw.

And now the gazing crew surround her,
   While, secure from all alarms,
Swift as a ball from a nine-pounder,
   They dart into each other's arms.

THE SIGNAL TO ENGAGE.

THE signal to engage shall be
    A whistle and a hollow,
Be one and all but firm, like me,
    And conquest soon will follow.
You, Gunnel, keep the helm in hand —
    Thus, thus, boys! steady, steady,
'Till right a-head you see the land,
    Then, soon as we are ready,
        The signal, &c.

Keep, boys, a good look out, d'ye hear!
    'Tis for Old England's honour;
Just as you brought your lower tier
    Broadside to bear upon her,
        The signal, &c.

All hands then, lads, the ship to clear;
    Load all your guns and mortars;
Silent as death th' attack prepare;
    And, when you're all at quarters,
        The signal, &c.

SOUNDING THE BOWL.

IF, my hearty, you'd not like a lubber appear,
You must very well know how to hand, reef, and steer;
Yet a better manœuvre 'mongst seamen is found,
'Tis the tight little maxim to know how to sound:
Which a sailor can tell from a bay to a shoal,
But the best sort of sounding is sounding the bowl.

I've sounded at land, and I've sounded at sea,
. I've sounded a-weather, and sounded a-lee,
I've sounded my quine at the randivoo-house,
· And I've sounded my purse without finding a souse:
What then? we've a brother in each honest soul,
And sailors can ne'er want for sounding the bowl.

All men try for soundings wherever they steer,
Your nabobs for soundings strive hard in Cape Clear,
And there is not a soul from the devil to the pope,
That could live but for sounding the Cape of Good Hope:
No fear, then, nor danger, our hearts shall control,
Though at sea we're in soundings, while sounding the
   bowl.

THE SAILOR'S SHEET-ANCHOR.

SMILING grog is the sailor's best hope, his sheet anchor,
 His compass, his cable, his log,
That gives him a heart which life's care cannot canker;
   Though dangers around him
   Unite to confound him,
 He braves them, and tips off his grog.
  'Tis grog, only grog,
  Is his rudder, his compass, his cable, his log,
  The sailor's sheet-anchor is grog.

   What though he to a friend in trust
    His prize-money convey,
   Who, to his bond of faith unjust,
    Cheats him, and runs away:

What's to be done ?   He vents a curse
  'Gainst all false hearts ashore ;
Of the remainder clears his purse,
   And then to sea for more.
     There smiling grog, &c.

What though his girl, who often swore
  To know no other charms,
He finds, when he returns ashore,
  Clasp'd in a rival's arms :
What's to be done ?   He vents a curse,
  And seeks a kinder she ;
Dances, gets groggy, clears his purse,
  And goes again to sea.

To crosses born, still trusting there,
The waves less faithless than the fair ;
There into toils to rush again,
And stormy perils brave —what then ?
    Smiling grog, &c.

THE GOOD SHIP THE KITTY.

I sail'd in the good ship the Kitty,
  With a smart blowing gale and rough sea ;
Left my Polly, the lads call so pretty,
  Safe here at an anchor—Yo, Yea !

She blubber'd salt tears when we parted,
  And cried, " Now be constant to me !"
I told her not to be down-hearted,
  So up went the anchor—Yo, Yea !

And from that time, no worse nor no better,
   I've thought on just nothing but she;
Nor could grog nor flip make me forget her,
   She's my best bower-anchor—Yo, Yea!

When the wind whistled larboard and starboard,
   And the storm came on weather and lee,
The hope I with her should be harbour'd
   Was my cable and anchor—Yo, Yea!

And yet, my boys, would you believe me?
   I return'd with no rhino from sea;
Mistress Polly would never receive me,
   So again I heav'd anchor—Yo, Yea!

THE JOLLY YOUNG WATERMAN.

AND did you not hear of a jolly young waterman,
   Who at Blackfriars bridge used for to ply?
He feather'd his oars with such skill and dexterity,
   Winning each heart, and delighting each eye.
He look'd so neat, and he row'd so steadily,
The maidens all flock'd to his boat so readily;
And he eyed the young rogues with so charming an air,
That this waterman ne'er was in want of a fare.

What sights of fine folks he oft row'd in his wherry,
   'Twas clean'd out so nice, and so pa nted withal:
He was always first oars when the fine city ladies
   In a party to Ranelagh went, or Vauxhall.

And oftentimes would they be giggling and leering,
But 'twas all one to Tom their gibing and jeering,
For loving or liking he little did care,
For this waterman ne'er was in want of a fare.

And yet but to see how strangely things happen,
   As he row'd along thinking of nothing at all,
He was ply'd by a damsel so lovely and charming,
   That she smiled, and so straightway in love he did fall.
And would this young damsel but banish his sorrow,
He'd wed her to-night, before to-morrow.
And how should this waterman ever know care,
When he's married and never in want of a fare?

WHEN LAST FROM THE STRAITS.

WHEN last from the Straits we had fairly cast anchor,
   I went, bonny Kitty to hail,
With quintables stored, for our voyage was a spanker,
   And bran new was every sail:

But I knew well enough how, with words sweet as honey,
   They trick us poor tars of our gold,
And when the sly gipsies have finger'd the money,
   The bag they poor Jack give to hold.

So I chased her, d'ye see, my lads, under false colours,
   Swore my riches were all at an end,
That I'd sported away all my good-looking dollars,
   And borrow'd my togs of a friend.

MISS KITTY & THE BAG.

Oh then, had you seen her, no longer " my honey,"
   'Twas varlet, audacious, and bold,
Begone from my sight ! now you've spent all your money,
   For Kitty the bag you may hold.

With that I took out double handfuls of shiners,
   And scornfully bid her good bye ;
'Twould have done your heart good, had you then seen
      her fine airs,
   How she'd leer, and she'd sob, and she'd sigh.
But I stood well the broadside ; while jewel and honey
   She call'd me, I put up the gold,
And bearing away, as I sack'd all the money,
   Left the bag for Ma'am Kitty to hold.

AT SEA.

If tars of their money are lavish,
   I say, brother, take this from me,
'Tis because we're not muck-worms, nor slavish,
   Like lubbers who ne'er go to sea.
What's cunning, and such quivication,
   And them sly manœuvres to we ?
To be roguish is no valuation
   To hearties who plough the salt sea.

As for cheating—light-weights, and short-measures,
   And corruption, and brib'ry, d'ye see,
They never embitter the pleasures
   Of good fellows who plough the salt sea.

You've ashore actions, writs, cesseraries,
 And regiments of counsel to fee;
Jack knows not of such-like vagaries—
 We never trust lawyers at sea.

'Tis said that with grog and our lasses,
 Because jolly sailors are free,
Our money we squander like asses
 Which like horses we earn'd when at sea.
But let them say this, that, or t'other,
 In one thing they're forced to agree,
Honest hearts find a friend and a brother
 In each worthy that ploughs the salt sea.

THE HEART OF A TAR.

Yet though I've no fortune to offer,
 I've something to put on a par;
Come, then, and accept of my proffer,
 'Tis the kind honest heart of a tar.

Ne'er let such a trifle as this is,
 Girls, be to my pleasure a bar,
You'll be rich, though 'tis only in kisses,
 With the kind honest heart of a tar.

Besides, I am none of your ninnies;
 The next time I come from afar
I'll give you a lapful of guineas,
 With the kind honest heart of a tar.

Your lords, with such fine baby faces,
    That strut in a garter and star,
Have they, under their tambour and laces,
    The kind honest heart of a tar?

I've this here to say, now, and mind it,
    If love, that no hazard can mar,
You are seeking, you'll certainly find it,
    In the kind honest heart of a tar.

THE FORECASTLE MAN.

Your finiking sirs may in finery appear,
Disdaining such tars as can hand, reef, and steer,
On the decks, spruce as tailors may cautiously tread,
And live at the stern, without minding the head.
    Old tough experienced sailors know,
        Where'er they take their trip,
    Whether rising on mountains, or sinking below,
        The forecastle man's the ship.

Your delicate fresh-water masters may treat
With dainties, and like guttling aldermen eat,
Turn cabins to drawing-rooms—sleep on a bed,
And despise English biscuit, to nibble French bread
    Old tough, &c.

c

LIFE'S TROUBLED SEA.

This life is like a troubled sea,
Where helm a-weather or a-lee,
The ship will neither stay nor wear,
But drives, of every rock in fear.

All seamanship in vain we try,
We cannot keep her steadily;
But just as fortune's wind may blow,
The vessel's tosticated to and fro;
Yet, come but love on board,
Our hearts with pleasure stored,
No storm can overwhelm,
   Still blows in vain
   The hurricane,
While love is at the helm.

BROTHER SOLDIERS, WHY CAST DOWN?

Brother soldiers, why cast down?
   Never, boys, be melancholy:
You say our lives are not our own,
   But therefore should we not be jolly?
This poor tenement, at best,
   Depends on fickle chance: meanwhile,
Drink, laugh, and sing; and for the rest
   We'll boldly brave each rude campaign;
   Secure, if we return again,
   Our pretty landlady shall smile.

Fortune his life and yours commands,
  And this moment, should it please her
To require it at your hands,
  You can but die, and so did Cæsar.
Our span, though long, were little worth,
  Did we not time with joy beguile :
Laugh, then, the while you stay on earth,
  And boldly brave, &c.

Life's a debt we all must pay,
  'Tis so much pleasure, which we borrow,
Nor heed, if on a distant day
  It is demanded, or to-morrow.
The bottle says we're tardy grown,
  Do not the time and liquor spoil,
Laugh out the little life you own,
  And boldly brave, &c.

EACH BULLET HAS ITS COMMISSION.

WHAT argufies pride and ambition ?
  Soon or late death will take us in tow :
Each bullet has got its commission,
  And when our time's come we must go.
Then drink and sing—hang pain and sorrow,
  The halter was made for the neck ;
He that's now 'live and lusty—to-morrow
  Perhaps may be stretch'd on the deck.

There was little Tom Linstock of Dover
  Got killed, and left Polly in pain :
Poll cried, but her grief was soon over,
  And then she got married again.
     Then drink, &c.

Jack Junk was ill-used by Bet Crocker,
  And so took to guzzling the stuff,
Till he tumbled in old Davy's locker,
  And there he got liquor enough.
     Then drink, &c.

For our prize-money then to the proctor,
  Take of joy while 'tis going our freak ;
For what argufies calling the doctor
  When the anchor of life is a-peak ?
     Then drink, &c.

LOVELY POLLY.

A SAILOR's love is void of art,
Plain-sailing to his port, the heart,
  He knows no jealous folly :
'Tis hard enough at sea to war
With boisterous elements that jar—
  All's peace with lovely Polly.

Enough that, far from sight of shore,
Clouds frown, and angry billows roar,
  Still is he brisk and jolly :
And while carousing with his mates,
Her health he drinks—anticipates
  The smiles of lovely Polly.

Should thunder on the horizon press,
Mocking our signals of distress,
   E'en then dull melancholy
Dares not intrude :—he braves the din,
In hopes to find a calm within
   The snowy arms of Polly.

A HERO'S TRUE GLORY.

When last, in the Dreadful, your honour set sail,
On Newfoundland banks, there came on a hard gale,
There was thunder, red lightning, and cold whistling
     hail,
   Enough the old gemman to scare :
One who threaten'd your life, dash'd below by a wave,
Your own hand I saw snatch'd from a watery grave ;
And you said 'twas well done, for that still with the
     brave
   The noblest of glory 's to spare.

When yard-arm and yard-arm 'long side of a foe,
When the blood from the scuppers rain'd on us below,
When crippled enough to be taken in tow,
   To strike we saw Mounseer prepare :
If a broadside below, or a volley above,
The men were all ready to give her for love,
How oft has your honour cried, not a hand move,
   A hero's true glory 's to spare.

GROG AND GIRLS.

A SAILOR, and an honest heart,
Like ship and helm, are ne'er apart;
For how should one stem wind and tide
If t'other should refuse to guide?
With that she freely cuts the waves:
And so the tar,
When clashing waves around him jar,
Consults his heart, and dangers braves
Where duty calls; nor asks for more
Than grog aboard, and girl ashore.

'Tis not a thousand leagues from home
More horrid that the billows foam;
'Tis not that gentler is the breeze
In Channel than in distant seas—
Danger surrounds him far and near;
But honest tar,
Though winds and water round him jar,
Consults his heart, and scorns to fear;
The risks he runs endear him more
To grog aboard, and girl ashore.

'Tis not that in the hottest fight
The murd'rous ball will sooner light
On him than any other spot,
To face the cannon is his lot;
He must of danger have his share.
But honest tar,
Though fire and winds, and water jar,
Consults his heart and shakes off care;
And when the battle's heat is o'er,
In grog aboard, drinks girl ashore.

POLL & MY PARTNER JOE.

POLL AND PARTNER JOE.

I was, d'ye see, a waterman,
  As tight and spruce as any,
    'Twixt Richmond town
    And Horsleydown
  I earn'd an honest penny;
None could Fortune's favours brag
  More than cou'd lucky I,
My cot was snug, well fill'd my cag,
  My grunter in the sty.
    With wherry tight
    And bosom light
I cheerfully did row;
  And, to complete this princely life,
  Sure never man had friend and wife
Like my Poll and my partner Joe.

I roll'd in joys like these awhile,
  Folks far and near caress'd me,
    'Till, woe is me!
    So lubberly,
  The press-gang came and press'd me.
How could I all these pleasures leave?
  How with my wherry part?
I never so took on to grieve—
  It wrung my very heart.
    But when on board
    They gave the word
To foreign parts to go,
  I rued the moment I was born
  That ever I should thus be torn
From my Poll and my partner Joe.

I did my duty manfully
  While on the billows rolling;
    And, night or day,
    Could find my way,
Blindfold, to the main-top bowling.
Thus all the dangers of the main,
  Quicksands, and gales of wind
I braved, in hopes to taste again
  The joys I left behind.
    In climes afar,
    The hottest war,
Pour'd broadsides on the foe,
  In hopes these perils to relate,
  As by my side attentive sate
My Poll and my partner Joe.

At last it pleased his Majesty
  To give peace to the nation,
    And honest hearts
    From foreign parts
Came home for consolation.
Like lightning (for I felt new life,
  Now safe from all alarms)
I rush'd, and found my friend and wife
  Lock'd in each other's arms!
    Yet fancy not
    I bore my lot
Tame, like a lubber—no;
  For, seeing I was fairly trick'd,
  Plump to the devil I finely kick'd
My Poll and my partner Joe.

THE SAILOR.

THAT girl who fain would choose a mate,
　　Should ne'er in fondness fail her,
May thank her lucky stars if fate
　· Should splice her to a sailor.
He braves the storm, the battle's heat,
　　The yellow boys to nail her;
Diamond, if diamonds she could eat,
　　Would seek her honest sailor.

If she'd be constant, still his heart
　　She's sure will never fail her?
For, though a thousand leagues apart,
　　Still faithful is her sailor.
If she be false, still he is kind, ·
　　And, absent, does bewail her;
Her trusting as he trusts the wind,
　　Still faithless to the sailor.

A butcher can provide her prog,
　　Three threads to drink, a tailor;
What's that to biscuit and to grog,
　　Procured her by her sailor?
She who would such a mate refuse,
　　The devil sure must ail her;
Search round, and, if you're wise, you'll choose
　　To wed an honest sailor.

JACK RATLIN.

JACK RATLIN was the ablest seaman,
None like him could hand, reef, and steer;
No dangerous toil but he'd encounter
With skill, and in contempt of fear.
In fight a lion; the battle ended,
Meek as the bleating lamb he'd prove:
Thus Jack had manners, courage, merit;
Yet did he sigh—and all for love.

Tho song, the jest, the flowing liquor,
For none of these had Jack regard:
He, while his messmates were carousing,
High sitting on the pendant-yard,
Would think upon his fair one's beauties,
Swear never from such charms to rove;
That truly he'd adore them living,
And, dying, sigh—to end his love.

The same express the crew commanded,
Once more to view their native land,
Among the rest, brought Jack some tidings,
Would it had been his love's fair hand!
Oh, fate! her death defaced the letter;
Instant his pulse forgot to move;
With quiv'ring lips, and eyes uplifted,
He heaved a sigh—and died for love!

YEO, HEAVE, HO!

The boatswain calls, the wind is fair,
The anchor heaving,
Our sweethearts leaving,
We to duty must repair,
  Where our stations well we know.
Cast off halliards from the cleets,
Stand by well, clear all the sheets;
Come, my boys!
Your handspikes poise,
And give one general huzza.
Yet sighing, as you pull away,
For the tears ashore that flow;
To the windlass let us go,
With yo, heave, ho!

The anchor coming now apeak,
Lest the ship, striving,
Be on it driving,
That we the tap'ring yards must seek,
  And back the foretop-sail well we know.
A pleasing duty! From aloft
We faintly see those charms, where oft,
When returning,
With passion burning,
We fondly gaze; those eyes that seem,
In parting, with big tears to stream.
But come! lest ours as fast should flow,
To the windlass once more go,
With yo, heave, ho!

Now the ship is under weigh,
The breeze so willing
The canvass filling,
The press'd triangle cracks the stay,
  So taught to haul the sheet we know.
And now in trim we gaily sail,
The massy beam receives the gale;
While freed from duty,
To his beauty
(Left on the less'ning shore afar)
A fervent sigh heaves every tar;
To thank those tears for him that flow,
That from his true love he should go,
With yo, heave, ho!

THE SOLDIER'S GRAVE.

Of all sensations pity brings
  To proudly swell the ample heart,
From which the willing sorrow springs,
  In others' woe that bears a part.
Of all sad sympathy's delights,
  The manly dignity of grief,
A joy in mourning that excites,
  And gives the anxious mind relief:
Of these would you the feeling know,
  Most gen'rous, noble, greatly brave,
That ever taught a heart to glow,
  'Tis the tear that bedews a soldier's grave.

For hard and painful is his lot,
   Let dangers come he braves them all;
Valiant perhaps to be forgot,
   Or undistinguish'd doom'd to fall:
Yet wrapt in conscious worth secure,
   The world that now forgets his toil,
'He views from a retreat obscure,
   And quits it with a willing smile.
Then, trav'ller, one kind drop bestow,
   'Twere graceful pity, nobly brave;
Nought ever taught the heart to glow
   Like the tear that bedews a soldier's grave.

SATURDAY NIGHT.

'Tis said we vent'rous die-hards, when we leave the shore,
    Our friends should mourn,
    Lest we return
To bless their sight no more.
    But this is all a notion
     Bold Jack can't understand,
    Some die upon the ocean,
     And some upon the land.
     Then since 'tis clear,
     Howe'er we steer,
No man's life's under his command;
     Let tempests howl,
     And billows roll
    And dangers press:
Of those in spite, there are some joys
   Us jolly tars to bless,
For Saturday night still comes, my boys,
   To drink to Poll and Bess.

One seaman hands the sails, another heaves the log,
  The purser swops
  Our pay for slops,
The landlord sells us grog :
  Then each man to his station,
   To keep life's ship in trim.
  What argufies noration ?
   The rest is all a whim.
    Cheerly, my hearts!
    Then play your parts,
  Boldly resolved to sink or swim ;
    The mighty surge
    May ruin urge,
  And danger press :
    Of these in spite, &c.

For all the world just like the ropes aboard a ship
   Each man's rigg'd out
   A vessel stout,
To take for life a trip.
  The shrouds, the stays, the braces,
   Are joys, and hopes, and fears ;
  The halliards, sheets, and traces,
   Still, as each passion veers,
    And whim prevails,
    Direct the sails,
  As on the sea of life he steers.
    Then let the storm
    Heaven's face deform,
  And dangers press :
    Of these in spite, &c.

THE GREENWICH PENSIONER.

'TWAS in the good ship Rover
  I sail'd the world around,
And for three years and over,
  I ne'er touch'd British ground;
At length in England landed,
  I left the roaring main,
Found all relations stranded,
  And went to sea again.

That time bound straight to Portugal,
  Right fore and aft we bore;
But, when wee'd made Cape Ortugal,
  A gale blew off the shore:
She lay, so did it shock her,
A log upon the main,
  Till, sav'd from Davy's locker,
We stood to sea again.

Next in a frigate sailing,
  Upon a squally night,
Thunder and lightning hailing
  The horrors of the fight;
My precious limb was lopped off,
  I, when they'd eas'd my pain,
Thank'd God I was not popped off,
  And went to sea again.

Yet still am I enabled
  To bring up in life's rear,
Although I am disabled
  And lie in Greenwich tier;
The king, God bless his royalty,
  Who saved me from the main,
I'll praise with love and loyalty,
  But ne'er to sea again.

THE FLOWING CAN.

A SAILOR'S life's a life of woe,
  He works now late now early,
Now up and down, now to and fro,
  What then, he takes it cheerly:
Blest with a smiling can of grog,
    If duty call,
    Stand, rise, or fall,
To fate's last verge he'll jog:
    The cadge to weigh,
    The sheets belay,
He does it with a wish!
    To heave the lead,
    Or to cat-head
The pondrous anchor fish:
  For while the grog goes round,
  All sense of danger drown'd,
    We despise it to a man:

We sing a little, we laugh a little,
And work a little, and swear a little,
And fiddle a little, and foot it a little,
  And swig the flowing can.

If howling winds and roaring seas
  Give proof of coming danger,
We view the storm, our hearts at ease,
  For Jack's to fear a stranger;
Blest with the smiling grog we fly,
    Where now below
    We headlong go,
Now rise on mountains high:

    Spite of the gale,
    We hand the sail,
Or take the needful reef,
    Or man the deck
    To clear the wreck,
To give the ship relief;
    Though perils threat around,
    All sense of danger drown'd,
We despise it to a man,
    We sing a little, &c.

But yet think not our fate is hard,
  Though storms at sea thus treat us,
For coming home, a sweet reward,
  With smiles our sweethearts greet us!
Now too the friendly grog we quaff,
    Our am'rous toast,
    Her we love most,
And gaily sing and laugh:

D

The sails we furl,
  Then for each girl
The petticoat display;
  The deck we clear,
  Then three times cheer,
As we their charms survey;
  And then the grog goes round,
  All sense of danger drown'd,
We despise it to a man:
  We sing a little, &c.

SWEETHEARTS AND WIVES.

'Twas Saturday night, the twinkling stars
  Shone on the rippling sea;
No duty call'd the jovial tars,
  The helm was lash'd a-lee;
The ample can adorn'd the board,—
  Prepar'd to see it out,
Each gave the girl that he ador'd,
  And push'd the grog about.

Cried honest Tom, my Peg I'll toast,
  A frigate neat and trim,
All jolly Portsmouth's favourite boast:
  I'd venture life and limb—
Sail seven long years, and ne'er see land,
  With dauntless heart and stout,
So tight a vessel to command:
  Then push the grog about.

I'll give, cried little Jack, my Poll,
   Sailing in comely state,
Top-gan't sails set, she is so tall,
   She looks like a first-rate:
Ah! would she take her Jack in tow,
   A voyage for life throughout,
No better berth I'd wish to know:
   Then push the grog about.

I'll give, cried I, my charming Nan,
   Trim, handsome, neat, and tight;
What joy so fine a ship to man,
   She is my heart's delight!
So well she bears the storms of life,
   I'd sail the world throughout,
Brave ev'ry toil for such a wife:
   Then push the grog about.

Thus to describe Poll, Peg, or Nan,
   Each his best manner tried;
Till, summon'd by the empty can,
   They to their hammocks hied:
Yet still did they their vigils keep,
   Though the huge can was out,
For, in soft visions, gentle sleep
   Still push'd the grog about.

BONNY KATE.

THE wind was hush'd, the fleecy wave
Scarcely the vessel's sides could lave,
When in the mizen-top his stand
Tom Clueline, taking, spied the land.

Oh, sweet reward for all his toil !
Once more he views his native soil—
Once more he thanks indulgent Fate,
That brings him to his bonny Kate.

Soft as the sighs of Zephyr flow,
Tender and plaintive as her woe,
Serene was the attentive eve,
That heard Tom's bonny Kitty grieve.
" Oh what avails," cried she, " my pain?
He's swallow'd in the greedy main :
Ah, never shall I welcome home,
With tender joy, my honest Tom !"

Now high upon the faithful shroud,
The land awhile that seem'd a cloud,
While objects from the mist arise,
A feast presents Tom's longing eyes.
A riband near his heart which lay,
Now see him on his hat display,
The given sign to show that Fate
Had brought him safe to bonny Kate.

Near to a cliff, whose heights command
A prospect of the shelly strand,
While Kitty Fate and Fortune blamed,
Sudden with rapture she exclaim'd,
" But see, oh Heaven ! a ship in view—
My Tom appears among the crew ;
The pledge he swore to bring safe home
Streams in his hat—'tis honest Tom !"

What now remains were easy told :
Tom comes, his pockets lined with gold ;
Now rich enough no more to roam,
To serve his king he stays at home ;
Recounts each toil, and shows each scar,
While Kitty and her constant tar
With rev'rence teach to bless their fates
Young honest Toms and bonny Kates.

BEN BACKSTAY.

BEN BACKSTAY loved the gentle Anna,
  Constant as purity was she,
Her honey words, like succ'ring manna,
  Cheer'd him each voyage he made to sea.
One fatal morning saw them parting,
  While each the other's sorrow dried,
They, by the tear that then was starting,
  Vow'd to be constant till they died.

At distance from his Anna's beauty,
  While howling winds the sky deform,
Ben sighs, and well performs his duty,
  And braves, for love, the frightful storm.
Alas, in vain !   The vessel batter'd,
  On a rock splitting, open'd wide ;
While, lacerated, torn, and shatter'd,
  Ben thought of Anna, sigh'd, and died.

The semblage of each charming feature
  That Ben had worn around his neck,
Where art stood substitute for nature,
  A tar, his friend, saved from the wreck.
In fervent hope, while Anna, burning,
  Blush'd as she wish'd to be a bride,
The portrait came—joy turn'd to mourning—
  She saw, grew pale, sunk down, and died.

LITTLE BEN.

RESPLENDENT gleam'd the ample moon,
  Reflected on the glitt'ring lee,
The bell proclaim'd night's awful noon,
  And scarce a ripple shook the sea.
When thus, for sailors, nature's care,
  What education has denied,
Are of strong sense, a bounteous share,
  By observation well supplied.
While thus, in bold and honest guise,
  For wisdom moved his tongue,
Drawing from reason comfort's drop
  In truth and fair reflection wise,
    Right cheerfully sung
Little Ben that kept his watch on the main-top.

Why should the hardy tar complain?
  'Tis certain true he weathers more,
From dangers on the roaring main,
  Than lazy lubbers do ashore.

Ne'er let the noble mind despair,
 Though roaring seas run mountains high,
All things are built with equal care,
 First-rate or wherry, man or fly.
If there's a Power that never errs,
 And certainly 'tis so—
For honest hearts what comforts drop—
 As well as kings and emperors,
  Why not take in tow
Little Ben that keeps his watch in the main-top?

What though to distant climes I roam,
 Far from my darling Nancy's charms,
The sweeter is my welcome home,
 To blissful moorings in her arms.
Perhaps she on that sober moon
 A lover's observation takes,
And longs that little Ben may soon
 Relieve that heart which sorely aches.
Ne'er fear: that Power that never errs,
 That guards all things below—
For honest hearts what comforts drop—
 · As well as kings and emperors,
  Will surely take in tow
Little Ben that keeps his watch in the main-top.

THE TAR FOR ALL WEATHERS.

I SAIL'D from the Downs in the Nancy,
 My jib how she smack'd through the breeze;
She's a vessel as tight to my fancy
 As ever sail'd on the salt seas.

So adieu to the white cliffs of Britain,
  Our girls, and our dear native shore!
For if some hard rock we should split on,
  We shall never see them any more.
But sailors were born for all weathers,
  Great guns let it blow high, blow low,
Onr duty keeps us to our tethers,
  And where the gale drives we must go.

When we enter'd the Gut of Gibraltar,
  I verily thought she'd have sunk,
For the wind so began for to alter,
  She yaw'd just as thof she was drunk.
The squall tore the mainsail to shivers,
  Helm a-weather the hoarse boatswain cries;
Brace the foresail athwart; see she quivers,
  As through the rough tempest she flies.
    But sailors, &c.

The storm came on thicker and faster,
  As black just as pitch was the sky,
When truly a doleful disaster
  Befel three poor sailors and I.
Ben Buntline, Sam Shroud, and Dick Handsail,
  By a blast that came furious and hard,
Just while we were furling the mainsail,
  Were ev'ry soul swept from the yard.
    But sailors, &c.

Poor Ben, Sam, and Dick cried peccavi;
  As for I, at the risk of my neck,
While they sunk down in peace to old Davy,
  Caught a rope and so landed on deck.

Well, what would you have? We were stranded,
   And out of a fine jolly crew
Of three hundred that sail'd, never landed
   But I and, I think, twenty-two.
      But sailors, &c.

After thus we at sea had miscarried,
   Another guess way set the wind,
For to England I came, and got married
   To a lass that was comely and kind.
But whether for joy or vexation,
   We know not for what we were born:
Perhaps I may find a kind station,
   Perhaps I may touch at Cape Horn.
      For sailors, &c.

TOM BOWLING.

HERE, a sheer hulk, lies poor Tom Bowling,
   The darling of our crew;
No more he'll hear the tempest howling,
   For death has broach'd him to.
His form was of the manliest beauty,
   His heart was kind and soft,
Faithful, below, he did his duty,
   But now he's gone aloft.

Tom never from his word departed,
   His virtues were so rare,
His friends were many and true-hearted,
   His Poll was kind and fair:

And then he'd sing so blithe and jolly,
  Ah, many's the time and oft!
But mirth is turn'd to melancholy,
  For Tom is gone aloft.

Yet shall poor Tom find pleasant weather,
  When He, who all commands,
Shall give, to call life's crew together,
  The word to pipe all hands.
Thus Death, who kings and tars despatches,
  In vain Tom's life has doff'd,
For, though his body's under hatches,
  His soul is gone aloft.

A DROP OF THE CREATURE.

To ask would to come for to go
  How a true-hearted tar you'd discern,
He's as honest a fellow, I'd have you to know,
  As e'er stepp'd between stem and stern:
  Let furious winds the vessel waft,
  In his station amidships, or fore, or aft,
  He can pull away,
  Cast off, belay,
  Aloft, alow,
  Avast, yo ho!
  And hand, reef, and steer,
  Know each halliard and gear,
  And of duty every rig;
  But his joy and delight
  Is, on Saturday night,
  A drop of the creature to swig.

The first voyage I made to sea,
　One day as I hove the lead,
The main-top gallant-mast went by the lee,
　For it blew off the Devil's Head.
　Tumble up there, bear a hand, turn to,
　While I, the foremost of the crew,
　Soon could pull away,
　Cast off, belay,
　Aloft, yo ho !
　And hand, reef, and steer,
　Know each halliard and gear,
　And of duty every rig;
　But my joy and delight
　Was, on Saturday night,
　A drop of the creature to swig.

There was Kit with a cast in his eye,
　And Tom with a timber toe,
And shambling Will, for he hobbled awry,
　All wounded a-fighting the foe:
　Three lads, though crazy grown and crank,
　As true as ever bumbo drank,
　For they'd pull away,
　Cast off, belay,
　Aloft, alow,
　Avast, yo ho!
　And hand, reef, and steer,
　Know each halliard and gear,
　And of duty every rig;
　But their joy and delight
　Was, on Saturday night,
　A drop of the creature to swig.

Then over life's ocean I'll jog,
  Let the storm or the Spaniards come on,
So but sea-room I get and a skin full of grog,
  I fear neither devil nor Don:
  For I am the man that's spract and daft,
  In my station amidships, or fore, or aft,
  I can pull away,
  Cast off, belay,
  Aloft, alow,
  Avast, yo ho!
  And hand, reef, and steer,
  Know each halliard and gear,
  And of duty every rig;
  But my joy and delight
  Is, on Saturday night,
  A drop of the creature to swig.

THE SOLDIER'S ADIEU.

Adieu, adieu, my only life!
  My honour calls me from thee;
Remember thou'rt a soldier's wife,
  Those tears but ill become thee:
What though by duty I am call'd
  Where thund'ring cannons rattle,
Where Valour's self might stand appall'd,
  When on the wings of thy dear love
To heaven above
Thy fervent orisons are flown,
The tender prayer
Thou put'st up there
Shall call a gardian-angel down
  To watch me in the battle.

My safety thy fair truth shall be,
　　As sword and buckler serving,
My life shall be more dear to me,
　　Because of thy preserving:
Let perils come, let horror threat,
　　Let thund'ring cannons rattle,
I'll fearless seek the conflict's heat,
　　Assured, when on the wings of love,
　　　　To heaven above, &c.

Enough: with that benignant smile
　　Some kindred god inspired thee,
Who knew thy bosom void of guile,
　　Who wonder'd and admired thee:
I go assured, my life, adieu!
　　Though thund'ring cannons rattle,
Though murd'ring carnage stalk in view,
　　When, on the wings of thy true love,
　　　　To heaven above, &c.

NAUTICAL PHILOSOPHY.

I BE one of they sailors who think 'tis no lie,
That for every wherefore of life there's a why,
That be fortune's strange weather, a calm or a squall,
Our berths, good or bad, are chalk'd out for us all:
That the stays and the braces of life will be found
To be some of 'em rotten, and some of 'em sound,
That the good we should cherish, the bad never seek,
For death will too soon bring each anchor apeak.

When astride on the yard they top-lifts they let go,
And I com'd, like a shot, plump among 'em below,
Why I cotch'd at a halliard, and jump'd upon deck,
And so broke my fall to save breaking my neck:
Just like your philosophers, for all their jaw,
Who less than a rope gladly catch at a straw;
Thus the good we should cherish, the bad never seek,
For death will too soon bring each anchor apeak.

Why, now, that there cruise that we made off the
      Banks,
Where I pepper'd the foe, and got shot for my thanks,
What then? She soon struck; and though crippled on
      shore,
And laid up to refit, I had shiners galore.
At length live and looking I tried the false main,
And to get more prize-money got shot at again;
Thus the good we should cherish, the bad never seek,
For death will too soon bring each anchor apeak.

Then just as it comes take the bad with the good;
One man's spoon's made of silver, another's of wood;
What's poison for one man's another man's balm,
Some are safe in a storm, and some lost in a calm;
Some are rolling in riches, some not worth a souse,
To-day we eat beef, and to-morrow lobs-scouse:
Thus the good we should cherish, the bad never seek,
For death will too soon bring each anchor apeak.

HAPPY JERRY.

I was the pride of all the Thames,
  My name was natty Jerry,
The best of smarts and flashy dames
  I've carried in my wherry:
For then no mortal soul like me
  So merrily did jog it,
I lov'd my wife and friend, d'ye see,
  And won the prize of Dogget:
In coat and badge, so neat and spruce,
  I row'd, all blithe and merry,
And every waterman did use
  To call me Happy Jerry.

But times soon chang'd, I went to sea,
  My wife and friend betray'd me,
And in my absence treacherously
  Some pretty frolics play'd me:
Return'd, I used them like a man,
  But still, 'twas so provoking,
I could not joy my very can,
  Nor even fancy smoking;
In tarnish'd badge, and coat so queer,
  No longer blithe and merry,
Old friends now pass'd me with a sneer,
  And call'd me Dismal Jerry.

At sea, as with a dangerous wound,
  I lay under the surgeons,
Two friends each help I wanted found
  In every emergence:

Soon after my sweet friend and wife
  Into this mess had brought me,
These two kind friends who sav'd my life
  In my misfortunes sought me :
We're come, cried they, that once again
  In coat and badge so merry,
Your kind old friends, the watermen,
  May hail you Happy Jerry.

I'm Peggy, once your soul's desire,
  To whom you prov'd a rover,
Who since that time, in man's attire,
  Have sought you the world over ;
And I, cried t' other, am that Jack,
  When boys, you used so badly,
Though now the best friend to your back,—
  Then prithee look not sadly.
Few words are best, I seiz'd their hands,
  My grateful heart grew merry,
And now in love and friendship's bands
  I'm once more Happy Jerry.

JACK IN HIS ELEMENT.

Bold Jack the sailor here I come,
  Pray how d'ye like my nib,
My trousers wide, my trampers rum,
  My nab and flowing jib :
I sails the seas from end to end,
  And leads a joyous life,
In every mess I find a friend,
  In every port a wife.

I've heard them talk of constancy,
   Of grief, and such-like fun;
I've constant been to ten, cried I,
   But never, grieved for one :
The flowing sails we tars unbend,
   To lead a jovial life,
In every mess to find a friend,
   In every port a wife.

I've a spanking wife at Portsmouth Gates,
   A pigmy at Goree,
An orange-tawny up the Straits,
   A black at St. Lucie :
Thus, whatsomedever course I bends,
   I leads a jovial life,
In every mess I find a friend,
   In every port a wife.

Will Gaft by Death was ta'en aback,
   I came to bring the news,
Poll whimper'd sore, but what did Jack?
   Why, stood in William's shoes :
She cut, I chased, but in the end
   She lov'd me as her life,
And so she got an honest friend,
   And I a loving wife.

Thus be we sailors all the go,
   On fortune's sea we rub,
We works and loves, and fights the foe,
   And drinks the generous bub.
Storms that the masts to splinters rend,
   Can't shake our jovial life,
In every mess we find a friend,
   In every port a wife.

E

VICTORY'S LAUREL.

HARK that din of distant war,
  How noble in the clangor,
Pale Death ascends his ebon car,
  Clad in terrific anger:
A doubtful fate the soldier tries,
  Who joins the gallant quarrel:
Perhaps on the cold ground he lies,
No wife, no friend, to close his eyes,
Though nobly mourn'd,
Perhaps return'd,
  He's crown'd with victory's laurel.

How many who, disdaining fear,
  Rush on the desperate duty,
Shall claim the tribute of the tear
  That dims the eye of Beauty?
  A doubtful fate, &c.

What nobler fate can fortune give?
  Renown shall tell our story
If we should fall, but if we live,
  We live our country's glory.
    'Tis true a doubtful fate, &c.

BUXOM NAN.

THE wind was hush'd, the storm was over,
  Unfurl'd was every flowing sail,
From toil released, when Dick of Dover
  Went wtih his messmates to regale:

All danger's o'er, cried he, my neat hearts,
  Drown care then in the smiling can,
Come bear a hand, let's toast our sweethearts,
  And first I'll give you buxom Nan.

She's none of those that's always gigging,
  And stem and stern made up of art;
One knows a vessel by her rigging.
  Such ever slight a constant heart:
With straw hat and pink streamers flowing,
  How oft to meet me has she ran;
While for dear life would I be rowing,
  To meet with smiles my buxom Nan.

Jack Jollyboat went to the Indies,
  To see him stare when he came back,
The girls were all off of the hinges,
  His Poll was quite unknown to Jack:
Tant masted all, to see who's tallest,
  Breastworks, top-ga'ant sails, and a fan;
Messmate, cried I, more sail than ballast:
  Ah still give me my buxom Nan.

None in life's sea can sail more quicker,
  To show her love or serve a friend:
But hold, I'm preaching o'er my liquor;
  This one word then, and there's an end:
Of all the wenches whatsomedever,
  I say then, find me out who can,
One half so tight, so kind, so clever,
  Sweet, trim, and neat, as buxom Nan.

FORETOP MORALITY.

Two real tars, whom duty call'd
　　To watch in the foretop,
Thus one another overhaul'd,
　　And took a cheering drop :
I say, Will Hatchway, cried Tom Tow,
　　Of conduct what's your sort,
As through the voyage of life you go,
　　To bring you safe to port ?

Cried Will, you lubber, don't you know ?
　　Our passions close to reef,
To steer where honour points the prow,
　　To hand a friend relief:
These anchors get but in your power,
　　My life for't, that's your sort;
The bower, the sheet, and the best bower,
　　Shall bring you up in port.

Why then you're out, and there's an end,
　　Tom cried out blunt and rough,
Be good, be honest, serve a friend,
　　Be maxims well enough :
Who swabs his bows at other's woe,
　　That tar's for me your sort;
His vessel right a-head shall go
　　To find a joyful port.

Let storms of life upon me press,
    Misfortunes make me reel,
Why, dam'me, what's my own distress?
    For others let me feel.
Ay, ay, if bound with a fresh gale
    To heaven, this is your sort,
A handkerchief's the best wet sail
    To bring you safe to port.

SWIZZY.

If bold and brave thou can'st not bear
Thyself from all thou lovest to tear,—
If, while winds war and billows roll,
A spark of fear invade thy soul,—
If thou'rt appall'd when cannons roar,
I prithee, messmate, stay ashore:
    There, like a lubber,
    Whine and blubber,
Still for thy ease and safety busy,
    Nor dare to come
    Where honest Tom,
    And Ned, and Nick,
    And Ben, and Phil,
    And Jack, and Dick,
    And Bob, and Bill,
All weathers sing, and drink the swizzy.

If, shouldst thou lose a limb in fight,
She who made up thy heart's delight
(Poor recompence that thou art kind)
Shall prove inconstant as the wind,—
If such hard fortune thou'dst deplore,
I prithee messmate, stay ashore:
    There, like a lubber, &c.

If, pris'ner in a foreign land,
No friend, no money at command,
That man thou trusted hadst alone
All knowledge of thee should disown,—
If this should vex thee to the core,
I prithee, messmate, stay ashore.
    There, like a lubber, &c.

SOLDIER DICK.

WHY, don't you know me by my scars?
I'm soldier Dick come from the wars;
Where many a head without a hat
Crowds honour's bed—but what of that?
Beat drums, play fifes, 'tis glory calls,
What argufies who stands or falls?
Lord, what should one be sorry for?
Life's but the fortune of the war:
Then rich or poor, or well or sick,
Still laugh and sing shall soldier Dick.

I used to look two ways at once,
A bullet hit me on the sconce,
And dows'd my glim : d'ye think I'd wince?
Why, lord, I've never squinted since.
    Beat drums, &c.

Some distant keep from war's alarms,
For fear of wooden legs and arms,
While others die safe in their beds
Who all their lives had wooden heads.
    Beat drums, &c.

Thus gout or fever, sword or shot,
Or something, sends us all to pot;
That we're to die, then, do not grieve,
But let's be merry while we live.
   Beat drums, &c.

THE SHIPWRECK.

Avert yon omen, gracious Heaven!
   The ugly scud,
By rising winds resistless driven,
   Kisses the flood.
How hard the lot for sailors cast,
   That they should roam
For years, to perish thus at last
   In sight of home!
For if the coming gale we mourn
   A tempest grows,
Our vessel's shatter'd so and torn,
   That down she goes!

The tempest comes, while meteors red
   Portentous fly;
And now we touch old Ocean's bed,
   Now reach the sky!
On sable wings, in gloomy flight,
   Fiends seem to wait,
To snatch us in this dreadful night,
   Dark as our fate:
Unless some kind, some pitying power
   Should interpose,
She labours so within this hour,
   Down she goes.

But see, on rosy pinions borne,
 O'er the mad deep,
Reluctant beams the sorrowing morn,
 With us to weep.
Deceitful sorrow, cheerless light,
 Dreadful to think,
The morn is risen, in endless night
 Our hopes to sink!
She splits! she parts!—through sluices driven,
 The water flows;
Adieu, ye friends,—have mercy, Heaven!
 For down she goes!

THE GIRL ASHORE.

The tar's a jolly tar that can hand, reef, and steer,
 That can nimbly cast off and belay,
Who in darkest of nights finds each halliard and gear,
 And dead reck'ning knows well and lee-way:
  But the tar to please me
  More jolly must be,
 He must laugh at the waves as they roar;
  He must rattle,
  And in battle
  Brave danger and dying,
  Though bullets are flying,
 And fifty things more:
  Singing, quaffing,
  Dancing, laughing,
  Take it cherrily
  And merrily,
 And all for the sake of his girl ashore.

The tar's a jolly tar who his rhino will spend,
  Who up for a messmate will spring,
For we sailors all think he that's true to his friend
  Will never be false to his king.
     But the tar to please me
     More jolly must be,
   He must venture for money galore:
     Acting duly,
     Kind and truly,
     And nobly inherit
     A generous spirit,
   A prudent one more;
     Singing, laughing,
     Dancing, quaffing,
     Take it cherrily and merrily,
   And save up his cash for his girl ashore.

The tar's a jolly tar who loves a beauty bright,
  And at sea often thinks of her charms,
Who toasts her with glee on a Saturday-night,
  And wishes her moor'd in his arms.
     But the tar to please me
     More jolly must be;
   Though teased at each port by a score,
     He must, sneering
     At their leering,
     Never study to delight 'em,
     But scorn 'em and slight 'em,
   Still true to the core:
     Singing, laughing,
     Dancing, quaffing,
     Take it cherrily and merrily,
   And constant return to his girl ashore.

TRUE ENGLISH SAILOR.

Jack dances and sings, and is always content,
   In his vows to his lass he'll ne'er fail her,
His anchor's a-trip when his money's all spent—
   And this is the life of a sailor.

Alert in his duty he readily flies,
   Where the winds the tired vessel are flinging,
Though sunk to the sea-gods, or toss'd to the skies,
   Still Jack is found working and singing.

'Longside of an enemy, boldly and brave,
   He'll with broadside on broadside regale her,
Yet he'll sigh to the soul o'er that enemy's grave,
   So noble's the mind of a sailor.

Let cannons roar loud, burst their sides let the bombs,
   Let the winds a dread hurricane rattle,
The rough and the pleasant he takes as it comes,
   And laughs at the storm and the battle.

In a fostering Power while Jack puts his trust,
   As fortune comes, smiling he'll hail her,
Resign'd, still, and manly, since what must be must,—
   And this is the mind of a sailor.

Though careless and headlong if danger should press,
   And rank'd 'mongst the free list of rovers,
Yet he'll melt into tears at a tale of distress,
   And prove the most constant of lovers.

To rancour unknown, to no passion a slave,
   Nor unmanly, nor mean, nor a railer,
He's gentle as mercy, as fortitude brave,—
   And this is a true English sailor.

BILL BOBSTAY.

TIGHT lads have I sail'd with, but none e'er so sightly
   As honest Bill Bobstay, so kind and so true,
He'd sing like a mermaid, and foot it so lightly,
   The forecastle's pride, and delight of the crew!
But poor as a beggar, and often in tatters,
   He went, though his fortunes was kind without end:
For money, cried Bill, and them there sort of matters,
   What's the good on't, d'ye see, but to succour a friend?

There's Nipcheese, the purser, by grinding and squeezing,
   First plund'ring, then leaving the ship, like a rat,
The eddy of fortune stands on a stiff breeze in,
   And mounts, fierce as fire, a dog-vane in his hat.
My bark, though hard storms on life's ocean should rock
     her,
   Though she roll in misfortune and pitch end for end,
No, never shall Bill keep a shot in the locker,
   When by handing it out he can succour a friend.

Let them throw out their wipes, and cry, " Spite of their
     crosses,
   And forgetful of toil that so hardly they bore,
That sailors, at sea, earn their money like horses,
   To squander it idly like asses ashore."

Such lubbers their jaw would coil up, could they measure,
　　By their feelings, the gen'rous delight without end
That gives birth in us tars to that truest of pleasure,
　　The handing our rhino to succour a friend.

Why what's all this nonsense they talks of, and pother,
　　About rights of man?　What a plague are they at?
If they mean that each man to his messmate's a brother,
　　Why, the lubberly swabs! every fool can tell that.
The rights of us Britons we know 's to be loyal,
　　In our country's defence our last moments to spend,
To fight up to the ears to protect the blood royal,
　　To be true to our wives, and to succour a friend.

CHARITY.

Why, good people all, at what do you pry?—
　　Is't the stump of my arm or my leg?
Or the place where I lost my good-looking eye?
　　Or is it to see me beg?
Lord love you, hard fortune is nothing at all,
　　And he's but a fool and a dunce
Who expects, when he's running full butt 'gainst a wall,
　　Not to get a good rap on the sconce.
If beg, borrow, or steal, be the choice of mankind,
　　Surely I choose the best of the three;
Besides, as times go, what a comfort to find
　　That in this bad world there's some charity!

For a soldier I listed, to grow great in fame,
　　And be shot at for sixpence a-day;
Lord help the poor poultry wherever I came,
　　For how could I live on my pay?

I went to the wars to fight the king's foes,
    Where the bullets came whistling by,
Till they swiv'led three ribs, broke the bridge of my nose,
    Queer'd my napper, and knock'd out my eye.
Well, what of all this? I'd my legs and my arms,
    And at Chelsea to lay up was free,
Where my pipe I could smoke, talk of battles and storms,
    And bless his good majesty's charity.

But thinking it shameful to live at my ease,
    Away while the frolic was warm,
In search of good fortune I sails the salt seas,
    And so loses my leg and my arm.
With two strings to my bow, I now thought myself sure;
    But such is the fortune of war,
As a lobster at Greenwich they show'd me the door,
    At Chelsea they call'd me a'tar :
So falling to nothing betwixt those two stools,
    I, the whole world before me, was free
To ask comfort from misers, and pity from fools,
    And live on that air, men's charity.

And what now of all this here patter at last?
    How many who hold their heads high,
And in fashion's fine whirligig fly round so fast,
    Are but beggars as well as I!
The courtier he begs for a snug sinecure,
    For a smile beg your amorous elves,
Churchwardens hand the plate, and beg round for the poor,
    Just to pamper and fatten themselves.
Thus we're beggars throughout the whole race of mankind,
    As by daily experience we see ;
And, as times go, what a comfort to find
    That in this bad world there is some charity.

POOR PEGGY.

Poor Peggy loved a soldier lad
   More, far more, than tongue can tell ye,
Yet was her tender bosom sad
   Whene'er she heard the loud reveilez.
The fifes were screech-owls to her ears,
   The drums like thunder seem'd to rattle,
Ah! too prophetic were her fears,
   They call'd him from her arms to battle!
There wonders he against the foe
   Perform'd, and was with laurels crown'd,
Vain pomp! for soon death laid him low
   On the cold ground.

Her heart all love, her soul all truth,
   That none her fears or flight discover,
Poor Peg, in guise a comely youth,
   Follow'd to the field her lover.
Directed by the fife and drum
   To where the work of death was doing,
Where of brave hearts the time was come,
   Who, seeking honour, grasp at ruin;
Her very soul was chill'd with woe,
   New horror came in every sound,
And whisper'd death had laid him low
   On the cold ground.

With mute affliction as she stood
   Did her weak woman's fears confound her;
While terror all her soul subdued,
   A mourning train came thronging round her.

The plaintive fife and muffled drum
　The martial obsequies discover,
His name she heard, and cried I come,
　Faithful, to meet my murder'd lover!
Then heart-rent by a sigh of woe, 　　　•
　Fell, to the grief of all around,
Where death had laid her lover low
　On the cold ground.

JACK'S GRATITUDE.

I'vE sail'd round the world without fear or dismay,
　I've seen the wind foul, and I've seen the wind fair,
I've been wounded, and shipwreck'd, and trick'd of my
　　　pay,
　But a brave British sailor should never despair.

When in a French prison I chanced for lie,
　With no light from the heavens, and scarce any air,
In a dungeon, instead of in battle, to die,
　Was dismal, I own, but I did not despair.

But, Lord, this is nothing—my poor upper works
　Got shatter'd, and I was obliged to repair ;
I've been shot by the French, and a slave 'mong the
　　　Turks,
　But a brave British sailor should never despair.

But for all these misfortunes, I'd yet cut a dash,
　Laid snug up my timbers, and never know care,
If the agent had not run away with the cash,
　And so many brave fellows plunged into despair.

So coming 'longside of our bold royal tar,
   I told him the rights on't—for why should I care?
Of my wrongs and my hardships, and wounds in the war,
   And if how he would right me, I should not despair.

Says his highness, say he, such ill treatment as thine
   Is a shame, and henceforward thy fortune's my care;
So now, Blessings on him, sing out me and mine,
   And thus British seamen should never despair.

So straightway he got it made into a law
   That each tar of his rhino should have his full share,
And so agents, d'ye see, may coil up their slack jaw,
   For the duke is our friend, and we need not despair.

Then push round the grog, though we face the whole
      world,
   Let our royal tar's pennant but fly in the air,
And the sails of our navy again be unfurl'd,—
   We'll strike wond'ring nations with awe and despair.

THE SOLDIER'S LAST RETURN.

Alas! the battle's lost and won,
   Dick Flink's borne off the field
By Death, from whom the stoutest run,
   Who makes whole armies yield!
Dick well in honour's footsteps trod,
   Brav'd war and its alarms;
Now Death, beneath the humble sod,
   Has grounded his arms?

Dick's march'd before us on a rout
    Where ev'ry soldier's sent;
His fire is dead, his courage out,
    His ammunition spent:
His form so active now's a clod,
    His grace no longer charms,
For Death, beneath the humble sod,
    Has grounded his arms.

Come, fire a volley o'er his grave,
    Dead marches let us beat:
War's honours well become the brave,
    Who sound their last retreat.
All must obey Fate's awful nod,
    Whom life this moment warms;
Death soon or late, beneath the sod,
    Will ground the soldier's arms !

TACK AND TACK.

Adieu, my gallant sailor, obey thy duty's call,
    Though false the sea, there's truth ashore;
Till nature is found changing, thou'rt sure of constant
      Poll :
    And yet, as now we sever,
    Ah much I fear that never
Shall I, alas, behold thee more !

F

Jack kiss'd her, hitch'd his trousers, and hied him to
  begone,
 Weigh'd anchor, and lost sight of shore :
Next day a brisk south-wester a heavy gale brought on,—
  Adieu, cried Jack, for ever,
  For much I fear that never
 Shall I, sweet Poll, behold you more.

Poll heard that to the bottom was sunk her honest tar,
 And for a while lamented sore ;
At length, cried she, I'll marry ; what should I tarry for ?
  I may lead apes for ever,
  Jack's gone, and never, never
 Shall I, alas, behold him more !

Jack, safe and sound returning, sought out his faithful
  Poll :
 Think you, cried she, that false I swore ?
I'm constant still as ever, 'tis nature's chang'd, that's
  all ;
  And thus we part for ever
  For never, sailor, never
 Shall I behold you more !

If, as you say, that nature like winds can shift and veer,
 About ship for a kinder shore ;
I heard the trick you play'd me, and so, d'ye see, my
  dear,
  To a kind heart for ever
  I've spliced myself, so never
 Shall I, false Poll, behold you more.

GRIEVING'S A FOLLY.

SPANKING Jack was so comely, so pleasant, so jolly,
 Though winds blew great guns, still he'd whistle and
   sing,
For Jack lov'd his friend, and was true to his Molly,
 And, if honour gives greatness, was great as a king:
One night as we drove with two reefs in the main-sail,
 And the scud came on low'ring upon a lee shore,
Jack went up aloft for to hand the top-gantsail,
 A spray wash'd him off, and we ne'er saw him more:
  But grieving's a folly,
  Come let us be jolly;
If we've troubles on sea, boys, we've pleasures on shore.

Whiffling Tom still of mischief, or fun in the middle,
 Through life in all weathers at random would jog,
He'd dance, and he'd sing, and he'd play on the fiddle,
 And swig with an air his allowance of grog:
Long side of a Don, in the Terrible frigate,
 As yard-arm and yard-arm we lay off the shore,
In and out whiffling Tom did so caper and jig it,
 That his head was shot off, and we ne'er saw him
   more:
  But grieving's a folly, &c.

Bonny Ben was to each jolly messmate a brother,
 He was manly and honest, good-natur'd and free;
If ever one tar was more true than another
 To his friend and his duty, that sailor was he:

One day with the davit to weigh the kedge anchor
    Ben went in the boat on a bold craggy shore,
He overboard tipp'd, when a shark and a spanker
    Soon nipp'd him in two, and we ne'er saw him more :
        But grieving's a folly, &c.

But what of it all, lads? shall we be downhearted
    Because that mayhap we now take our last sup ?
Life's cable must one day or other be parted,
    And Death in safe moorings will bring us all up :
But 'tis always the way on't ; one scarce finds a brother
    Fond as pitch, honest, hearty, and true to the core,
But by battle, or storm, or some damn'd thing or other,
    He's popp'd off the hooks, and we ne'er see him more !
        But grieving's a folly, &c.

BLEAK WAS THE MORN.

BLEAK was the morn when William left his Nancy,
    The fleecy snow frown'd on the whiten'd shore,
Cold as the fears that chill'd her dreary fancy,
    While she her sailor from her bosom tore :
To his fill'd heart a little Nancy pressing,
    While a young tar the ample trousers ey'd,
In need of firmness in this state distressing,
    Will check'd the rising sigh, and fondly cried,
    Ne'er fear the perils of the fickle ocean,
    Sorrow's a notion,
        Grief all in vain ;
    Sweet love, take heart,
    For we but part
        In joy to meet again.

Loud blew the wind, when, leaning on that willow
 Where the dear name of honest William stood,
Poor Nancy saw, toss'd by a faithless billow,
 A ship dash'd 'gainst a rock that topp'd the flood :
Her tender heart with frantic thrilling,
 Wild as the storm that howl'd along the shore,
No longer could resist a stroke so killing,
 'Tis he, she cried, nor shall I see him more.
 Why did he ever trust the fickle ocean?
 Sorrow's my portion,
  Misery and pain !
 Break my poor heart,
 For now we part
  Never to meet again.

Mild was the eve, all nature was smiling,
 Four tedious years had Nancy pass'd in grief,
When, with her children the sad hours beguiling,
 She saw her William fly to her relief !
Sunk in his arms with bliss he quickly found her,
 But soon return'd to life, to love, and joy,
While her grown young ones anxiously surround her,
 And now Will clasps his girl, and now his boy.
 Did I not say, though 'tis a fickle ocean,
 Sorrow's all a notion,
  Grief all in vain ?
 My joy how sweet,
 For now we meet
  Never to part again !

HONESTY IN TATTERS.

This here's what I does,—I, d'ye see, forms a notion
  That our troubles, our sorrows, and strife,
Are the winds and the billows that foment the ocean,
  As we work through the passage of life.
And for fear, on life's sea lest the vessel should founder,
  To lament, and to weep, and to wail,
Is a pop-gun that tries to out-roar a nine-pounder,
  All the same as a whiff in a gale.
Why now I, though hard fortune has pretty near starv'd
      me,
  And my togs are all ragged and queer,
Ne'er yet gave the bag to the friend who had serv'd
      me,
  Or caus'd ruin'd beauty a tear.

Now there, t'other day, when my messmate deceiv'd
      me,
  Stole my rhino, my chest, and our Poll ;
Do you think in revenge, while their treachery griev'd
      me,
  I a court-martial call'd ?—Not at all.
This here on the matter was my way of arg'ing,—
  'Tis true they han't left me a cross ;
A vile wife and false friend though are gone by the
      bargain,
  So the gain d'ye see's more than the loss.
      For though fortune's a jilt, and has, &c.

The heart's all—when that's built as it should, sound,
    and clever,
  We go 'fore the wind like a fly,
But if rotten and crank, you may luff up for ever,
    You'll always sail in the wind's eye:
With palaver and nonsense, I'm not to be paid off,
    I'm adrift, let it blow then great guns,
A gale, a fresh breeze, or the old gemman's head off,
    I takes life rough and smooth as it runs:
      Content, though hard fortune, &c.

THE BLIND SAILOR.

COME, never seem to mind it,
  Nor count your fate a curse,
However sad you find it,
  Yet somebody is worse.
In danger some must come off short,
  Yet why should we despair?
For if bold tars are Fortune's sport,
  Still are they Fortune's care.

Why, when our vessel blew up,
  A fighting that there Don,
Like squibs and crackers flew up
  The crew, each mother's son.
They sunk,—some rigging stopp'd me short,
  While twirling in the air;
And thus, if tars are Fortune's sport,
  Still are they Fortune's care.

Young Peg of Portsmouth-common
  Had like to have been my wife,
'Longside of such a woman
  I'd led a pretty life:
A landsman, one Jem Davenport,
  She convoy'd to Horn-fair;
And thus, though tars are Fortune's sport,
  They still are Fortune's care.

A splinter knock'd my nose off,
  My bowsprit's gone, I cries,
Yet well it kept their blows off,
  Thank God 'twas not my eyes.
Chance if again their fun's that sort,
  Let's hope I've had my share.
Thus, if bold tars are Fortune's sport,
  They still are Fortune's care.

Scarce with these words I'd outed,
  Glad for my eyes and limbs,
When a cartridge burst, and douted
  Both my two precious glims.
Why, then, they're gone, cried I, in short,
  Yet Fate my life did spare;
And thus, though tars are Fortune's sport,
  They still are Fortune's care.

I'm blind, and I'm a cripple,
  Yet cheerful would I sing
Were my misfortunes triple,
  Cause why, 'twas for my king.
Besides, each Christian I exhort,
  Pleased, will some pittance spare;
And thus, though tars are Fortune's sport,
  They still are Fortune's care.

JACK AT THE WINDLASS.

Come, all hands ahoy to the anchor,
   From our friends and relations to go;
Poll blubbers and cries, devil thank her!
   She'll soon take another in tow.
This breeze, like the old one, will kick us
   About on the boisterous main;
And one day, if Death should not trick us,
   Perhaps we may come back again.
With a will-ho, then pull away, jolly boys,
   At the mercy of fortune we go;
We're in for't, then damme, what folly boys,
   For to be downhearted, yo ho!

Our Boatswain takes care of the rigging,
   More 'specially when he gets drunk;
The bobstays supply him with swigging,
   He the cable cuts up for old junk.
The studding-sail serves for his hammock,
   With the clew-lines he bought him his call,
While ensigns and jacks in a mammock
   He sold to buy trinkets for Poll.
      With a will-ho, &c.

Of the Purser this here is the maxim,—
   Slops, grog, and provision he sacks;
How he'd look if you was but to ax him
   With the captain's clerk who 'tis goes snacks.

Oh, he'd find it another guess story,
   That would bring his bare back to the cat,
If his Majesty's honour and glory
   Was only just told about that.
      With a will-ho, &c.

Our Chaplain's both holy and godly,
   And sets us for heaven agog ;
Yet to my mind he looks rather oddly
   When he's swearing and drinking of grog :
When he took on his knee Betty Bowser,
   And talk'd of her beauty and charms,
Cried I, which is the way to heaven now, sir ?
   Why, you dog, cried the Chaplain, her arms.
      With a will-ho, &c.

The Gunner's a devil of a bubber,
   The Carfindo can't fish a mast,
The Surgeon's a lazy land-lubber,
   The Master can't steer if he's ast ;
The Lieutenants conceit are all wrapp'd in,
   The Mates scarcely merit their flip,
Nor is there a swab, but the Captain,
   Knows the stem from the stern of the ship.
      With a will-ho, &c.

Now, fore and aft having abused them,
   Just but for my fancy and gig,
Could I find any one that ill-used them,
   Damn me, but I'd tickle his wig.
Jack never was known for a railer,
   'Twas fun ev'ry word that I spoke,
And the sign of a true-hearted sailor
   Is to give and to take a good joke.
      With a will-ho, &c.

CONSTANCY.

THE surge hoarsely murm'ring, young Fanny's grief
    mocking,
  The spray rudely dashing as salt as her tears;
The ship's in the offing, perpetually rocking,
  Too faithful a type of her hopes and her fears.
'Twas here, she cried out, that Jack's vows were so many,
  Here I bitterly wept, and I bitterly weep:
Her heart-whole he swore to return to his Fanny,
  Near the trembling pine that nods over the deep.

Ah! mock not my troubles, ye pitiless breakers;
  Ye winds, do not thus melt my heart with alarms;
He is your pride and mine, in my grief then partakers,
  My sailor in safety waft back to my arms.
They are deaf and ungrateful: these woes are too many;
  Here, here will I die, where I bitterly weep;
Some true lover shall write the sad fate of poor Fanny,
  On the trembling pine that hangs over the deep.

Thus, her heart sadly torn with its wild perturbation,
  No friend but her sorrow, no hope but the grave;
Led on by her grief to the last desperation,
  She ran to the cliff, and plung'd into the wave.
A tar saved her life—the fond tale shall please many,
  Who before wept her fate, now no longer shall weep:
'Twas her Jack, who, returning, had sought out his
    Fanny,
  Near the trembling pine that hangs over the deep.

EV'RY INCH A SAILOR.

The wind blew hard, the sea ran high,
The dingy scud drove 'cross the sky,
All was safe lash'd, the bowl was slung,
When careless thus Ned Haulyard sung:
   A sailor's life's the life for me,
   He takes his duty merrily;
   If winds can whistle, he can sing,
   Still faithful to his friend and king;
   He gets beloved by all the ship,
   And toasts his girl, and drinks his flip.

Down topsails, boys, the gale comes on,
To strike top-gallant yards they run,
And now to hand the sail prepared,
Ned cheerful sings upon the yard:
   A sailor's life, &c.

A leak, a leak!—come, lads, be bold,
There's five foot water in the hold;
Eager on deck see Haulyard jump,
And hark, while working at the pump:
   A sailor's life, &c.

And see! the vessel nought can save,
She strikes, and finds a wat'ry grave!
Yet Ned preserved, with a few more,
Sings as she treads a foreign shore:
   A sailor's life, &c.

And now—unnumber'd perils past,
On land, as well as sea—at last
In tatters to his Poll and home
See honest Haulyard singing come:
   A sailor's life, &c.

Yet for poor Haulyard what disgrace,—
Poll swears she never saw his face;
He damns her for a faithless she,
And singing goes again to see:
   A sailor's life, &c.

THE TOKEN.

The breeze was fresh, the ship in stays,
Each breaker hush'd, the shore a haze,
When Jack, no more on duty call'd,
His true-love's tokens overhaul'd:
The broken gold, the braided hair,
The tender motto, writ so fair,
Upon his 'bacco-box he views,
Nancy the poet, Love the muse:
   "If you loves I as I loves you,
   No pair so happy as we two."

The storm—that like a shapeless wreck
Had strew'd with rigging all the deck,
That tars for sharks had given a feast,
And left the ship a hulk—had ceased;

When Jack, as with his messmates dear
He shared the grog, their hearts to cheer,
Took from his 'bacco-box a quid,
And spelt, for comfort, on the lid,
  " If you loves I as I loves you,
  No pair so happy as we two."

The battle—that with horror grim,
Had madly ravaged life and limb,
Had scuppers drench'd with human gore,
And widow'd many a wife—was o'er :
When Jack to his companions dear
First paid the tribute of a tear,
Then, as his 'bacco-box he held,
Restored his comfort, as he spelld',
  " If you loves I as I loves you,
  No pair so happy as we two."

The voyage-—that had been long and hard,
But that had yielded full reward;
That brought each sailor to his friend,
Happy and rich—was at an end ;
When Jack, his toils and perils o'er,
Beheld his Nancy on the shore,
He then the 'bacco-box display'd,
And cried, and seized the willing maid,
  " If you loves I as I loves you,
  No pair so happy as we two."

JACK'S FIDELITY.

JACK'S FIDELITY.

If ever a sailor was fond of good sport
   'Mongst the girls, why that sailor was I.
Of all sizes and sorts, I'd a wife at each port,
   But, when that I saw'd Polly Ply,
I hail'd her my lovely, and gov'd her a kiss,
   And swore to bring up once for all,
And from that time black Barnaby spliced us to this,
   I've been constant and true to my Poll.

And yet now all sorts of temptations I've stood,
   For I afterwards sail'd round the world,
And a queer set we saw of the devil's own brood,
   Wherever our sails were unfurl'd:
Some with faces like charcoal, and others like chalk,
   All ready one's hearts to o'erhaul;
"Don't you go to love me, my good girl," said I—" walk;
   I've sworn to be constant to Poll."

I met with a squaw out at India, beyond,
   All in glass and tobacco-pipes dress'd,
What a dear pretty monster! so kind and so fond,
   That I ne'er was a moment at rest.
With her bobs at her nose, and her quaw, quaw, quaw,
   All the world like a Bartlemy doll;
Says I, "You Miss Copperskin, just hold your jaw,—
   I've sworn to be constant to Poll."

Then one near Sumatra, just under the Line,
   As fond as a witch in a play ;
" I loves you," says she, " and just only be mine,
   Or by poison I'll take you away."
"Curse your kindness," says I, " but you can't frighten
      me ;
   You don't catch a gudgeon this haul ;
If I do take your ratsbane, why then, do you see,
   I shall die true and constant to Poll."

But I 'scaped from them all, tawny, lilly, and black,
   And merrily weather'd each storm,
And, my neighbours to please, full of wonders came
    back,
   But, what's better, I'm grown pretty warm.
And so now to sea I shall venture no more,
   For you know, being rich, I've no call ;
So I'll bring up young tars, do my duty ashore,
   And live and die constant to Poll.

THE SOLDIER'S FUNERAL.

The martial pomp, the mournful train,
Bespeak some honour'd hero slain !
The obsequies denote him brave ;
Hark the volley o'er his grave :
The awful knell sounds low and lorn,
Yet cease, ye kindred brave, to mourn.

HEAVING THE LEAD.

The plaintive fife and muffled drum
The man may summon to his silent home!
The soldier lives:—his deeds to trace,
Behold the Seraph Glory place
An ever-living laurel round his sacred tomb.
Nor deem it hard, ye thoughtless gay,
Short's man's longest earthly stay;
Our little hour of life we try,
And then depart: we're born to die.
Then lose no moment dear to fame,—
They longest live who live in name.
　　　The plaintive fife, &c.

TACK AND HALF-TACK.

THE Yarmouth roads are right ahead,
　The crew with ardour burning,
Jack sings out as he heaves the lead,
　On tack and half-tack turning;
　　By the dip eleven!
Lash'd in the chains, the line he coils,
　Then round his head 'tis swinging;
And thus to make the land he toils,
　In numbers quaintly singing,
　　By the mark seven!
And now, lest we run bump ashore,
He heaves the lead, and sings once more,
　Quarter less four!
About ship, lads, tumble up there, can't you see?
Stand by, well; hark, hark; helm's a-lee!
Here she comes, up tacks and sheets, haul, mainsail haul,
Haul of all!

And, as the long-lost shore they view,
Exulting shout the happy crew;
Each singing, as the sail he furls,
Hey for the fiddles and the girls

The next tack we run out to sea,
 Old England scarce appearing:
Again we tack, and Jack with glee
  Sings out as land we're nearing,
   By the dip eleven!
And as they name some beauty dear
  To tars of bliss the summit,
Jack joins the jest, the jibe, the jeer,
  And heaves the ponderous plummet;
   By the mark seven!
And now, while dangerous breakers roar,
 Jack cries, lest we run bump ashore,
 Quarter less four!
About ship, lads, tumble up there, can't you see?
Stand by, well; hark, hark; helm's a-lee!
Here she comes, up tacks and sheets, haul, mainsail haul,
Haul of all!
 And, as the long-lost shore they view,
 Exulting shout the happy crew;
 Each singing, as the sails he furls,
 Hey for the fiddles and the girls.

Thus tars at sea, like swabs at home,
 By tack and tack are biass'd,
The furthest way about we roam,
 To bring us home the nighest;
  By the dip eleven!

TOM TACKLE.

For one tack more, and 'fore the wind,
 Shall we, in a few glasses,
Now make the land both true and kind,
 To find our friends and lasses:
  By the mark seven!
Then heave the lead, my lad, once more,
Soon shall we gaily tread the shore,
 And a half four!
About ship, lads, tumble up there, can't you see?
Stand by, well; hark, hark; helm's a-lee!
Here she comes, up tacks and sheets, haul, mainsail haul,
Overhaul all!
 And as the long-lost shore they view,
 Exulting shout the happy crew;
 Each singing, as the sails he furls,
 Hey for the fiddle and the girls.

TOM TACKLE WAS POOR.

Tom Tackle was noble, was true to his word;
If merit bought titles, Tom might be my lord;
How gaily his bark through Life's ocean would sail,
Truth furnish'd the rigging, and Honour the gale.
Yet Tom had a failing, if ever man had,
That, good as he was, made him all that was bad;
He was paltry and pitiful, scurvy and mean,
And the sniv'lingest scoundrel that ever was seen:
For so said the girls and the landlords 'longshore.
Would you know what his fault was—Tom Tackle was
  poor!

'Twas once on a time when we took a galloon,
And the crew touch'd the agent for cash to some tune,
Tom a trip took to jail, an old messmate to free,
And four thankful prattlers soon sat on his knee.
Then Tom was an angel, downright from heaven sent!
While they'd hands he his goodness should never repent:
Return'd from next voyage, he bemoan'd his sad case,
To find his dear friend shut the door in his face!
Why d'ye wonder? cried one, you're served right, to be
       sure;
Once, Tom Tackle was rich—now Tom Tackle is poor!

I ben't, you see, versed in high maxims and sitch;
But don't this same honour concern poor and rich?
If it don't come from good hearts, I can't see where from,
And dam'me, if e'er tar had a good heart, 'twas Tom.
Yet, some how or 'nother, Tom never did right:
None knew better the time when to spare or to fight:
He, by finding a leak, once preserved crew and ship,
Saved the Commodore's life—then he made such rare
       flip!
And yet for all this, no one Tom could endure;
I fancies as how 'twas—because he was poor.

At last an old shipmate, that Tom might hail land,
Who saw that his heart sail'd too fast for his hand,
In the riding of comfort a mooring to find,
Reef'd the sails of Tom's fortune, that shook in the wind:
He gave him enough through Life's ocean to steer,
Be the breeze what it might, steady, thus, or no near;
His pittance is daily, and yet Tom imparts
What he can to his friends—and may all honest hearts,
Like Tom Tackle, have what keeps the wolf from the
       door,
Just enough to be generous—too much to be poor.

LOVELY NAN.

Sweet is the ship that, under sail,
Spreads her white bosom to the gale;
　　Sweet, oh! sweet the flowing can;
Sweet to poise the labouring oar,
That tugs us to our native shore
　　When the boatswain pipes the barge to man;
Sweet sailing with a fav'ring breeze;
But oh! much sweeter than all these,
　　Is Jack's delight—his lovely Nan!

The needle, faithful to the north,
To show of constancy the worth,
　　A curious lesson teaches man:
The needle time may rust, the squall
Capsize the binnacle and all,
　　Let seamanship do all it can:
My love in worth shall higher rise,
Nor time shall rust, nor squalls capsize,
　　My faith and truth to lovely Nan.

When in the bilboes I was penn'd,
For serving of a worthless friend,
　　And every creature from me ran;
No ship performing quarantine,
Was ever so deserted seen,
　　None hail'd me, woman, child, nor man;
But though false friendship's sails were furl'd,
Though cut adrift by all the world,
　　I'd all the world in lovely Nan.

I love my duty, love my friend,
Love truth and merit to defend,
   To moan their loss who hazard ran;
I love to take an honest part,
Love beauty, with a spotless heart,
   By manners love to show the man;
To sail through life by honour's breeze—
'Twas all along of loving these
   First made me dote on lovely Nan.

THE VETERANS.

Dick Dock, a tar at Greenwich moor'd,
One day had got his beer on board,
When he a poor maim'd pensioner from Chelsea saw;
   And all to have his jeer and flout,
   For the grog once in, the wit's soon out,
Cried, How, good master Lobster, did you loose your claw?
   Was't that time in a drunken fray?
   Or t'other, when you ran away?
But hold you, Dick, the poor soul has one foot in the
      grave;
   'Fore slander's wind too fast you fly;
   D'ye think it fun?—you swab, you lie;
Misfortune ever claim'd the pity of the brave.

Old Hannibal, in words as gross,—
For he, like Dick, had got his dose.—
To try a bout at wrangling quickly took a spell;
   If I'm a Lobster, master Crab,
   By the information on your nab,
In some scrimmage or other, why they crack'd your shell;

THE VETERANS.

And then, why, how you hobbling go
On that jury-mast, your timber toe,
A nice one to find fault, with one foot in the grave
But halt, old Hannibal, halt, halt!
Distress was never yet a fault,
Misfortune ever claim'd the pity of the brave.

If Hannibal's your name, d'ye see,
As sure as they Dick Dock call me,
As once it did fall out, I ow'd my life to you:
Spilt from my horse, once when 'twas dark,
And nearly swallow'd by a shark,
You boldly plunged in, saved me, and pleased all the
crew.
If that's the case, then cease our jeers:
When boarded by the same Mounseers,
You, a true English lion, snatch'd me from the grave,
Cried " Cowards, do the man no harm,
Dam'me, don't you see he's lost his arm?"
Misfortune ever claim'd the pity of the brave.

Then broach a can before we part,
A friendly one, with all our heart,
And as we put the grog about, we'll cheerly sing,
At land and sea may Britons fight,
The world's example and delight,
And conquer every enemy of George our King:
'Tis he that proves the hero's friend,
His bounty waits us to our end,
Though crippled, and laid up, with one foot in the grave;
Then, Tars and Soldiers, never fear,
You shall not want compassion's tear;
Misfortune ever claim'd the pity of the brave.

DELIGHT OF THE BRAVE.

Say, soldier, which of glory's charms,
  That heroes' souls inflame,
Gives brightest lustre to their arms,
  Or best ensures their fame?
Is it her lion-mettled rage,
  Let loose from ardour's den,
Legion with legion to engage,
  And make men slaughter men?
Is it to a defenceless foe,
  Mild mercy to forbear,
And glut the call of vengeance? No!
  The brave delight to spare:
'Tis clemency, pale misery's friend,
  Foremost in glory's van,
To dry the starting tear, and blend
  The hero with the man.

Then on the wretch fall double shame
  Who, in foul slander lored,
Knows war alone by murder's name,
  The soldier by the sword:
As blessings out of evils come,
  Let once the conflict cease,
The eagle brings the halcyon home,
  War courts the smiles of peace:

Yet he to higher merit vaults
　Who glory's track hath trod,
Great generous merit that exalts
　A mortal to a god.
'Tis clemency, pale misery's friend,
　Ever in glory's van,
To dry the starting tear, and blend
　The hero with the man.

JACK JUNK.

'Twas one day at Wapping, his dangers o'erhauling,
　Jack Junk cock'd his jemmy and broach'd a full can,
While a posse of neighbours, of each different calling,
　Cried, Only but hear what a marvellous man.
Avast, cried out Jack, what's there marvellous in it?
　When our time's come the stoutest of hearts must
　　comply.

Why now, you master tallow-chandler, by way of
throwing a little light upon the subject, don't you think
'tis better to be extinguished when one's fighting in
defence of one's king and country, than to stay at home
lingering and go out like the snuff of a candle?

Then like men do your duty, we have all our minute,
And at sea or ashore we shall live till we die,
Hurraw, hurraw, hurraw, boys, let's live till we die.

Why now, you master plumber, that marvels at billows,
　I shall founder at sea, and you'll die in your bed;
What of that? some have sods and some waves for their
　　pillows,
　And 'tis likely enough we may both die of lead:
And as for the odds, all the difference that's in it,
I shall pop off at once, and you'll lingering lie.

Why, smite my crooked timbers, who knows but master Snip, there, may slip his cable and break his back with taking the ninth part of a fall off the shopboard into his own hell.

> Then like men, &c.

As for you, master bricklayer, to make out your calling
  A little like mine e'n't a matter that's hard;
Pray mayn't you from a ladder or scaffold be falling,
  As easy as I from a rattling or yard:
Then, for you, its commission a tile may bring in it,
  As soon as a shot or a splinter for I.

As for master doctor, the undertaker, and sexton—they don't want no wipe from me; they sends too many folks contented to their long home, not to know how to go there contentedly themselves.

> Then like men, &c.

And when Captain Death comes the reck'ning to settle,
  You may clear ship for action as much as you like,
And behave like a man, but he's such weight of mettle,
  At the very first broadside the bravest must strike.
And when you have said all you can, what's there in it?
  Who to scud 'gainst the storm but a lubber would try?

For as to qualms of conscience, cheating customers, betraying friends, and such like, being a set of honest tradesmen, I dare say you are perfectly easy about they sort of things.

> Then like men, &c.

TOM TRUELOVE'S KNELL.

Tom Truelove woo'd the sweetest fair
  That e'er to tar was kind,
Her face was of a beauty rare,
  More beautiful her mind.
His messmates heard ; while with delight
  He named her for his bride,
A sail appear'd, ah, fatal sight !
  For grief his love had died.
Must I, cried he, those charms resign,
  I loved so dear, so well ?
Would they had toll'd, instead of thine,
  Tom Truelove's knell.

Break heart at once, and there's an end,
  Thou all that heaven could give !
But, hold ! I have a noble friend—
  Yet, yet for him I'll live.
Fortune, who all her baleful spite
  Not yet on Tom had tried,
Sent news, one rough, tempestuous night,
  That his dear friend had died.
And thou too ! must I thee resign,
  Who honour loved so well ?
Would they had toll'd, instead of thine,
  Tom Truelove's knell.

Enough, enough, a salt-sea wave
  A healing balm shall bring ;
A sailor you, cried one, and brave ?
  Live still to serve your king !

The moment comes, behold the foe—
   Thanks, generous friend, he cried :
The second broadside laid him low ;
   He named his love, and died.
The tale, in mournful accents sung,
   His friends still sorrowing tell,
How, sad and solemn, three times rung
   Tom Truelove's knell.

THE SAILOR'S JOURNAL.

'Twas post meridian, half-past four,
   By signal I from Nancy parted,
At six she linger'd on the shore,
   With uplift hands and broken-hearted.
At seven, while taughtening the forestay,
   I saw her faint, or else 'twas fancy ;
At eight we all got under weigh,
   And bid a long adieu to Nancy!

Night came, and now eight bells had rung,
   While careless sailors, ever cheary,
On the mid watch so jovial sung,
   With tempers labour cannot weary.
I, little to their mirth inclined,
   While tender thoughts rush'd on my fancy,
And my warm sighs increased the wind,
   Look'd on the moon, and thought of Nancy!

And now arrived that jovial night
   When every true-bred tar carouses ;
When, o'er the grog, all hands delight
   To toast their sweethearts and their spouses.

Round went the can, the jest, the glee,
　　While tender wishes fill'd each fancy;
And when, in turn, it came to me,
　　I heaved a sigh, and toasted Nancy!

Next morn a storm came on at four,
　　At six the elements in motion
Plunged me and three poor sailors more
　　Headlong within the foaming ocean.
Poor wretches! they soon found their graves;
　　For me—it may be only fancy,—
But love seem'd to forbid the waves
　　To snatch me from the arms of Nancy!

Scarce the foul hurricane was clear'd,
　　Scarce winds and waves had ceased to rattle,
When a bold enemy appear'd,
　　And, dauntless, we prepared for battle.
And now, while some loved friend or wife
　　Like light'ning rush'd on every fancy,
To Providence I trusted life,
　　Put up a prayer, and thought of Nancy!

At last,—'twas in the month of May,—
　　The crew, it being lovely weather,
At three A. M. discover'd day
　　And England's chalky cliffs together.
At seven up Channel how we bore,
　　While hopes and fears rush'd on my fancy,
At twelve I gaily jump'd ashore,
　　And to my throbbing heart press'd Nancy!

WHO CARES?

If lubberly landsmen, to gratitude strangers,
  Still curse their unfortunate stars,
Why, what would they say, did they try but the dangers
  Encounter'd by true-hearted tars?
If life's vessel they put 'fore the wind, or they tack her,
  Or whether bound here or there,
Give 'em sea-room, good fellowship, grog, and tobacker,
  Well then, damme if Jack cares where.

Then your stupid Old Quidnuncs, to hear them all
      clatter,
  The devil can't tell you what for,
Though they don't know a gun from a marlinspike,
      chatter
  About and concerning of war.
While for king, wife, and friend, he's through every-
      thing rubbing,
  With duty still proud to comply,
So he gives but the foes of Old England a drubbing,
  Why then, damme if Jack cares why.

And then, when good fortune has crown'd his endeavours,
  And he comes home with shiners galore,
Well, what if so be he should lavish his favours
  On every poor object 'long shore?
Since money's the needle that points to good nature,
  Friend, enemy, false, or true,
So it goes to relieve a distress'd fellow-creature,
  Well then, damme if Jack cares who.

Don't you see how some diff'rent thing ev'ry one's
    twigging,
  To take the command of a rib,
Some are all for the breast-work, and some for the rig-
    ging,
  And some for the cut of her jib.
Though poor, some will take her in tow, to defend her,
  And again, some are all for the rich;
As to I, so she's young, her heart honest and tender,
  Why, then, damme if Jack cares which.

Why now, if they go for to talk about living,
  My eyes—why a little will serve:
Let each a small part of his pittance be giving,
  And who in this nation can starve?
Content's all the thing—rough or calm be the weather,
  The wind on the beam or the bow;
So honestly he can splice both ends together,
  Why then, damme if Jack cares how.

And then for a bring-up, d'ye see, about dying,
  On which such a racket they keep,
What argufies if in a churchyard you're lying,
  Or find out your grave in the deep?
Of one thing we're certain, whatever our calling,
  Death will bring us all up—and what then?
So his conscience's tackle will bear overhauling,
  Why then, damme if Jack cares when.

ALL GIRLS.

No more of waves and winds the sport,
Our vessel is arrived in port ;
At anchor see she safely rides,
And gay red ropes adorn her sides ;
The sails are furl'd, the sheets belay'd,
The crimson petticoat's display'd,
Deserted are the useless shrouds,
And wenches come aboard in crowds.
Then come, my lads, the flip put round,
While safely moor'd on English ground,
    With a jorum of diddle,
    A lass and a fiddle,
Ne'er shall care in the heart of a tar be found :
And, while upon the hollow deck,
   To the sprightly jig our feet shall bound,
Take each his charmer round the neck,
    And kiss in time to the merry sound.

Bess hears the death of honest Jack,
Who swore he'd safe and sound come back ;
She calls him scurvy, lying swab,
And then she kindly takes to Bob.
Ben asks the news of bonny Kate,
Who said she'd prove a constant mate ;
But winds and girls are false, for she
Took Ned the morn Ben went to sea.
Well, come, says Ben, the flip put round,
While safely moor'd on English ground,
    With a jorum of diddle,
    A lass and a fiddle,
Ne'er shall care in the heart of a tar be found :

George Cruikshank.

TARS CAROUSING.

And while, upon the hollow deck,
 To the sprightly jig our feet shall bound,
Take each his charmer round the neck,
 And kiss in time to the merry sound.

By will and power, when last ashore,
His rhino Tom to Poll made o'er;
Poll touch'd the prize-money and pay,
And with the agent ran away:
And Jenny, just as 'cute a trick,
His back once turn'd, play'd whistling Dick;
Dick left her clothes to cut a flash,
She sold 'em all and spent the cash.
But come, says Dick, the flip put round,
While safely moor'd on English ground,
  With a jorum of diddle,
  A lass and a fiddle,
Ne'er shall care in the heart of a tar be found;
And while, upon the hollow deck, &c.

While feet and tongues like light'ning go,
With—What cheer, Suke? and How do, Joe?
Dick Laniard chooses Peg so spruce,
And buxom Nell takes Kit Caboose.
Thus, 'mongst the girls they left behind,
A lot of true and false they find;
While they bewail those shot or drown'd,
And welcome home the safe and sound;
Still thankful, while the flip goes round,
They're safely moor'd on English ground,
  With a jorum of diddle,
  A lass and a fiddle,
Ne'er shall care in the heart of a tar be found:
And while, upon the hollow deck, &c.

H

MOORINGS.

I've heard, cried out one, that you tars tack and tack,
  And at sea what strange hardships befel you;
But I don't know what's moorings. What, don't you?
      said Jack;
  Man your ear-tackle, then, and I'll tell you:—
Suppose you'd a daughter quite beautiful grown,
  And, in spite of her prayers and implorings,
Some scoundrel abused her, and you knock'd him down,
  Why, d'ye see, he'd be safe at his moorings.

In life's voyage should you trust a false friend with the
      helm,
  The top-lifts of his heart all akimbo,
A tempest of treachery your bark will o'erwhelm,
  And your moorings will soon be in limbo;
But if his heart's timbers bear up against pelf,
  And he's just in his reckonings and scorings,
He'll for you keep a look-out the same as himself,
  And you'll find in his friendship safe moorings.

If wedlock's your port, and your mate, true and kind,
  In all weathers will stick to her duty,
A calm of contentment shall beam in your mind,
  Safe moor'd in the haven of beauty:
But if some frisky skiff, crank at every joint,
  That listens to vows and adorings,
Shape your course how you will, still you'll make Cuck-
      old's Point,
  To lay up a beacon at moorings.

A glutton's safe moor'd, head and stern, by the gout,
   A drunkard's moor'd under the table,
In straws drowning men will Hope's anchor find out,
   While a hare's a philosopher's cable:
Thus mankind are a ship, life a boisterous main,
   Of Fate's billows where all hear the roarings,
Where for one calm of pleasure we've ten storms of pain,
   Till death brings us all to our moorings.

SUFFERINGS PAST.

THOUGH hard the valiant soldiers' life,
   They some sweet moments know;
Joy ne'er was yet unmix'd with strife,
   Nor happiness with woe.
'Tis hard when friend, when children, wife,
   Reluctant from him part,
While fancy paints the muffled drum,
   The mournful fife,
And the loud volley o'er his grave,
The solemn requiem to the brave:
    All this he hears,
    Yet calms their fears
With smiles while horror's in his heart:
But when the smiling hour shall come,
   To bring him home at last,
How sweet his constant wife to greet,
   His children, friends,
And in their circling arms to find amends
   For all his sufferings past.

'Tis hard when, desolation spread,
   Death whirls the rapid car,
And those invaded hear and dread
   The thunder of the war :
Ah! then, indeed, friend, children, wife,
   Have you true cause to fear!
Too soon, alas! the muffled drum,
   The mournful fife,
And the loud volley o'er the grave
   Shall sound sad requiems to the brave,
     While those alive
     Faint joy revive,
And blend Hope's smile with Pity's tear :
But when the smiling hour shall come
   To bring him home at last,
How sweet his constant wife to greet,
   His children, friends,
And in their circling arms to find amends
   For all his sufferings past.

COMELY NED.

Give ear to me, both high and low,
   And, while you mourn hard fate's decree,
Lament a tale right full of woe
   Of comely Ned that died at sea.
His father was a commodore,
   His king and country served had he ;
But now his tears in torrents pour
   For comely Ned that died at sea.

His sister Peg her brother loved,
   For a right tender heart had she,
And often to strong grief was moved
   For comely Ned that died at sea.
His sweetheart Grace, once blythe and gay,
   That led the dance upon the lea,
Now wastes in tears the' lingering day
   For comely Ned that died at sea.

His friends, who loved his manly worth
   (For none more friends could boast than he),
To mourn now lay aside their mirth
   For comely Ned that died at sea.
Come then and join, with friendly tear,
   The song that, midst of all our glee,
We from our hearts chant once a-year
   For comely Ned that died at sea.

NANCY DEAR.

WHY should the sailor take a wife,
   Since he was born to roam,
And lead at sea a wand'ring life,
   Far from his friends and home?
When fate comes riding in the gale,
And dreadful hurricanes assail
   The tar's astonish'd ear,
How could he resolution form,
How, whistling, mock the roaring storm,
   But for his Nancy dear?

For battle should the ship be clear'd,
   As death when all is still,
Save from some tar a murmuring's heard,
   Who sighs and makes his will :—
" My watch, my 'bacco-pouch, I give
To Tom for her, should I not live,
   To my fond heart so near."
Nor could he smile, the fight grown hot,
And, whistling, mock the flying shot,
   But for his Nancy dear.

When hissing flames now reach the sky,
   Now in the ocean dip,
And, as to climb the shrouds they fly,
   Grasp the devoted ship ;—
How, while a yawning watery grave,
Sole chance from fire the crew to save,
   Threats, could he calm appear?
How quit the vessel, scarce afloat—
How, whistling, board the crowded boat,
   But for his Nancy dear?

When shipwreck'd many leagues from home,
   The remnant of the crew
Bewail some Dick, or Jack, or Tom,
   Whom well they loved and knew:
And, while by strangers kindly fed,
Who, as they hear the story, spread
   Their hospitable cheer,—
How could he on such misery think,
Yet, whistling, put about the drink,
   But for his Nancy dear?

And last, when hungry, faint, and sore,
  Through danger and delay,
Forced, hard extreme! from door to door,
  To beg his vagrant way. ·
But see, his toils are all forgot;
Hark, hark! within her humble cot,
  In accents sweet and clear,
She sings the subject of her pain,
He, whistling, echoes back the strain
  He taught his Nancy dear.

JACK'S CLAIM TO POLL.

Would'st know, my lad, why every tar
  Finds with his lass such cheer?
'Tis all because he nobly goes
  And braves each boist'rous gale that blows,
To fetch, from climates near and far,
  Her messes and her gear:
For this around the world sails Jack,
  While love his bosom warms;
For this, when safe and sound come back,
  Poll takes him to her arms.

Ere Poll can make the kettle boil
  For breakfast, out at sea
Two voyages long her Jack must sail,
  Encountering many a boisterous gale,
For the sugar to some western isle,
  To China for the tea.
To please her taste thus faithful Jack
  Braves dangers and alarms;
While grateful, safe and sound come back,"
  Poll takes him to her arms.

Morocco shoes her Jack provides
  To see her lightly tread;
Her petticoat of orient hue
  And snow-white gown in India grew;
Her bosom Barcelona hides,
  Leghorn adorns her head.
Thus round the world sails faithful Jack
  To deck his fair one's charms;
Thus grateful, safe and sound come back,
  Poll takes him to her arms.

THE LADS OF THE VILLAGE.

WHILE the lads of the village shall merrily ah,
  Sound their tabors, I'll hand thee along;
And I say unto thee, that, verily ah,
  Thou and I will be first in the throng.

Just then, when the youth who last year won the dow'r
  And his mate shall the sports have begun,
When the gay voice of gladness resounds from each
    bow'r,
  And thou long'st in thy heart to make one;
    While the lads, &c.

Those joys that are harmless what mortal can blame?
  'Tis my maxim that youth should be free;
And to prove that my words and my deeds are the same,
  Believe thou shalt presently see;
    While the lads, &c.

THE SAILOR'S MAXIM.

OF us tars 'tis reported again and again,
That we sail round the world yet know nothing of men;
And, if this assertion is made with a view
To prove sailors know nought of men's follies, 'tis true;
How should Jack practise treachery, disguise, or foul art,
In whose honest face you may read his fair heart?
Of that maxim still ready example to give,
Better death earn'd with honour than ignobly to live.

How can *he* wholesome truth's admonitions defy,
On whose manly brow never sat a foul lie?
Of the fair born protector, how virtue offend?
To a foe how be cruel? how ruin a friend?
If danger he risk in professional strife,
There his honour is safe though he venture his life;
Of that maxim still ready example to give,
Better death earn'd with honour than ignobly to live.

But to put it at worst, from fair truth could he swerve,
And betray the kind friend he pretended to serve,
While snares laid with craft his fair honour trepan,
Man betray him to error, himself but a man:
Should repentance and shame to his aid come too late,
Wonder not if in battle he rush on his fate;
Of that maxim still ready example to give,
Better death earn'd with honour than ignobly to live.

MEG OF WAPPING.

'Twas landlady Meg that made such rare flip;
　Pull away, pull away, hearties!
At Wapping she lived, at the sign of the Ship,
　Where tars meet in such jolly parties.
She'd shine at the play, and she'd jig at the ball,
　All rigg'd out so gay and so topping;
For she married six husbands, and buried them all,—
　Pull away, pull away, pull away! I say;
What d'ye think of my Meg of Wapping?

The first was Old Bluff, with a swingeing purse;
　Pull away, pull away, jolly boys!
He was cast away. Said Meg, Who cares a curse?
　As for grieving, why, Lord, that's a folly, boys!
The second in command was blear-eyed Ned:
　While the surgeon his limb was a lopping,
A nine-pounder came, and smack went his head,—
　Pull away, pull away, pull away! I say;
Rare news for my Meg of Wapping!

Then she married to Sam, and Sam loved a sup;
　Pull away, pull away, brother!
So groggy Sam got, and the ship he blew up,
　And Meg had to look for another.

MᶜEG OF WAPPING.

The fourth was bold Ben, who at danger would smile,
  'Till his courage a crocodile stopping,
Made his breakfast on Ben on the banks of the Nile ;—
  Pull away, pull away, pull away! I say;
What a fortunate Meg of Wapping!

Stay, who was the fifth? Oh, 'twas Dick so neat;
  Pull away, pull away, so merry!
And the savages Dick both kill'd and eat,
  And poor Meg she was forced to take Jerry.
Death again stood her friend, for, kill'd in a fray,
  He also the grave chanced to pop in;
So now with my song I shall soon belay ;—
  Pull away, pull away, pull away! Belay!
The six husbands of Meg of Wapping.

But I didn't tell you how that she married seven;
  Pull away, pull away, no neatly!
'Twas honest Tom Trip, and he sent her to heaven,
  And her strong box rummaged sweetly;
For Meg, growing old, a fond dotard proved,
  And must after a boy needs be hopping;
So she popp'd off, and Tom, with the girl that he loved:
  Pull away, pull away, pull away! I say—
Spent the shiners of Meg of Wapping.

POOR SHIPWRECK'D TAR.

Escaped with life, in tatters,
　Behold me safe ashore;
Such trifles little matters,
　I'll soon get togs galore:
For Poll swore when we parted
　No chance her faith should jar,
And Poll's too tender hearted
　To slight a Shipwreck'd Tar.

To Poll his course straight steering,
　He hastens on apace;
Poor Jack can't get a hearing,—
　She never saw his face.
From Meg, Doll, Sue, and Kitty,
　Relief is just as far.
Not one has the least pity
　For a poor Shipwreck'd Tar.

This, whom he thought love's needle,
　Now his sad misery mocks,
That wants to call the beadle
　To set him in the stocks.
Cried Jack, This is hard dealing;
　The elements at war
Than this had kinder feeling—
　They spared a Shipwreck'd Tar.

But all their taunts and fetches
   A judgment are on me;
I, for these harden'd wretches,
   Dear Nancy, slighted thee.
But see, poor Tray assails me,
   His mistress is not far,
He wags his tail and hails me,
   Though a poor Shipwreck'd Tar.

'Twas faithful love that brought him,—
   Oh, lesson for mankind!
'Tis one, cried she, I taught him;
   For on my constant mind
Thine image, dear, was graven;
   And now, removed each bar,
My arms shall be the haven
   For my poor Shipwreck'd Tar.

Heaven and my love reward thee!
   I'm shipwreck'd, but I'm rich;
All shall with pride regard thee,—
   Thy love shall so bewitch
With wonder each fond fancy,
   That children near and far
Shall lisp the name of Nancy,
   Who saved her Sihpwrecked Tar!

A DOSE FOR THE DON.

DEARLY as the stream that guides its vital motion,
   Be cherish'd by each grateful British heart
The great event that gave the lordly ocean
   To English tars fresh laurels to impart.
     Valentine's-day in smiles came on,
     Love fill'd the seaman's anxious mind,
     Delighted with past scenes so sweet,
While ardent hope kept every pulse alive,
Sweet hope some glorious moment might arrive,
   To serve the wife and king and friend he left behind,
     When Jervis, with his gallant fleet,
   Discover'd the proud Don.

Strange signal-guns all night distinctly hearing,
   When day's faint dawn presented first the shore,
We, anxious, on the starboard tack were steering,
   While east by north eight leagues Cape Vincent
       bore.
     Near ten, propitious hope came on;
     Our signal for a large fleet flew;
     When instant with a press of sail,
Form'd in two lines, onward we gaily stood;
Till boldly dashing through the yielding flood,
   While honour fired each ship's determined crew,
     We proudly bore up within hail
   Of the astonish'd Don.

Ships twenty-seven now bid a bold defiance;
 Fifteen our number, and of smaller size.
So towering elephants look down on lions,
 Till of their courage they become the prize.
  For now the trying hour came on,
  That each must act a gallant part;
  Fate on one grand manœuvre hinged,—
One mighty stroke, prompt, dangerous, and bold.
But what of English tars the courage can withhold?
 We broke their straggling line, scared every heart,
  And Jack the tawny whiskers singed
 Of the astonish'd Don.

Here might I dwell on this unequall'd action
 That soars beyond example out of sight,—
That gain'd four ships—that broke a dangerous faction;
 But English seamen never brag,—they fight.
  Then let perfidious France come on,
  Aided by Holland and by Spain,
  In the deep a watery grave to meet.
Fair England proudly with one voice shall sing
The worth and virtues of a patriot king;
 While some such heroes lead the glorious strain
  As Jervis and his gallant fleet,
 That humbled the proud Don.

JERVIS FOR EVER!

 I've sail'd the salt seas pretty much,
  And rough'd it in all weathers,
 The French, the Spanish, and the Dutch,
  To buckle to their tethers.

And in these voyages I must need,
  You see, have known some service;
But all I've know'd and all I've seed
  Is now outdone by Jervis!

You've heard, I s'pose, the people talk
  Of Benbow and Boscawen,
Of Anson, Pocock, Vernon, Hawke,
  And many more then going;
All pretty lads, and brave, and rum,
  That seed much noble service;
But, Lord, their merit's all a hum,
  Compared to Admiral Jervis!

Now there's the famous ninety-two,
  That made so great a bustle,
When the Rising Sun and her whole crew
  Were all sent down by Russell:
A glorious sight, I've heard them say,
  And pretty was the service,
But not like that on Voluntun's-day,
  Led on by valiant Jervis!

Bold Rodney did the kingdom thank
  For that brush in the West Indies,
And Parker, on the Dogger Bank,
  The Dutch beat off the hinges.
Van Tromp said how he'd sweep the sea,
  'Till Blake show'd him some service;
Fine fellows all, but don't tell me
  That they're the likes of Jervis!

Howe made the Frenchmen dance a tune,
   An admiral great and glorious—
Witness for that the first of June,
   Lord, how he was victorious!
A noble sight as e'er was seen,
   And did the country service;
But twenty-seven beat with fifteen
   None ever did but Jervis!

As for that same equality,
   That this battle well was fighted,
In England, high and low degree
   Are equally delighted.
'Tis in the mouths of all one meets,
   All praise this noble service;
And ballad-singers in the streets
   Roars—Admirable Jervis!

They say that he's become a lord,
   At his Majesty's desire;
He always was a king aboard,—
   How can they lift him higher?
'Tis noble, that must be confess'd,
   And suits such worthy service;
But the title he'll be known by best
   Will be—gallant Admiral Jervis!

To Thompson let the bumbo pass,
   Grey, Parker, Walgrave, Caulder,—
Nelson, that took St. Nicholas,—
   My timbers, how he maul'd her!

I

But we a freight of grog might start,
    To drink all on that service,—
Here's blessings on each noble heart
    That fought with valiant Jervis!

And bless the king, and bless the queen,
    And bless the fam'ly royal;
Let Frenchmen come, 'twill soon be seen
    That British hearts are loyal.
Let Dutch and Spaniards join their hosts,
    They'll see some pretty service;
Zounds! who's afraid, while England boasts
    Such Admirals as Jervis?

THE NANCY.

MAYHAP you have heard that as dear as their lives
All true-hearted tars love their ships and their wives;
To their duty like pitch sticking close till they die,
And whoe'er wants to know it I'll tell 'em for why:—
One through dangers and storms brings me safely ashore,
T'other welcomes me home when my danger is o'er;
Both smoothing the ups and the downs of this life,
For my ship's called the Nancy, and Nancy's my wife.

When Nancy my wife o'er the lawn scuds so neat
And so light, the proud grass scarcely yields to her feet,
So rigg'd out and so lovely, t'ent easy to trace
Which is reddest—her top-knot, her shoes, or her face;

While the neighbours, to see her, forget all their cares,
And are pleased that she's mine, though they wish she
   was theirs.
Marvel not, then, to think of this joy of my life—
I my ship calls the Nancy, for Nancy's my wife.

As for Nancy my vessel, but see her in trim,
She seems through the ocean to fly, and not swim ;
'Fore the wind, like a dolphin, she merrily plays,
She goes anyhow well, but she looks best in stays.
Scudding, trying, or tacking, 'tis all one to she,
Mountain high, or sunk low in the trough of the sea ;
She has saved me from many hard squeaks for my life,
So I call'd her the Nancy, 'cause Nancy's my wife.

When so sweet in the dance careless glides my heart's
   queen,
She sets out, and sets in, far the best on the green ;
So, of all the grand fleet my gay vessel's the flower,
She outsails the whole tote by a knot in an hour.
Then they both sail so cheerful through life's varying breeze,
All hearts with such pilots must be at their ease ;
Thus I've two good protectors to watch me through life,
My good ship the Nancy, and Nancy my wife.

Then these hands from protecting them who shall debar ?
Ne'er ingratitude lurk'd in the heart of a tar ;
Why, everything female from peril to save
Is the noblest distinction that honours the brave.
While a rag, or a timber, or compass I boast,
I'll protect the dear creatures against a whole host ;
Still grateful to both to the end of my life,—
My good ship the Nancy, and Nancy my wife.

DUNCAN AND VICTORY!

Again the willing trump of fame,
Receives from bounteous heav'n a claim,
Around glad nature's sons to call,
And wake with wonder the terrestrial ball :
Strike shuddering France and harrow'd Spain
With Duncan's thunder, and Britannia's reign,
Confirm'd anew her empire o'er the main.
Sing, Britons, sing, prizing what fate has given,
 Union,content, and gratitude to heav'n !

October the eleventh, at nine,
Neptune beheld the British line ;
And, lest his honours, so long worn,
Should from our ever-conquering flag be torn,
Dismay to France, horror to Spain,
Bad Duncan's thunder great Britannia's reign
Proclaim anew—the sovereign of the main !
    Sing, Britons, sing, &c.

Fate warr'd on that momentous day,—
Three hours nine ships saw captured lay ;
Vain Holland's dream of power's no more !
Her conquer'd fleet shall grace the British shore.
Droop, fearful France ! sink, trembling Spain !
Duncan, in thunder, great Britannia's reign
Proclaims anew—the sovereign of the main !
    Sing, Britons, sing, &c.

A SALT EEL FOR MYNHEER.

WHY, Jack, my fine fellow, here's glorious news,—
   Lord, I could have told 'em as much,
That the devil himself durst not stand in their shoes,
   If Duncan fell in with the Dutch !
What heart in the kingdom can now feel dismay ?
   Nine sail of the line ! not amiss :
While they shrug up their shoulders and snuff it away,
   How the mounseers will jabber at this.
No ! while English bosoms boast English hearts,
   We'll tip 'em all a round touch,
While with ardour each starts that nothing can quench,
      We'll bang the Spaniards,
      Belabour the Dutch,
   And block up and laugh at the French.

Now the French, while in harbour so snug and so sly,
   'Bout their courage they make a fine rout;
If they'd have the whole world not believe it a lie,
   Then, damme, why don't they come out?
Because, though they brag that so boldly they feel,
   They are all of them trembling for fear,
Lest from Bridport they get such another salt eel
   As brave Duncan prepared for Mynheer.
      For while, &c.

Let French, Spanish, and Dutch, lay together their heads,
   And of beating the English brag,
That they'll sail up the Thames, take us all in our beds,
   And hoist on the Tower their flag.

" Oui, oui," cries Mounseer, " Si, signor," says the Don,
  Mynheer smokes his pipe and cries " Yaw ;"
But when Jervis, or Duncan, or Bridport come on,
  They are damnably sick in the craw.
      No, while, &c.

Your true honest maxim I've heard 'em commend
  Is the nation you live in to sing;
Where your property, children, your wife, and your
      friend,
  Are the care of their father the king.
The man, then, so blest, who disseminates strife,
  Deserves, while he sinks in disgrace,
Neither king to protect him, to love him a wife,
  Nor children to smile in his face.
      No, while, &c.

WELL IT'S NO WORSE.

I WENT to sea all so fearlessly,
Broach'd my grog all so carelessly,
By and by, in a brush, I lost my arm,
    Tol de rol, de rol de ri !
    So, says I,
'Twas well 'twas no worse harm :
Man's but man, and there's an end ;
    And since 'tis so,
    E'en let it go ;
I ne'er shall lift it 'gainst a friend.

Next, a squall a tempest led off,
Enough to blow the devil's head off;
I got spilt, and that way lost my leg:
  Tol de rol, de rol de ri!
  So, says I,
I must now be forced to beg.
Well, man's but man, that's all I say;
  So in this plight,
  If I can't fight,
For certain I can't run away.

So, as if Old Nick was in it,
Something happen'd every minute,
Till, at last, poor I! they doused my glims;
  Tol de rol, de rol de ri!
  So, says I,
Why, I've lost my eyes and limbs.
Well, the sails of life by time are furl'd!
  'Twas fate's decree,
  That I may'nt see
The treachery of this wicked world.

Things grew worser still and worser;
Fortune, I had cause to curse her;
Coming home, I found I'd lost my wife:
  Tol de rol, de rol de ri!
  So, says I,
I'd rather lost my life:
But we're all mortal—she was old;
  Then why take on?
  If so be she's gone,
I ne'er again shall hear her scold.

Now laid up in Greenwich quarter,
Chatham chest my right, by charter,
Being old, I've lost all but my tongue :
    Tol de rol, de rol de ri!
    So, says I,
'Twas not so when I was young ;
But, then, says I again, you dunce !
    Be fear afar
    From every tar ;
Damme, a man can die but once !

ALL'S ONE TO JACK.

THOUGH mountains high the billows roll,
And angry ocean's in a foam,
The sailor gaily slings the bowl,
And thinks on her he left at home :
Kind love his guardian spirit still,
His mind's made up, come what come will;
Tempests may masts to splinters tear,
Sails and rigging go to rack,
So she loves him he loves so dear,
    'Tis all one to Jack.

His friend in limbo should he find,
His wife and children brought to shame,
To everything but kindness blind,
Jack signs his ruin with his name.

Friendship the worthy motive still,
His mind's made up, come what come will;
The time comes round, by hell-hounds press'd,
Goods, clothes, and person go to rack;
But, since, he succour'd the distress'd,
  'Tis all one to Jack.

Once more at sea prepared to fight,
A friendly pledge, round goes the can;
And though large odds appear in sight,
He meets the danger like a man:
Honour his guardian spirit still,
His mind's made up, come what come will;
Like some fierce lion, see him go
Where horror grim marks the attack!
So he can save a drowning foe,
  'Tis all one to Jack.

And when at last (for tars and kings
Must find in death a peaceful home)
The shot its sure commission brings,
And of poor Jack the time is come,—
Cheerful his duty to fulfil,
His mind's made up, come what come will;
The cannon's poised, from its fell jaws
A fatal shot takes him aback;
But since he died in honour's cause,
  'Twas all one to Jack.

BRITONS UNITED.

THE French are all coming, for so they declare,
Of their floats and balloons all the papers advise us ;
They're to swim through the ocean and ride on the air,
In some foggy evening, to land and surprise us :
Their army's to come and plant liberty's tree,
Call'd the army of England, what matchless presumption!
Let them come ; those who meet not with agues at sea
Will on shore first get fevers and then a consumption :
Poor fools ! by the finger of fate they're invited,
      For our freedom and laws
      Come on, in this cause,
They no longer are Britons who are not united.

The old women and children report such strange things
Of their grand preparations, their routs, and their rackets,
One army they tell us is furnish'd with wings,
And another's accoutred, they say, in cork jackets !
Well, so much the better : their luck let 'em try ;
Come here how they will we shall damnably nim 'em :
'Tent the first time, my lads, we have made the French fly ;
And as for their jackets, we'll curiously trim 'em.
      Poor fools, &c.

Then they'll fasten a rope from the Land's-End to France,
On which, when their wonderful project's grown riper,
They'll all to the tune of the carmagnol dance,
Determined to make Jack Rosbiff pay the piper.

But let 'em take care we don't come athawt hause:
If we should, they'll just fancy the devil has got 'em,
For they'll get from their horses so decent a toss,
That capsiz'd will soon send them a dance to the bottom,
    Poor fools, &c.

Yet who knows how far their mad liberty scheme
May succeed? of man's wrongs the supposed panacea;
They have often come here, kill'd us all in a dream,
And afterwards eat us all up—in idea.
And let 'em dream on that they're cutting our throats,
'Till, devoted to danger they're little aware on,
They wake from their sleep, change their flat-bottom'd
    boats
For a voyage o'er the Styx in the boat of old Charon.
    Poor fools, &c.

But jesting apart, we their pride must chastise,
Though we'd no other hold on our hearts and our duty
Than their insolent boast that they'll seize as their prize,
In their purse English gold, in their arms English beauty;
English beauty for them! The infernals scaled Heaven,
That soon hurl'd to fate their audacious malignity;
So shall they, to their fate by a virtuous frown driven,
Own that females of Britain possess British dignity.
    Poor fools, &c.

Then rouse, Britons, rouse! while this vapouring crew
Are deluding their own and belying our nation,
Let us noble, unanimous, loyal, and true,
To their folly give pity, their threats indignation.

Our freedom's not riot, nor uproar run wild,
To honour, to virtue, to dignity treason;
A rational blessing, just, temp'rate, and mild;
The freedom of England's the freedom of reason.
        Poor fools, &c.

CHANGE FOR A GUINEA.

JACK BINACLE met with an old shipmate
  That sail'd with him board of the Thunder,
And they talk'd of their pranks at a pretty round rate,
  And made all the hearkeners wonder:
For though brave at sea, when you get him ashore,
  A tar often turns out a ninny,
      For now he must jog,
      His leave's out with his grog;
Here, house, what's to pay? come sport us the score,
  Hand us over the change for a guinea:
For a sailor's life is a roaring life,
He laughs while the winds and the waves are at strife,
      So safe on shore
      He can pay his score,
  And sport the splendid guinea.

The landlord's sweet daughter now comes in his view,
  Up to tars when they get into harbour;
Her shoes are morocco, her petticoat's blue,
  Her wig's just come home from the barber:

Jack stares in her face with a whimsical phiz,
  Reviews her, and looks like a ninny,
      For each chalk on his score
        She counts two or more,
He fix'd on her eyes, while she penetrates his,
And cheats him while changing his guinea :
For a sailor's life is a careless life,
He sings while the waves and the winds are at strife,
      To be cheated on shore,
      While to pay his score
He sports the splendid guinea.

Here's two eighteen-pen'orths, that's five and a kick,—
  Three pen'orths of 'bacco, a shilling,
For a sixpenny 'bacco-box, quite span and spick,
Half a crown, and a tizzy the filling;
Jack hears not a word, chucks her under the chin,—
  Lord, how can you be such a ninny?
      Let me reckon your score,—
      For two sixpen'orths more,
Two hogs and three simons for what's to come in,
  So there's three shillings out of a guinea :
For a sailor's life is a roaring life,
He whistles while billows and winds are at strife,
      From the landlords 'long shore,
      For a five-shilling score,
To get three shillings out of a guinea.

Well, well, cries out Jack, you know figures and such,
  I dare say you're right, mistress Moggy ;
All my wonderment is we should tip off so much
  In the time, and yet never get groggy :

But no sailor at toss-pot e'er yet play'd amiss,
 Then he's cunning and never a ninny ;
   Come, put round the grog,
   For away we must jog,
So now, my dear girl, if you'll give me a kiss,
 You may pocket your change for a guinea.
For a sailor's life is a careless life,
He minds neither billows nor winds at strife,
   But pays his score
   With spirit on shore,
 And that's all the use of a guinea.

NELSON AND WARREN.

I SAY, my heart, why here's your works !
 The French have it now with the gravy ;
Why, what between the English and Turks,
 They'll lose both their army and navy.
Bold Nelson went out with determinate view
 To keep up our national glory ;
So of thirteen large ships he left Mounseer but two
 Just to tell the Directory the story.
Then of England and England's brave tars let us sing,
 As true as the keel to the kelson ;
Let's be loyal to honour, to truth, and the king,
 And drink to the Navy and Nelson.

To destroy, burn, and sink his orders were,
 And by heart he so perfectly got 'em,
That some he took, some blow'd up in the air,
 And some he sent to the bottom.

So you see the despatches was easily stow'd,
   'Twas no use with a history to charge 'em ;
He'd occasion for only the old-fashion mode,
   Taken, burnt, and destroy'd as per marjum.
       Then of England, &c.

So, ship to ship, was next the word ;
   Master Brueys, how sweet they did sarve him !
For when a bold Briton sits down to his bird,
   He pretty well knows how to carve him :
Thus with one of his precious limbs shot away,
   Bold Nelson know'd well how to nick 'em ;
So as for the French, 'tis as much as to say
   We can tie up one hand and lick 'em.
       Then of England, &c.

But with France 'tis all up, they are meeting their fate ;
   They've thrown down their basket of crockery,
And vengeance like this will o'ertake soon or late,
   All who make of religion a mockery.
Then of England, that wonderful country, sing,
   Where we've thousands of joy, if we need 'em ;
Mild laws that protect us, a Protestant King,
   Lovely women, grog, biscuit, and freedom.
       Then of England, &c.

But while we're about it, let's loudly blend
   The names of bold Nelson and Warren,
And be thankful to heav'n there must soon be an end
   To wars both domestic and foreign.
While fame shall sing out the glad news with a smile,
   Let the thundering roar of our cannon
Speak our valorous acts, from the mouth of the Nile,
   All the way to the banks of the Shannon.

TRUE COURAGE.

Why, what's that to you, if my eyes I'm a wiping?
 A tear is a pleasure, d'ye see, in its way;
'Tis nonsense for trifles, I own, to be piping;
 But they that han't pity, why I pities they.
Says the captain, says he (I shall never forget it),
 "If of courage you'd know, lads, the true from the
  sham,
'Tis a furious lion in battle, so let it,
 But, duty appeased, 'tis in mercy a lamb."

There was bustling Bob Bounce, for the old one not
  caring,
 Helter skelter, to work, pelt away, cut and drive;
Swearing he, for his part, had no notion of sparing,
 And as for a foe, why he'd eat him alive.
But when that he found an old prisoner he'd wounded,
 That once saved his life as near drowning he swam,
The lion was tamed, and, with pity confounded,
 He cried over him just all as one as a lamb.

That my friend Jack or Tom I should rescue from
  danger,
 Or lay my life down for each lad in the mess,
Is nothing at all,—'tis the poor wounded stranger,
 And the poorer the more I shall succour distress:
For however their duty bold tars may delight in,
 And peril defy, as a bugbear, a flam,
Though the lion may feel surly pleasure in fighting,
 He'll feel more by compassion when turn'd to a lamb.

The heart and the eyes, you see, feel the same motion,
    And if both shed their drops, 'tis all to the same end;
And thus 'tis that every tight lad of the ocean
    Sheds his blood for his country, his tears for his
        friend.
If my maxim's disease, 'tis disease I shall die on,—
    You may snigger and titter, I don't care a damn!
In me let the foe feel the paw of a lion,
    But, the battle once ended, the heart of a lamb.

MAGNANIMITY.

WHEN once the din of war's begun
That heroes so delight in,
Armies are conquer'd, cities won,
By bloodshed and brave fighting.
The trumpet sounds! the columns march,
    Friends from dear friends are sunder'd;
Prepared is the triumphal arch,
    And the fall'n foe is plunder'd.
All this, I own, deserves a name,
And truly in the rolls of fame
    Portrays a marking feature:
Yet give me bravery from the heart,
From self divested and apart,
    Exceeding mortal nature,
That rushes through devouring waves,
And, like a guardian angel, saves
    A sinking fellow-creature.

K

In equal balance to maintain
The barriers of each nation,
Thus ever did stern Fate ordain
Slaughter should thin creation.
The trumpet sounds! his native land
    Each tries to save from slavery;
While in the contest, hand in hand,
    Walk clemency and bravery.
All this, I own, deserves a name,
And stands in the records of fame
    A truly marking feature:
Yet give me bravery from the heart,
From self divested, and apart,
    Type of celestial nature,
That rushes, &c.

NANCY.

You ask how it comes that I sing about Nancy
    For ever, yet find something new;
As well may you ask why delight fills the fancy
    When land first appears to the crew.
When, safe from the toils of the perilous ocean,
    In each heart thanks of gratitude spring;
Feel this, and you'll have of my joy a faint notion
    When with rapture of Nancy I sing.

You and I nature's beauties have seen the world over,
    Yet never knew which to prefer;
Then why should you wonder that I am no rover,
    Since I see all those beauties in her?

Why, you'll find about ships all you've known and been
    hearing,
  On their different bearings to bring;
Though they all make their ports, they all vary in
    steering,
  So do I when of Nancy I sing.

Could a ship round the world, wind and weather per-
    mitting,
  A thousand times go and come back,
The ocean's so spacious 'twould never be hitting
  For leagues upon leagues the same tack:
So her charms are so numerous, so various, so clever,
  They produce in my mind such a string,
That, my tongue once let loose, I could sing on for ever,
  And vary the oftener I sing.

Shall I tell you the secret? you've but to love truly,
  Own a heart in the right place that's hung;
And, just as the prow to the helm answers duly,
  That heart will lend words to the tongue.
No art do I boast of, no skill I inherit,
  Then do not of my praises ring.;
But to love and to nature allow all the merit
  That taught me of Nancy to sing.

TOL DE ROL.

Of all the lives that e'er was lived,
  A sailor's life for I;
Hap what hap may, he's never grieved,
  But works and bungs his eye.

To do his duty never loth,
In danger's face he'll fly,
Though certain sure to get popp'd off,
Tol de liddle liddle tol tol lol tol diddle liddle
liddle li.

Why, when to hand that sail we'd got
All shiver'd by the foe,
Scarce up aloft, a second shot
Mast, yards, and all laid low.
At the risk of every precious neck,
By the run we comed, but I
Only broke my arm against the deck,
Tol di riddle, &c.

Now there when I left Poll ashore,
Well stored with togs and gold,
And went to sea to fight for more,
A jolly tar and bold,
A wounded prisoner soon I lay,
In a dismal plight was I;
Comed home, I found Poll flow'd away,
Tol di riddle, &c.

Then, when my precious leg they lopp'd,
Just for a bit of fun,
I took it up, on t'other hopp'd,
And ramm'd it in a gun.
What's that for? cries my messmate Dick;
What for, you fool! said I;
Why, to give mounseer another kick!
Tol di riddle, &c.

I owns this crazy hull of mine
   At sea has had its share ;
Shipwreck'd three times, and wounded nine,
   And blow'd up in the air!
But somebody must pay the cost,—
   I've yet my leg and my eye ;
The rest I for my country lost,
   Tol di riddle, &c.

PEACE.

Hark, hark of war, the dreadful clangour!
   Oh that men, who brothers are,
With no one private cause of anger,
   Dire fate should force to murderous war!

See, see, those heaps of dead and dying!
   Hark, what shrieks are heard afar!
No quarter suffer'd to the flying ;—
   Oh, the horrid trade of war!

Yet think not, with thy blood-stain'd laurel,
   Bellona, long to hurl thy car ;
Time soon shall heal the sanguine quarrel,
   And stay the fell effects of war.

Soon lovely peace, her balm applying,
   Of suffering hearts shall close each scar ;
The living cheer, lament the dying,
   And rid the world of cruel war.

THE PRIDE OF THE OCEAN.

SEE the shore lined with gazers, the tide comes in fast,
The confusion but hear! bear a hand there, avast!
The blocks and the wedges the mallets obey,
And the shores and the stanchions are all cut away :
While with head like a lion, built tight fore and aft,
Broad amidships, lean bows, and taper abaft;
In contempt of all danger from quicksands and rocks,
The pride of the ocean is launch'd from the stocks.

Now the signal is flying, and, fleet in her course,
She chases a sail, far superior her force;
And now the brisk broadside is merrily pour'd,
And splinters, cut ropes, and masts go by the board :
Next yard-arm-and-yard-arm entangled they lie,
The tars loudly swearing to conquer or die ;
Till hull'd and cut up, getting more than she likes,
To the pride of the ocean the enemy strikes.

The prize is sent home, and, alert in a trice,
They make gaskets and points, and they knot and they
          splice ;
While knowing Jack tars of their gallantry talk,
Tell who served well Boscawen, and Anson, and Hawke ;
Till, all of a sudden, a calm, then a scud,
A tempest brings on that the face of the flood
The thunder and lightning and wind so deform,
The pride of the ocean scarce lives out the storm.

And now, having nobly defended the cause
Of the nation, of freedom, religion, and laws,
Her timbers all crazy, all open her seams,
Torn and: wounded her planks, and quite rotten her
      beams,
To the last humbly fated her country to aid,
Near the very same slip where her keel was first laid,
No trace of her rate but her ports and her bulk,
The pride of the ocean's cut down a sheer hulk.

NATURE AND NANCY.

Let swabs with their wows, their palaver, and lies,
    Sly flattery's silk sails still be trimming,
Swear their Polls be all angels dropp'd down from the
    skies,—
    I your angels don't like,—I loves women.
And I loves a warm heart and a sweet honest mind,
    Good as truth, and as lively as fancy;
As constant as honour, as tenderness kind;
    In short, I loves Nature and Nancy.

I read in a song about Wenus, I thinks,
    All rigg'd out with her Cupids and graces;
And how roses and lilies, carnations and pinks,
    Was made paint to daub over their faces.
They that loves it may take all such art for their pains,
    For mine 'tis another guess fancy;
Give me the rich health, flesh and blood, and blue veins
    That pays the sweet face of my Nancy.

Why, I went to the play, where they talk'd well at least,
　　As to act all their parts they were trying;
They were playing at soldiers, and playing at feast,
　　And some they was playing at dying.
Let 'em hang, drown, or starve, or take poison, d'ye see,
　　All just for their gig and their fancy;
What to them was but jest is right earnest to me,
　　For I live and I'd die for my Nancy.

Let the girls then, like so many Algerine Turks,
　　Dash away, a fine gay-painted galley,
With their Jacks and their pennants and gingerbread
　　　　works,
　　All for show, and just nothing for value,—
False colours throw out, deck'd by labour and art,
　　To take of pert coxcombs the fancy;
They are all for the person, I'm all for the heart,—
　　In short, I'm for Nature and Nancy.

GRATITUDE.

He lives! propitious pow'rs, he lives!
　　What though the tear
From every eye involuntary start?
　　　Indulgent Heav'n, continually that gives
　　New blessings to delight this happy land,
　　Has snatch'd from the assassin's hand that life
　　　To ev'ry Briton dear!
That source from whence life flows to ev'ry heart.
　　Britons, exult and rally round the throne!
　　　To pious airs
　　　Breathe grateful pray'rs—
　Your monarch's safety is your own.

Of joy and horror, what a scene!
Behold the king,
In fortitude and virtue find a host!
Heaven beaming comfort on the pious queen,
And her angelic progeny around;
Dire murder and fell treason to confound,
See Providence like lightning spring.
Be cherish'd in each heart the loyal boast!
Britons, exult, &c.

To Heaven, that still permits
For mortals' good,
Now pour we out our grateful hearts in pray'r:
And as each virtue high enthroned that sits
In his great mind has long transcended praise,
So be the hour, in calendars and lays,
To unborn Britons understood,
That proved great George high Heaven's especial care.
Britons, exult, &c.

THUS WE SOLDIERS LIVE.

Thus, my lads, we soldiers live:
We live a life
Like man and wife,—
Now making love—now in a row;
A noble, glorious trade we drive;
From morn to night
We love and fight,
And follow the noisy rowdydowdydow

Now courting honour in some trench—
And now some willing comely wench;
To victory leading now the way—
Now leading at some ball the hey:
To the fair now kneeling for some boon—
Now at the head of a platoon;
Ever equally delighting,—
Now in love, and now in fighting.

Charge the enemy's right flank! My dear angel, how I adore you! They fly! follow up the pursuit. My life, my love, my soul! Permit me to lay my laurels at your feet.

   Thus, my lads, &c.

In peace the sprightly fife and drum
Diffuse delight where'er we come.
The serjeant first, neat as my nail,
With brandish'd cane, and dangling tail,
Careless around saluting all,
With te di rero ree, and tol, lol, lol;
While wonder sits on every face
Throughout the astonish'd market-place.
Did you ever see the like of this?
To mamma, in raptures, cries out Miss.
While clodpole cries, with chizzled phiz,
What a nice way of walking marching is!

I zay, zarjint, if it were not for the wooden legs and arms, I wish I may die if I don't think I should list.— Wooden legs and arms! my fine fellow; what signifies such trifles as those? Why you have made a shift all your life with a wooden head. Come, my angel, prevail upon your sweetheart to go with us. Come, my lads, if you are for honour and fame, follow us to the field; where you shall be all covered with wounds and glory; and where, if you should chance to get killed, damme, you'll live for ever.

Thus, my lads, &c.

> But when the trumpet sounds afar,
> And we let slip the dogs of war, .
> Then to see the dead and dying,
> Hear bullets whistle as they're flying;
> Oh! what delights, so sweet, so glorious,
> That proudly cover the victorious!
> Hacking, hewing, cutting, slashing,
> Killing, wounding, mincing, mashing;
> While drums and fifes and cannons loud
> Upon the astonish'd senses crowd,
> And strike the ears with hideous yell,
> As if it were the yawn of hell,
> Of the dying to sound out the knell.

Ods wounds and fire, sarjint, what comical things you soldiers do see! See! why, sir, I once saw a cannon-ball take off a steeple with eight men ringing the bells. Cannon! dom't, I do believe that cannon be a gun. But the drollest thing I ever saw in my life was a lawyer's head that was knocked off and placed upon a tailor's shoulders. Ruined poor dear Snip,—the poor devil has never spoken a word of truth since.

Thus, my lads, &c.

ANNA, ANNE, NAN, NANCE, OR NANCY.

My love's a vessel trim and gay,
  Rigg'd out with truth and stored by honour;
As through life's sea she cuts her way,
  All eyes with rapture gaze upon her :
Built every wondering heart to please,—
  The lucky shipwrights Love and Fancy;
From stem to stern she moves with ease,
  And at her launch they call'd her Nancy.

When bearing up against life's gales,
  So well she stems the dangerous trouble,
I call her Anna,—as she sails,
  Her form's so grand, her air's so noble.
When o'er the trembling wave she flies,
  That plays and sports as she advances,
Well said, my Nan ! I fondly cries,
  As my full heart in concert dances.

In studding-sails before life's breeze
  So sweetly gentle is her motion,
She's Anne,—for as she moves with ease,
  She seems the queen of all the ocean.
But when on Sundays rigg'd in stays,
  Like beauty gay, and light as fancy,
She wins my heart a thousand ways ;
  I then delight to call her Nancy.

When laying on a tack so neat,
  The breeze her milk-white bosom filling,
She skims the yielding waves so fleet,
  I call her Nance, my bosom thrilling.
Thus is she precious to my heart,
  By whate'er name comes o'er my fancy;
Graceful or gay, grand, neat, or smart,
  Or Anna, Anne, Nan, Nance, or Nancy.

JACK AT GREENWICH.

WE tars are all for fun and glee,—
  A hornpipe was my notion;
Time was I'd dance with any he
  That sails the salt sea ocean;
I'd tip the roll, the slide, the reel,
  Back, forward, in the middle;
And roast the pig, and toe and heel,
  All going with the fiddle:
But one day told a shot to ram,
  To chase the foe advancing,
A splinter queer'd my larboard gam,
  And, damme, spoilt my dancing.

Well, I'm, says I, no churlish elf;
  We messmates be all brothers;
Though I can't have no fun myself,
  I may make fun for others.
A fiddle soon I made my own,
  That girls and tars might caper,—
Learnt Rule Britannia, Bobbing Joan,
  And grow'd a decent scraper.

But just as I'd the knack on't got,
  And did it pretty middling,
I lost my elbow by a shot,
  And, damme, spoilt my fiddling.

So sometimes, as I turn'd my quid,
  I got a knack of thinking
As I should be an inwalid,
  And then I took to drinking.
One day call'd down my gun to man,
  To tip it with the gravy,
I gave three cheers, and took the can
  To drink the British Navy:
Before a single drop I'd sipp'd,
  Or got it to my muzzle,
A langridge off my daddle whipp'd,
  And, damme, spilt the guzzle.

So then I took to taking snuff,
  'Cause how my sorrows doubled;
And pretty pastime 'twas enough,
  D'ye see, when I was troubled:
But Fortune, that mischievous elf,
  Still at some fun or other,—
Not that I minds it for myself,
  But just for Poll and mother,—
One day, while lying on a tack,
  To keep two spanking foes off,
A broadside comes, capsizes Jack,
  And, damme, knocks my nose off.

So in misfortune's school grown tough,—
  In this same sort of knowledge,
Thinking, mayhap, I'd not enough,
  They sent me here to college.

And here we tell old tales and smoke,
   And laugh while we are drinking;
Sailors, you know, will have their joke,
   E'en though the ship were sinking.
For I, while I get grog to drink
   My wife, or friend, or king in,
'Twill be no easy thing, I think,
   Damme, to spoil my singing.

BROTHER JACK.

If the good old maxim's true,
That sons of Eve should all be brothers,
Tars have it to their hearts in view,
For their first good's the good of others ;
Nay, Jack such narrow love derides,
'Midst every danger still contented,
He the whole family provides
With every good that Heaven invented ;
And, leaving caution to the wind,
Risks every chance to serve mankind.

Away to India, cries the fair ;
To Beauty's voice obedient listen !
The vessel cuts the yielding air,
And muslins wave, and diamonds glisten :
Should winter, in its bleak array,
With chilling frosts and winds alarm her,
Jack points the prow to Hudson's Bay,
And comely furs both deck and warm her ;
And, gaily leaving care behind,
Ransacks the world to serve mankind.

Would cits the rich, voluptuous treat,—
Amidst the bustle and the hurry,
To make the bill of fare complete,
Jack brings the turtle and the curry:
He fetches tea for maiden aunts,
Finery and fashions for our spouses,
Feeds, clothes us, and supplies our wants,
And even furnishes our houses:
What thanks for those then shall we find,
Who thus adventure for mankind?

Then be the friendly toast we pass,
As honest hearts and Nature's freemen,—
Excluding daylight from the glass,—
Prosperity to English seamen!
On danger's brink who careless found,
For others make their lives a slavery;
The very wine that now goes round
We owe to their adventurous bravery.
Then drink to those, with grateful mind,
Who risk their lives to serve mankind.

THE UNION.

Come, join ev'ry heart, let the air loudly ring,
Of a people united and mighty we sing;
To the ends of the earth while the tidings are heard,
Be their fame, like Fate's fiat, applauded and fear'd.
Now, that joy ev'ry bosom receives and imparts,
Come, join this blest union of hands and of hearts:

St. George, and St. Andrew, St. Patrick shall join,
The league fix'd as fate, and the compact divine;
While the world's admiration and fear are excited,
To see Ireland, and Scotland, and England united.

The Tripod of old had the power to inspire
The priests with poetic and national fire;
On the pivot of commerce our tripod shall move,
Whence we prophesy plenty and brotherly love.
Now, that joy ev'ry bosom receives and imparts,
Come, join this blest union of hands and of hearts:
The Thames, and the Tweed, and the Shannon shall
   join,
And myriads of ships to each other consign;
While the world's admiration and fear are excited,
To see Scotland, and England, and Ireland united.

Old Shakspeare predicted we nothing could rue,
While England resolv'd to herself to prove true;
Come against us the world, then, what risk can we run,
Now that England and Scotland, and Ireland are one?
Now, that joy ev'ry bosom receives and imparts,
Come, join this blest union of hands and of hearts;
The rose, thistle, and shamrock, as graceful they join,
The fair in a wreath for each hero shall twine;
While the world's admiration and fear are excited,
To see England, and Ireland, and Scotland united.

THE CANARY-BIRD.

Since fate of sailors hourly varies,
　　Lest doubts should wound my anxious breast,
This pretty bird, from the Canaries
　　Jack brought, to set my heart at rest:
His life is charm'd, and when with sadness,
　　Cried he, his notes he mournful gives,
　　　　Then cherish care,
　　　　Indulge despair;
But sweetly, if they thrill with gladness,
　　Rejoice, and know your lover lives:
　　　　Attentive mark!
　　　　Hark! hark!
Rejoice, and know your lover lives.

Each hour, while my poor bosom flutters,
　　Relying on my lover's word,
Anxious to hear the song he utters,
　　I listen to my pretty bird:
But, thanks to Heaven, never with sadness
　　Has he yet mourn'd; even now he gives
　　　　(To silence care, and chase despair,)
His sprightly notes with joy and gladness;
　　And thus I know my lover lives:
　　　　Attentive mark!
　　　　Hark! hark!
　　'Tis thus I know my lover lives.

But see, he's here! my heart's contented;
  Sweet warbler, truly didst thou speak.
Dear love, cried Jack, 'twas all invented,
  Lest thy poor heart my fate might break.
Love taught the cheat, to cheer thy sadness,
  And cheats of love true love forgives;
      This anxious care
      Heal'd thy despair;
Birds always sing with joy and gladness;
  Thy love to thee and honour lives:
      Attentive mark!
      Hark! hark!
Thy love to thee and honour lives.

THE TRUMPETS SOUND.

THOUGH forward stands the soldier's name,
  'Midst prospects rude and steril,
To where high tow'rs the fane of fame,
  The steps are toil and peril.
How keen the pang when friends must part,
  Fierce glory's fire suspending,
An angel wife pours out that heart
  Which killing fears are rending.
  But vain are sympathetic sighs,
  Uplifted hands, and streaming eyes.
Beckon'd by fate, behold the bands,
  The drums at distance rattle.
Hark! the charge, 'tis honour commands,
  The trumpets sound to battle.

Death's work's begun; in honour's bed
  Promiscuous heaps are lying;
Appall'd the living, and the dead
  Lamented by the dying;
While memory added torture gives,
  That tenderest thoughts awaken,
See groups of mothers, children, wives,
  By feeble hope forsaken.
But vain are sympathetic sighs,
  Imploring hands, and streaming eyes:
Again appear the martial bands,
  The drums at distance rattle, &c.

Avaunt, grim war! sweet peace is ours,—
  The hero's noblest capture;
Joy gaily leads the dancing hours,
  And misery's lost in rapture.
Beneath her horn gay Plenty bends,
  Proud bards record the quarrel,
And in her temple Fame attends,
  To place the well-earn'd laurel.
  Yet but in trust he holds this meed;
  For should his aid his country need,
Then shall he cry, draw out the bands,
  When drums at distance rattle, &c.

VOYAGE OF LIFE.

A voyage at sea and all its strife,
  Its pleasure and its pain,
At every point resembles life,—
  Hard work for little gain.

The anchor's weigh'd, smooth is the flood,
   Serene seems every form,
But soon, alas! comes on the scud,
   That speaks the threatening storm.
The towering masts in splinters shivering!
The useless sails in tatters quivering!
Thunder rolling, lightning flashing,
Waves in horrid tumult dashing
   Foam along the dreary shore :
Still, while tars sit round so jolly,
The sprightly flute calls care a folly.
Aloft, alow, afloat, aground,
Let but the smiling grog go round,
   And storms are heard no more.

The voyage through life is various found,
   The wind is seldom fair ;
Though to the straights of pleasure bound,
   Too oft we touch at care.
Impervious danger we explore ;
   False friends, some faithless she :
Pirates and sharks are found ashore
   As often as at sea.
A low'ring storm, from envy brewing,
Shall at a distance menace ruin ;
While slander, malice, and detraction,
A host of fiends shall bring in action,
   And plant care's thorns at every pore.
Yet, roused to sweet domestic duty,
Some manly imp, or infant beauty,
Clings round his neck, or climbs his knees,—
Each thorn's pluck'd out, pain's turn'd to ease,
   And storms are heard no more.

The ship towers gaily on the main,
    To fight its country's cause,
And bid the obedient world maintain
    Its honours and its laws.
Nor from surrounding danger shrinks
    Till, sacrifice to fame,
Death dealing round, she nobly sinks
    Only to live in name.
And so the man,—his ample measure
Fill'd with alternate pain and pleasure,
Till, long in age and honour giving,
Life's strength worn out, a lesson giving
    To those he leaves his well-got store.
Mild hope and resignation greeting,
The playful soul, in circles fleeting,
Makes onward to its native skies,
While gasping nature pants and dies,
    And storms are heard no more.

JACK AT THE OPERA.

AT Wapping I landed, and call'd to hail Mog;
    She had just shaped her course to the play.
Of two rums and one water I order'd my grog,
    And to speak her soon stood under way.
But the Haymarket I for Old Drury mistook,
    Like a lubber so raw and so soft,
Half a George handed out, at the change did not look,
    Mann'd the ratlins, and went up aloft.

As I mounted to one of the uppermost tiers,
    With many a coxcomb and flirt,
Such a damnable squalling saluted my ears,
    I thought there'd been somebody hurt;

But the devil a bit—'twas your outlandish rips
    Singing out with their lanterns of jaws;
You'd a 'swored you'd been taking of one of they trips
    'Mongst the Caffres or wild Catabaws.

What's the play, Ma'am? says I, to a good-natured tit.
    The play! 'tis the *uproar* you quiz.
My timbers, cried I, the right name on't you've hit,
    For the devil an uproar it is,
For they pipe and they squeal, now alow, now aloft;
    If it wa'nt for the petticoat gear,
With their squeaking so mollyish, tender, and soft,
    One should scarcely know ma'am from mounseer.

Next at kicking and dancing they took a long spell,
    All springing and bounding so neat,
And spessiously one curious Madamaselle,—
    Oh, she daintily handled her feet.
But she hopp'd, and she sprawl'd, and she spun round
        so queer,
    'Twas, you see, rather oddish to me;
And so I sung out, Pray be decent, my dear;
    Consider I'm just come from sea.

Ten't an Englishman's taste to have none of these goes,
    So away to the playhouse I'll jog,
Leaving all your fine Bantums and Ma'am Parisoes,
    For old Billy Shakspeare and Mog.
So I made for the theatre, and hail'd my dear spouse;
    She smiled as she saw'd me approach;
And, when I'd shook hands and saluted her bows,
    We to Wapping set sail in a coach.

THE MANES OF THE BRAVE.

Now that war has, in human distress, done its best;
Now that, glutted with mischief, fell slaughter's at rest;
Now that smiling content crowns the peasant's clean
    board,
And the industrious ploughshare takes place of the
    sword;
In this season what care o'er the fancy shall brood?
What sigh press for vent, or what tear shall intrude?
Ah! indulge and reflect on each glorious grave—
A sigh and a tear to the manes of the brave.

Now that loud acclamations expand through the air,
And the brows of the brave are adorn'd by the fair;
Now that bands of musicians so gaily advance,
In the concert to join or enliven the dance;
At one grateful idea the tumult shall end,
The soft flute the sad cadence alone shall suspend;
And, while fancy leads on to the cold hallow'd grave,
Shall echo a sigh to the manes of the brave.

Proud award of those heroes for glory who burn,
Alike nobly honour'd the arch and the urn;
Surviving, or dying, such fame who achieve,
'Tis joy to regret, and 'tis pleasure to grieve.
Then our rapturous bosoms let gratitude swell,
While those sons of renown, who so gloriously fell,
Shall from heav'n cheer those mourners who throng near
    each grave,
And dry up their tears for the manes of the brave.

THE LETTER N.

Up from a loblolly-boy none was so cute,
    Of knowing things most sort I follard;
Ben Binacle learn'd me to read and dispute,
    For Ben was a bit of a scholard.
Of the whole criss-cross row I in time know'd the worth;
    But the dear letter N for my fancy;
For N stands for nature, and noble, and north,
    Neat, nimble, nine, nineteen, and Nancy.

She soon was my wife, and I sail'd round the world,
    To get prize-money where I could forage;
And for love, wheresoever our Jack was unfurl'd,
    I daunted them all with my courage:
For I now read in books about heroes and fame,
    And for all sorts of rows got a fancy;
Sticking still to dear N, for N stands for name,
    Note, novel, neck, nothing, and Nancy.

In the midst of this bustle I lost my poor friend,
    And each object around me grew hateful;
For I know'd not false heart with a fair face to blend,
    Nor had larning yet made me ungrateful.
I liked my friend well, and deplored him;—what then?
    My wife was the first in my fancy;
For, though B stands for buck, brother, bottom, and Ben,
    Yet N stands for needle and Nancy.

Well, I've weather'd life's storms, and till laid a sheer
    hulk
  Will my absence again never shock her;
Thanks to Fortune, at sea I've no need to break bulk,
  For I've plenty of shot in the locker.
Our kids play around us, and still to pursue
  The letter so dear to my fancy,
Though nineteen twice told noons and nights but renew
  The nice natty notion of Nancy.

EACH HIS OWN PILOT.

I was saying to Jack, as we talk'd t'other day
  About lubbers and snivelling elves,
That if people in life did not steer the right way,
  They had nothing to thank but themselves.
Now, when a man's caught by those mermaids the girls,
  With their flatt'ring palaver and smiles,
He runs, while he's list'ning to their fal de rals,
  Bump ashore on the Scilly Isles.
Thus, in steering in life, as in steering with us,
  To one course in your conduct resort,—
In foul winds, leaving luff and no near, keep her thus ;
      In honour's line ready,
      When fair, keep her steady,
  And neither to starboard incline nor to port.

If he's true in his dealings, life's wind to defy,
  And the helm has a trim and right scope,
Not luffing, but keeping the ship full and by,
  He may weather the Cape of Good Hope.

JACK COME HOME.

But if he steer's wide in temptation's high sea,
  And to pleasure gives too much head-way,
Hard a-port goes the helm, the ship's brought by the lee,
  And she founders in Botany Bay.
        Thus in, &c.

In wedlock so many wrong courses are made,
  They part convoy so oft and so fast,
Till so fond they are grown of that same Guinea-trade,
  Cape Farewell is their anchorage at last.
Some men, I must own, to be dubb'd may be born;
  But this, for the wives, I will say,
They seldom or ever bear down for Cape Horn
  'Till the husbands have show'd them the way.
        Thus in, &c.

As to mutinous spirits that through the world roll,
  If we had 'em aboard, Jack, with we,
They should make No Man's Land, and skulk through
        Lubber's Hole,
  And at last be laid in the Red Sea;
But fine honest fellows, to honour so dear,
  Shall, in this world by nothing perplex'd,
Of False Bay get to windward, bring up in Cape Clear,
  And bespeak a snug berth in the next.
        Thus in, &c.

JACK COME HOME.

Jack come home, his pockets lined,
  In search of Poll, his only pleasure,
To Pickle Stairs his course inclined,
  In her fair lap to pour his treasure:

But scarce arriv'd at fam'd Rag-fair,
  Where the keen Jew the clodpole fleeces,
His whistle turn'd into a stare,
  At " Come, who'll buy my water-cresses ?"

He starts and trembles at the sound,
  Which now is heard, and now obstructed;
And now his hopes are all aground,
  And now 'tis to his ear conducted.
" Zounds!" cried out Jack, " I know that phiz,—
  But then, such togs—they're all to pieces!
Why, it can't be! damme, it is—
  'Tis Poll a-bawling water-cresses!"

And now she's in his arms, while he
  Bids her relate fortune's reverses;
The world finds faithless as the sea,
  And loads false friends, in troops, with curses.
" They took," cried she, " my very bed;
  The sticks they seiz'd, and sold in pieces ;
So, to get a bit of honest bread,
  I cries, Who'll buy my water-cresses?"

" Still art thou rich, my girl," cried Jack,
  "And still shall taste each earthly pleasure ;
Thou'rt true, though rags are on thy back,
  And honour, Poll, 's a noble treasure.
In this gay tog-shop rigg'd so neat,
  Ill fortune from this moment ceases :"
This said, he scatter'd in the street
Basket, and rags, and water-cresses.

LOVE ME EVERMORE.

In either eye a lingering tear,
    His love and duty well to prove,
Jack left his wife and children dear,
    Impell'd by honour and by love ;
And as he loiter'd, wrapp'd in care,
    A sapling in his hand he bore,
Curiously carv'd, in letters fair—
    " Love me ; ah, love me, evermore ! "

At leisure to behold his worth,
    Tokens, and rings, and broken gold,
He plung'd the sapling firm in earth,
    And o'er and o'er his treasure told ;
The letters spelt, the kindness traced,
    And all affection's precious store,
Each with the favourite motto graced—
    " Love me ; ah, love me, evermore ! "

While on this anxious task employ'd,
    Tender remembrance all his care,
His ears are suddenly annoy'd,
    The bostswain's whistle cleaves the air :
'Tis duty calls, his nerves are braced,
    He rushes to the crowded shore,
Leaving the sapling in his haste,
    That bids him love for evermore.

The magic branch thus unreclaim'd,
    Far off at sea, no comfort near,
His thoughtless haste he loudly blamed
    With many a sigh and many a tear ;

Yet why act this unmanly part?
  The words the precious relic bore,
Are they not mark'd upon my heart?—
  " Love me; ah, love me, evermore!"

Escap'd from treacherous waves and winds,
  That three years he had felt at sea,
A wondrous miracle he finds,—
  The sapling is become a tree!
A goodly head that graceful rears,
  Enlarged the trunk, enlarged the core!
And on the rind, enlarged, appears
  " Love me; ah, love me, evermore!"

While gazing on the spell-like charms
  Of this most wonderful of trees,
His Nancy rushes to his arms,
  His children cling about his knees.
Increased in love, increased in size,
  Taught from the mother's tender store,
Each little urchin, lisping, cries,
  " Love me; ah, love me, evermore!"

Amazement seiz'd the admiring crowd;
  " My children," cried a villager seer,
" These signs, though mute, declare aloud
  The hand of Providence is here—
Whose hidden, yet whose sure decrees,
  For those its succour who implore,
Can still the tempest, level seas,
  And crown true love for evermore."

THREE CHEERS.

WHEN to weigh the boatswain's calling,
 The tops all mann'd,
 The fading land,
Throng'd with hearty friends appears,
 Then the sailor, though on duty,
 Seeks fondly for some distant beauty,
Whose token on his heart he wears;
Nor can his moisten'd eye withdraw:
But rous'd, his courage overhauling,
 The grog goes round,
 He hails the sound,
The toast—a prosperous voyage—three cheers !
And jolly tars sing out Houraw !

When light'ning, winds, and waves are jarring,
 And madly rove,
 Enough to move
Aught but a British seaman's fears;
 Then the tar, on duty flying,
 The yards, the shrouds, the pump is plying—
Belay, casts off tacks, halliards, jears,
Watches each cranny and each flaw:
But, ceas'd this elemental warring,
 The grog goes round,
 He hails the sound;
The toast—Great Britain's fleets—three cheers !
And jolly tars sing out Houraw !

When the wild tumultuous battle,
  With horrid roar
  Laves decks with gore—
 When ranks the raking broadside clears—
  The tar, his country's cause espousing,
  Feels in his veins the lion rousing;
 And, as he Freedom's standard rears,
He gorges Death's insatiate maw:
But, quell'd the foe, ceas'd the loud rattle,
  The grog goes round,
  He hails the sound;
 The toast—humanity—three cheers!
And jolly tars sing out Houraw!

But when, his various perils ended,
  He views the shore,
  All hands to moor,
 With more than mortal bliss he hears,
  A heaven on earth the sailor fancies,
  Hails little Toms, and little Nancies,
 And realized he feels and hears
Her truth he in his dreams foresaw.
To fate thus grateful, thus befriended,
  The grog goes round,
  All hail the sound;
 The toast—Jack's welcome home—three cheers!
And jolly tars sing out Houraw!

ONE.

Up the Mediterranin,
  One day was explaining
The chaplain and I about poets and bards;
  For I'm pretty discarning,
  And loves about larning
To know, and all notions that such things regards:
Then to hear him sing out 'bout the islands around,
Tell their outlandish names, call them all classic ground,
Where the old ancient poets all formerly mess'd,
And wrote about love and the girls they caress'd;
Swore they thought 'em all goddesses, creatures divine;—
I thinks that he said each old gemman had nine.
  Cried I, Well said, old ones!
  These poets were bold ones;
But everything's vanity under the sun.
  Love's as good sport as any;
  But nine's eight too many;—
I have one worth all nine, and my Nancy's that one.

  Then we read, for their wishes,
  They turn'd to queer fishes,
To cocks and to bulls, in some verses they call
  Ovid Metaramorphus,
  And one Mr. Orphus
Went to hell for his wife—but that's nothing at all.
Some figary, each hour, set these codgers agog;
Old Nackron swigg'd off his allowance of grog;
Master Jove had his fancies and fine falderals,—
What a devil that god was for following the girls!

M

But what makes the curisest part of their lives,
They were always a-chasing of other men's wives.
   What nonsense and folly!
   'Tis quite melancholy
That a man can't be bless'd till his neighbour's undone;
   Why, 'tis wicked to ax um,—
   Take the world, that's my maxum,
So one be left me, and my Nancy that one.

   Then we'd hot work between us,
   'Bout Graces and Wenus,
With their fine red and white, and their eyes full of darts;
   To be sure, pretty faces
   Be well in their places;
But, your reverence, in love there be such things* as
       hearts!
'Tis unmanly to chatter behind people's back,
But 'tis pretty well known that the lady's a crack;
Besides, if these things about beauty be true,
That there is but one Wenus, why, I says there's two!
Say there is but one Nancy, you'll then not mistake,
For she's mine, and I'd sail the world round for her
       sake.
   Then no further norations,
   Or chatterifications,
'Bout Wenus, and Graces, and such pretty fun,
   That so runs in your fancy;—
   Just see but my Nancy,
You'll find all their charms spliced together in one.

HISTORY OF THE WAR.

'Twas all how and about and concerning the war,
　　And the glory of Britain's bold navy,
And the different brushes, and what 'twas all for,
　　That the whistle of Fame has sung out sea and shore;
　　For when British bull-dogs begin for to roar,
　　French, and Spaniards, and Dutch cry peccavi.

For the war, how it happen'd, and what 'twas about,
　　That's nothing to we—tars must do what they're bid;
So all I can tell you, the war once broke out,
　　They told us to lick 'em, and lick 'em we did.
As to order and such, you don't get that from me;
　　I shall, just as they come, speak of actions that's past;
So they did us but honour, as lords of the sea,
　　It don't matter a damn which came first or which last.

Why, now, there was Howe and the glorious first of
June; then there was Jarvis when he beat the Spaniards
fifteen to twenty-seven; Duncan with his hard blows
with the Dutch; Nelson and the Nile; but, lud, 'tis
nonsense to tell you about the grand affairs. Our great-
grandchildren and their great-grandchildren will read
about it, you know, in almanacs and things, just as
people read of the hard frost and the fire of London. It
is the neat little brushes that I intends to talk to you about.
There was Pellew and the Hamphin: don't you remember
pegging away at that seventy-four, just for all the world
like two schoolboys licking a great hulking fellow? Then
there was Fawkener—who would not have died like Faw-

M 2

kener?—and then there was Cooke, in the East Indies; he
fell nobly, too; damme if I would not as soon be Cooke
as Fawkener! But avast, avast! there was another brave
fellow,—indeed, there was plenty of brave fellows, if that
was all,—but I mean Hood in the Mars; just saw the Her-
cules strike, and died. Hollo! zounds, I shall be swab-
bing my bows if I go on at this rate; stay; what was there
else? Oh, there was the brush with the La Pomone; and
then, you know, Sir Sidney, he did some neat things; and
then there was Trollope in the Glatton, and there was,
you know, there was,—damme if I know what there was,
but

'Twas all how, &c.

As to me, I en't learnt, for I can't read or write:
    But what's writing or reading, or any such arts?
To find their due praise, for their country that fight
    We must read from our memories what's writ on our
        hearts.
Not that heroes e'er brag, or for flattery sue,—
    True bravery was never yet known to be vain;
And the thanks and the honours so nobly their due,
    By deeds, not by words, gallant Britons obtain.

Why, what could be so glorious, you know, as Pellew,
when he took the Cleopatra, boarded her, and struck
her colours? Then there was Saumarez, off Cherbourg,
taok the Re-union, killed and wounded a hundred and
twenty, without the loss of a single British seaman. Both
knighted and barow-knighted; that's right: some sense
to fight for a country like this. In short we worked
them; we took Neptune, and Fortune, and Victory; but,

for the matter of that, we had all this on our side before.
Then we took Liberty—that was just bringing coals to
Newcastle, you know; Glory, ditto repeated; after that,
we took Immortality, but they did not care much about
that; and then, at last, we took their Constitution. That
was nonsense—we had a good constitution of our own.
Then we took Resistance, and Freedom, and Fame, and
Concord,—damme, we took almost everything from them
but the perlarver, and that they are welcome too: well
then, we took all the saints from the Spaniards, and then
we took from the Dutch—I don't know what the devil
we took from the Dutch, with their cursed hard names,
but

'Twas all how and about and concerning the war,
   And the glory of Britain's bold navy;
And the different brushes, and what 'twas all for,
   That the whistle of Fame has sung out sea and shore;
  For, when British bull-dogs begin for to roar,
The prettiest shall soon cry peccavi.

BEN BLOCK.

WOULD you hear a sad story of woe,
   That tears from a stone might provoke?
'Tis concerning a tar, you must know,
   As honest as e'er biscuit broke:
His name was Ben Block, of all men
   The most true, the most kind, the most brave;
But harsh treated by fortune,—for Ben
In his prime found a watery grave.

His place no one ever knew more;
  His heart was all kindness and love;
Though on duty an eagle he'd soar,
  His nature had most of the dove.
He loved a fair maiden named Kate;
  His father, to interest a slave,
Sent him far from his love, where hard fate
  Plunged him deep in a watery grave.

A curse on all slanderous tongues!—
  A false friend his mild nature abused,
And sweet Kate of the vilest of wrongs
  To poison Ben's pleasure accused:—
That she never had truly been kind;
  That false were the tokens she gave;
That she scorn'd him, and wish'd he might find
  In the ocean a watery grave.

Too sure from this cankerous elf
  The venom accomplish'd its end:
Ben, all truth and honour himself,
  Suspected no fraud in his friend.
On the yard, while suspended in air,
  A loose to his sorrows he gave,—
Take thy wish, he cried, false, cruel fair,
  And plunged in a watery grave.

THE STANDING TOAST.

[The last Song written by Mr. Dibdin.]

THE moon on the ocean was dimm'd by a ripple,
  Affording a chequer'd delight,
The gay jolly tars pass'd the word for the tipple
  And the toast—for 'twas Saturday night:
Some sweetheart or wife that he loved as his life
  Each drank, while he wish'd he could hail her;
But the standing toast that pleased the most
  Was—The wind that blows, the ship that goes,
  And the lass that loves a sailor!

Some drank the king and his brave ships,
  And some the constitution,
Some, May our foes and all such rips
  Own English resolution!
That fate might bless some Poll or Bess,
  And that they soon might hail her;
But the standing toast, &c.

Some drank our queen, and some our land,
  Our glorious land of freedom!
Some that our tars might never stand
  For heroes brave to lead 'em!
That beauty in distress might find
  Such friends as ne'er would fail her;
But the standing toast, &c.

THE LOUD TATTOO.

This, this, my lad,'s a soldier's life,—
He marches to the sprightly fife,
And in each town, to some new wife,
   Swears he'll be ever true ;
He's here—he's there—where is he not ?
Variety's his envied lot,
He eats, drinks, sleeps, and pays no shot,
   And follows the loud tattoo.

Call'd out to face his country's foes,
The tears of fond domestic woes
He kisses off, and boldly goes
   To earn of fame his due.
Religion, liberty, and laws,
Both his are and his country's cause—
For these, through danger, without pause,
   He follows the loud tattoo.

And if, at last, in honour's wars,
He earns his share of danger's scars,
Still he feels bold, and thanks his stars
   He's no worse fate to rue :
At Chelsea, free from toil and pain,
He wields his crutch, points out the slain,
And, in fond fancy, once again
   Follows the loud tattoo.

TRUE GLORY.

What is glory,—what is fame?
That a shadow, this a name,
   Restless mortals to deceive.
Are they renown'd—can they be great,—
Who hurl their fellow-creatures' fate,
   That mothers, children, wives, may grieve?
Ask smiling honour to proclaim
What is glory, what is fame;
Hark! the glad mandate strikes the listening ear,—
"The truest glory to the bosom dear
Is when the soul starts soft compassion's tear."

   What are riches, pomp, and power?
   Gewgaws that endure their hour,
      Wretched mortals to allure.
   Can greatness reach the idly vain,
   Indulging in the princely fane, .
      Deaf to the miseries of the poor?
   Ask smiling reason to proclaim
   What is glory, what is fame;
Hark! the sweet mandate strikes the listening ear,—
"The truest glory to the bosom dear
Is when the soul starts soft compassion's tear."

THE CARFINDO.

I, that once was a ploughman, a sailor am now,—
   No lark that aloft in the sky
Ever flutter'd his wings to give speed to the plough
   Was so gay or so carelesss as I.

But my friend was a carfindo aboard a king's ship,
And he ax'd me to go just to sea for a trip;
And he talk'd of such things,
As if sailors were kings,
And so teazing did keep,
That I left my poor plough to go ploughing the deep:
No longer the horn
Call'd me up in the morn;
I trusted the carfindo and the inconstant wind,
That made me for to go and leave my dear behind.

I did not much like for to be aboard a ship;
   When in danger there's no door to creep out;
I liked the jolly tars, I liked bumbo and flip,
   But I did not like rocking about.
By-and-bye comes a hurricane,—I did not like that;
Next a battle, that many a sailor laid flat.
Ah! cried I, who would roam,
That, like me, had a home?
Where I'd sow and I'd reap,
Ere I left my poor plough to go ploughing the deep:
Where sweetly the horn
Call'd me up in the morn,
Ere I trusted the carfindo and the inconstant wind,
That made me for to go and leave my dear behind.

At last safe I landed, and in a whole skin,
   Nor did I make any long stay
Ere I found, by a friend, whom I ax'd for my kin,
   Father dead, and my wife run away.
Ah, who but thyself, said I, hast thou to blame?
Wives, losing their husbands, oft lose their good name.

Ah, why did I roam,
When so happy at home
I could sow and could reap,
Ere I left my poor plough to go ploughing the deep?
When so sweetly the horn
Call'd me up in the morn.
Curse light upon the carfindo and the inconstant wind,
That made me for to go and leave my dear behind.

Why, if that be the case, said this very same friend,
   And you ben't no more minded to roam,
Gis a shake by the fist, all your care's at an end,
   Dad's alive, and your wife safe at home.
Stark staring with joy, I leap'd out of my skin,
Buss'd my wife, mother, sister, and all of my kin.
Now, cried I, let them roam
Who want a good home;
I am well, so I'll keep,
Nor again leave my plough to go ploughing the deep:
Once more shall the horn
Call me up in the morn,
Nor shall any damn'd carfindo, nor the inconstant wind,
E'er tempt me for to go and leave my dear behind.

THE DRUMMER.

Dapper Ted Tattoo is my natty name,
   For a roll or a trevally,
Among the girls loud sounds my fame,
   When I their quarters rally.

For with fife and drum
I smirking come,
Leer, cock my hat,
Swear, and all that,
Nor never dread
A broken head
Where the cause of strife's a doxy;
But as for wars,
And wounds, and scars,
And fighting foes,
And thumps, and blows,
I'd rather fight by proxy.

When chiefs and privates mingled lie,
And gasp without assistance,
In baggage-waggon, perch'd up, I
Stand umpire at a distance;
And with fife and drum
I smirking come
'Mongst soldiers' wives,
Who lead merry lives,
Nor ever dread
A broken head
Where the cause of strife's a doxy.
Let their husbands go,
And 'gainst the foe
Gain glory's scars
In honour's wars,—
I'd rather fight by proxy.

Yet think ye I am not renown'd
In foreign wars and civil?
Why, sir, when safe at home and sound,
Zounds, I could fight the devil!

And with fife and drum
Can smirking come,
And cock my hat,
Leer, and all that;
Nor never dread
A broken head
When the cause of strife's a doxy.
Let others go
And 'gainst the foe
Gain glory's scars
In honour's wars,—
I'd rather fight by proxy.

Thus through the world I make a noise
Where'er I'm a sojourner,
The mighty wonder and surprise
Of every chimney-corner;
Where with fife and drum
I smirking come,
And rap out, Zounds!
And talk of wounds,
Nor ever dread
A broken head
Where the cause of strife's a doxy.
They're fools who go
And 'gainst the foe
In glory's wars
Gain honour's scars:
I'm wise, and fight by proxy.

THE DRUM-HEAD.

Come on, jolly lads! to the drum-head repair;
I beat up for recruits in the name of the fair—
Britain's fair, who, to beauty to add a new charm,
Send good wishes, and flannel, our soldiers to warm.
At the sound of the fife and the roll of the drum,
Come away, my lads, come!
At the sweet call of beauty to duty repair,
And worthily merit the gift of the fair.
What but vict'ry complete can result from those wars,
Where the cestus of Venus encircles each Mars.

At old Troy some kind goddess, by spell or by charm,
Condescending, preserved votive warriors from harm;
So Britons shall boast the same tutelary care,
Invuln'rable grown by the gift of the fair.
      At the sound of the fife, &c.

England's armour's her commerce—the woolsack is
      known
To take place, in this kingdom, of all but the throne;
The power of our arms, then, what force can withstand,
When wool's form'd to armour by beauty's fair hand?
      At the sound of the fife, &c.

'Tis allow'd through the world, as this nation's proud
      meed,
That the beauties of Britain all beauty exceed!
How then must that beauty each Briton enslave,
When it tenders its influence to succour the brave!
      At the sound of the fife, &c.

Complete then the work; for the brave and the bold
Let no fair in this land her assistance withhold;
What power to attack British soldiers shall dare,
Who are arm'd, cap-a-pie, by a generous fair?
    At the sound of the fife, &c.

MAD PEG.

The gloomy night stalk'd slow away,
The twilight spoke the doubtful day,
When on a rock poor Peg reclined,
Mad as the waves, wild as the wind.
Give me my love! she frantic scream'd;
I saw his ghost as by it gleam'd:
I'll dive, I'll search the briny gloom,
And snatch him from his coral tomb.
Ah! let me, Fate, his relics save,—
True lovers should find out one grave.

And now the tempest dims the sky,—
How many ways poor sailors die!
See, see, the stagg'ring vessel splits!
She's lost like Peg's poor shipwreck'd wits.
No, 'twas in battle that he died.
Would no power turn the ball aside?
I saw it as it rent his heart;
I heard him cry—And must we part?
For Peggy, ah! these relics save,—
True lovers should find out one grave.

Where on the deep the cavern yawn'd,
Now as the purple morning dawn'd,
The surge, in breakers loud and hoarse,
Her love casts up, a lifeless corse.
She raves, she screams, her hands she wrings,
The shock returning reason brings:
Reason returns, alas! too late;
She clasps her love, and yields to fate.
Their mourning friends their relics save,
And these two lovers find one grave.

THE CAMP.

On! the camp's delightful rigs,
    At which such crowds are peeping,
Where chaises, dillies, carts, and gigs
    Serve both to ride and sleep in.
Oh! the joys that there abound,
    Where, lured by the fine weather,
Warriors of every rank are found,
Who higgledy piggledy, on the ground,
    Like gipsies, pig together.
    The morning gun
    Begins the fun,
Reveillies next the drum beats,
    The sprightly fife
    So full of life,
And then the silver trumpets;
    And these, with all their might,
    Announce a fine sham fight;

Marches, retreats, attacks, and routs,
Proclaim'd by guns, and shrieks and shouts,
The air with various clangors fill;
   While ranks of foot, and troops of horse,
   Resistless in their headlong course,
   Bear down, while sliding, shifting, trimming,
   Beaux, belles, Jew pedlars, and old women;
   Who, left in topsy-turvy plight,
   Exhibit, O ye gods! a sight
That beggars Greenwich hill!
Now either army stilly stands,
   The neighing horses cease to prance,
   The trumpet, that erst cried Advance,
   Now sounds Retreat;
   Drums cease to beat;
Foes, turn'd to friends, eager shake hands,
   On neither side the winner:
No longer arm'd for a sham fight,
They tooth and nail unite
   ·To exterminate—the dinner.
      Oh! the camp's delightful rigs, &c.

Oh! for a muse of fire, to sing
   The conflict of the day!
Upon a plain, in form a ring,
   The foe within entrenchments lay;
   A cover'd way
Hid each division: at the sight,
The heroes, eager for the fight,
   Arm, and the enemy invest.
   Each charge fresh vigour brings:
They thin the ranks,
Attacking flanks
   And wings:

N

Legs, heads, and carcases around
They in one shapeless heap confound;
And, ris'n to such a savage heat,
Not only kill, but all they kill they eat!
And see, to urge their furious course,
Light troops the foe now reinforce;
On the instant, as they stand amazed,
New works are raised;
Like magic to their wond'ring eyes,
Bastions, redoubts, and rav'lins rise.

 Again the signal giv'n;
 Again with headlong fury driv'n;
 Comfits, now discomfited,
 Lie in promiscuous ruin spread;
Trifles, blanchmange, and jellies quake,
 While, as with rage they teem,
Whole islands they devour of cake,
 And drink whole seas of cream.
Again the general cries, Charge all!
 The word's—The king!
 Forward they spring,
And drink, in savage joy, the blood
Drawn from the grape, in purple flood;
And strew with mangled heaps the plain,
And fight the battle o'er again,
And slay the slain!
And now, the foe all kill'd or fled,
While those that can walk off to bed,—
The solemn trumpet slowly sounded,
Leave 's given to carry off the wounded,
 And bury all the dead.
  Oh! the camp's delightful rigs, &c.

ONE WHO WENT TO SEA.

Alas! where shall I comfort find ?
My peace is gone, distress'd my mind;
    My heart beats high,
    I know not why;
Poor heart! ah me, ah me!
So tender, artless, and so young,
I listen'd to his flatt'ring tongue;
    Nor did I e'er
    Suspect a snare
From one who went to sea.
For sailors kind and honest are;
They injur'd virtue make their care;
One, only one, did e'er depart
From that prov'd rule, and he,
Ah me!
Was born to break my simple heart.
    Alas, &c.

When absent from my longing arms,
Each hour was fraught with new alarms;
Each rising morn beheld my tears;
The softest breeze, in my fond fears,
Did the horizon straight deform,
And Zephyr grew into a storm :
Yet to be cheated of my bliss—
And was I then so kind for this?
    Alas, &c.

THE LOVER'S PROBATION.

'Tis said that love, the more 'tis tried,
  Grows firmer and lasts longer ;
And when distress the knot has tied
  'Tis closer knit and stronger.
She who with love's best joys would fain
  That fate should thus regale her,
Must share the peril and the pain
  That mark the gallant sailor.

To hope in vain, in vain to sigh,
  Deep sorrow to dissemble ;
To shudder at each lowering sky,
  At every breeze to tremble;
While neither wishes, prayers, nor tears,
  To ease her mind avail her ;—
These dreadful trials speak her fears
  Who loves a gallant sailor.

And now, her miseries to refine,
  To fate she's forced to yield him ;
For, with swoll'n eyes, she spells the line
  Where newspapers have kill'd him :
This is the last of her alarms ;
  Cease, lovers, to bewail her ;
He comes, and in her trembling arms
  She holds her gallant sailor.

DICK HOPEFUL.

Dick Hopeful from an honest stock
Born, his kind parents' hopes to mock,
Who chose him out a lovely mate,
But he resolv'd to brave his fate,
Spurn'd at content and went to sea.
Damme, says Dick, no wife for me !
'Twere better brave the tempest's strife ;—
Who's such a fool to value life?

Mad as the winds, to sea he went ;
Nor was there danger ever sent,
By sickness, water, fire, or air,
Combin'd, but he'd a precious share ;
Till shipwreck'd, flush'd with drink, at night,
He saw a female and a light ;
'Twas her who long'd to be his wife.
For once, said he, I value life.

The thankless wretch next swore, and reel'd,
That night he'd die, or she should yield ;
And now, on force and outrage bent,
Her window scaled : but mark the event!
He found her on her knees at prayer
That Heaven might make him still its care,
Protect him from the tempest's strife,
And teach him how to value life.

Confounded at the scene he saw,
He stood immoveable with awe;
And he, before who knew not shame,
A contrite penitent became.
Next morn he led the nuptial band,
She yielded up her willing hand:
She's call'd the pattern of a wife,
And Dick knows how to value life.

BEAUTY'S BANNER.

Since love is the hero's best duty,
    And the brave fight to merit the fair,
How sweet, when commaded by beauty,
    He flies every danger to dare.
Hark, hark! the loud drum
Cries come, come, come, come,
Another Britannia appears;
And while England's banners she gracefully rears,
    And sweetly addresses the band,
    And beauty and bravery salute,
And the flute mocks the trumpet, the trumpet the flute,
  The heroes receive the dear plege from her hand,
    And swear that they'll well
    Hostile boasters repel,
  Till honour and safety give peace to the land.

Thus the hero may well wear his armour,
   And, patient, count over his scars;
Venus' dimples, assuming the charmer,
   Shall smooth the rough furrows of Mars.
     Hark, hark! &c.

Then round with the health of the donor,
   While angels might look and approve;
Since love is the hero's best honour,
   Let each hero do honour to love.
     Hark, hark! &c.

KICKARABOO.

ONE negro say one ting, you no take offence,
Black and white be one colour a hundred year hence;
For when massa Death kick him into him grave,
He no spare neither massa, no buckra, nor slave.
Then dance and then sing, an a banger strum, strum,
He foolish to tink what a morrow may come;
Lily laugh and grow fat, a best ting you can do,
Time enough to be sad when you kickaraboo.

One massa, one slave, high and low, all degrees,
Can be happy, all sing, make all pleasure him please;
One slave be one massa if him good, honest, brave,
One massa bad, wicked, him worse um one slave:
If you heart tell you good, you all happy, all well;
If bad, he a plague, vex you worse dan um hell.
Let you heart make you merry den, good, honest true,
An you no care no farder for kickaraboo.

One game him see massa him play, an call chess;
King, queen, bishop, castle, knight, all in a mess;
King kill knight, queen kill bishop, men castle trow
    down,
Like card soldier all scatter an lay on a ground;
An when de game over, king, bishop, tag, rag,
Queen, knight, all agedder him go in a bag:
So in life's game o' chess, when no more him can do,
Massa Death bring one bag, and we kickaraboo.

Den be good, what you am never mind de degree;
Lily flower good for summat as well as big tree.
You one slave, he no use a be sulky and sly;
Worky, worky, you 'haps be one massa by'm by;
Savee good and be poor, make you act better part,
Dan be rich in a pocket and poor in a heart.
Though ever so low, do your duty,—for true
All you friend drop a tear when you kickaraboo.

JOLTERING GILES.

HARK! with what glee yon merry clown
    Reasons, remarks, and sows;
To pain and care alike unknown,
    He whistles as he goes.
From nature's lore to reason taught,
    He knows not subtle rules,
But ventures oft such pithy thought
    As might instruct the schools.

" This ground 's just like the world," cries he,
  " And thezum zeeds its cares."
" How 's that ?" says one. " Why, cant'e zee,
  As I be a zowing o' tares?

Tol de roll, &c.

" For drill or broadcast none do know
Better than Jolt'ring Giles to sow,
Be't beans, or whuts, or wheat or rye,
Or barley, you mun come to I."

· Tol de roll, &c.

Thus Jolt'ring Giles, the merry clown,
  Reasons, remarks, and sows ;
To pain and care alike unknown,
  He whistles as he goes.

One day some dashing sprigs came by,
  Imported neat from town ;
As they pass'd on Giles heard 'em cry—
  " I say, let's quiz the clown !"
And just as they their fun began
  An ass was heard to bray
Ichaw ! " Here, fellow, clown ! "—" Anon !
  One at a time, zur, pray !"
" We reap the fruit of all that's sown
  By fellows of your stamp."
" That's very likely, zur, I own,
  Vor I be a zow o' hamp."

Tol de rol, &c.

For drill or broadcast, &c.

A vriend to all the country round,
  My labours all regale;
'Twas I the barley put i' the ground
  That brew'd th' exciseman's ale;
The wheat I sow wi' even hand
  To thousands shall give bread;
There's never no king, nor 'squire o' th' land,
  Zo many mouths ha' ved:
I zaves zum zouls, vor aught I know—
  If how thou'st wish to larn—
The tithe of every grain I grow
  Goes into the parson's barn.
                    Tol de rol, &c.
    For drill or broadcast, &c.

But what at last be all my pains?
  Just like to wheat or rye,
A man comes vorward, counts his gains,
  And holds his head up high:
Then, scarcely full and ripe he's grown,
  However great he be,
Death, with his zickle, cuts un down,
  And there be's an end o' he.
Zo, while a body's here below
  Clean hands be zure to keep,
Vor, zure as death, as we do zow
  We zartainly shall reap!
                    Tol de rol, &c.
    For drill or broadcast, &c.

THE IRISH DRUMMER.

Sure en't I the drummer that goes to the fight?
Only hear me with joy, and you 'll be stunn'd with
    delight.
The likes of my fame sure no mortal enjoys,
For there's nobody makes such a dev'l of a noise.
With my rub a dub, row de dow, rattle away,
See the army all drawn out in battle array ;
How sweetly they come to the sound of my drum,
With my rub a dub, &c.

Advancing the last, and retreating the first,
When we're covered with smoke, and with glory, and
    dust ;
'Mongst heroes that follow and heroes that fly,
If a devil of a thundering you hear, why that's I !
    With my rub a dub, &c.

Then the fun that you'd see, wid delight and surprise,
If the devilish smoke did not put out your eyes.
In the lovely Dutch concert of shrieks and dismay,
Sure en't it, my soul, the first fiddle I play ?
    With my rub a dub, &c.

Then, like herrings all smoked, from the field when
    we're come,
And our battles abroad we are fighting at home,
My share I contend for wid body and breath,
Though I nobody kill'd, fait I stunn'd them to death,
    With my rub a dub, &c.

THE LADIES.

THERE was lady, a lady, a pretty lady,
　　The pride of Aurora!
Such a string of relations! a string of relations!
　　(*Ad libitum.*)
First cousin to Narcissus, Hyacinthus' cousin-german,
Heliotropus' niece, the sister of Myrtillos,
　　And the grand-daughter of Flora!
Alike she delighted the eyes and the nose,
She outblush'd the belles, and she charm'd all the beaux,
And thus we smelt out that her name was Rose.
And though she alternate gave pleasure and smart,
In my bosom I placed her, and nearest my heart;
Half seas over in love, of no danger afraid,
I thought, not remembering that roses would fade,
　　That for ever now fix'd, I had done with my rambles.
But alas! Heaven knows, this delicate rose,
Alas! Heaven knows, this delicate rose,
In Hymen's soft fetters I scarcely had bound,
When, by symptoms of scratching, I presently found
　　　That roses have brambles, have brambles, have bram-
　　　　　　bles,
　　　　That roses have brambles!
　　　　　Thus my pretty little Rose,
　　　　　When I put her to my nose,
　　Scratch'd my face with her beautiful brambles!

　　There was a lady, a lady, a pretty lady;
　　　Not the same, but another.
　　Oh, such an extraction! oh, such an extraction!
　　　(*Ad libitum.*)
She could count by the father's side all the way to
　　Methusaleh and Adam, and to Eve by the mother;

Call'd a Phœnix by bards, by her godmothers Grace ;
But, as if Madam Nature, in making her face,
Had got drunk, and so happen'd her charms to misplace,
Though she gave wherewithal admiration to get,
There was no want of lily, nor ruby, nor jet ;
But the jet was her teeth in irregular rows,
Her lips were the lily, the ruby her nose.

    But love attempts all things ; and I swore to win her.
And this Madam Grace, with her whimsical face,
And this Madam Grace, with her whimsical face,
A bride to the altar I surely had led,
Had she not bless'd another, who never had said
    Grace before dinner, before dinner, before dinner!
        Grace before dinner !
           What a pity such a Grace,
           With such a queer face,
      Should forget to say grace before dinner!

    There was a lady, a lady, a Spanish lady,
      A lovely Blondinella !
And they call'd her for shortness, they call'd her for
  shortness,
    (*Ad libitum.*)
Signora Flora di Guzman y Bazalos Pintenda Merceda
    Yolante Isabella !
So numerous the charms of this heavenly belle,
They bewitch'd my fond heart like a conjuror's spell ;
Had she been Orpheus' wife, he'd have fetch'd her from
    hell.
The lily, the rose, and the stars in the skies,
Were eclipsed by her lips, and her teeth, and her eyes ;
No peacock so stately, more graceful no swan ;
Thus full gallop my love and my raptures began !

Her charms and attractions so filling my napper.
But, alas! pretty belle, how it grieves me to tell,
Alas! pretty belle, how it grieves me to tell,
She'd one imperfection, a sort of a speck,—
A kind of deduction, a drawback, a check,—
My bell had a clapper, had a clapper, a clapper,
My bell had a clapper!
Oh, my pretty little bell,
I'd have loved her very well,
If she hadn't had a devil of a clapper!

THE WAGGONER.

When I comes to town with a load of hay,
Mean and lowly though I seem,
I knows pretty well how they figures away,
While I whistles and drives my team.
Your natty sparks and flashy dames,
How I do love to queer!
I runs my rigs,
And patters and gigs,
And plays a hundred comical games,
To all that I comes near.
Then in a pet
To hear 'em fret,
A-mobbing away they go,—
("The scoundrel deserves to be horse-whipp'd!"
"Who? me, Ma'am?")
Wo, Ball, wo!
So to mind them I never seem,
But whistles and drives my team!

So, as I seems thinking of nothing at all,
  And driving as fast as I can,
I pins a queer thing against a wall,
  Half a monkey and half a man!
The mob came round him to put up his blood;
  While he's trembling from top to toe,
    My whip it goes spank,
    I tips Ball on the flank,
Ball plunges, and paints him all over with mud,
  Queers his stockings, and spoils the beau!
    Then the sweet pretty dear,
    Ah, could you but hear,—
    ("Odds, curse! I'll make you know,
    You infernal villain!"
" Lord bless your baby face, I would not hurt your
  spindle shanks for the world!")
    Wo, Ball, wo!
So to mind them I never seem,
But whistles and drives my team.

And so I gets the finest fun
  And frisk that ever you saw;
Of all I meets I can queer every one
  But you gemmen of the law.
Though they can scarcely put me down:
  Says I, to their courts when I'm led,
    Where their tails of a pig
    They hide with a wig,
How many ways in London town
  They dresses a calf's head!
    Then ev'ry dunce
    To hear open at once,

Like mill-clacks their clappers go,
("Oh! that's the fellow I saw grinning through the
  horse-collar in the country."
" I fancy you are the fellow I saw grinning through
  the pillory in London!")
    Wo, Ball, wo!
So, to mind 'em I never seem,
But whistles and drives my team.

THE FAIR.

WOULD ye see the world in little,
  Ye curious, here repair;
We'll suit you to a tittle
  At this our rustic fair.
We've glitt'ring baits to catch you,
  As tempting as at court;
With whim for whim we'll match you,
  And give you sport for sport.
From a sceptre to a rattle,
  We've everything in toys;
For infants that scarce prattle,
  To men who still are boys.
Cock-horses and state-coaches
  In gingerbread are sold;
Cakes, parliament, gilt watches,
  And horns all tipp'd with gold.
Then, if for fine parade you go,
Come here and see our puppet-show.

Walk in here, ladies and gentlemen. Here you may
see the Queen of Sheba, and King Solomon in all his
glory. You think that figure's all alive; but he is no
more alive than I am!

> While the pipes and the tabors rend the air,
> Haste, neighbours, to the fair.

> What's your sweepstakes and your races,
>   And all your fighting cocks,
> To our horse-collar grimaces,
>   And girls that run for smocks?
> Our Hobs can swivle noses,
>   At single-stick who fight,
> As well as your Mendozas,
>   Though not quite so polite.
> In their deceptions neater
>   Are your keen rooks allow'd,
> Than is yonder fire-eater,
>   Who queers the gaping crowd?
> Then boast not tricks so noxious,
>   That genteel life bespeak,
> Our jugglers, hixious doxious,
>   Shall distance every Greek.
> Can Pharaoh and his host be found
> To match our nimble merry-go-round?

Put in, here, put in, put in!—Every blank a prize!—
Down with it and double it,—twenty can play as well as
one!

> While the pipes, &c.

O

Hear yon mountebank assure ye
  Of diseases by the score,
A single dose shall cure ye.
  Can Warwick-lane do more ?
Wid virligigs tetotums,
  Yon Jew's imposhing faish,
Shall cheat you here in no times,
  All one as in Duke's place.
Hark, yonder, making merry,
  Full many a happy clown !
For champaign who drink perry,
  As good as that in town.
Then, for sights, we've apes and monkies,
  Some on four legs, some on two ;
Tall women, dwarfs, cropp'd donkies,
  For all the world like you !
Then, would ye Ranelagh find out,
What d'ye think of our roundabont ?

Walk in, ladies and gentlemen ! the only booth in the fair ! Here ye may make the tour of the whole world ! Would ye ride in the caravan, the expedition, the land-frigate, or the dilly ? Fourteen miles in fifteen hours, ladies and gentlemen !

While the pipes, &c.

HUMANITY'S COT.

Of horns and of echoes that through the woods ring,
  And of lads full of spunk and of soul,
And of gay sporting boxes let other bards sing,
  Merely built for the chase or the bowl.

I bring you, of sportsmen, a true and tried knot,
Who sport a snug box call'd Humanity's Cot.

Is honour in danger, worth sunk by its fears,
   On those coursers, their wishes, they're borne,
To hunt vice to the toils, and to dry virtue's tears,
   As the sun melts the dew of the morn.
Then join of true sportsmen so noble a knot,
The good lads that inhabit Humanity's Cot.

What chase a delight can more glorious yield,
   Than to hunt in so noble a track ;
Vice and folly the game, wide creation the field,
   And the vot'ries of honour the pack?
Rejoice, then, ye sportsmen, who're thrown by Fate's lot,
'Mongst the lads that inhabit Humanity's Cot.

Return'd from their toil, with life's comforts well stored,
   Reflection their food gives a zest ;
Health seasons the viand that smokes on the board,
   A clear conscience invites them to rest.
And sweet are the slumbers that fall to the lot
Of the lads that inhabit Humanity's Cot.

Then let each English sportsman these maxims embrace,
   Who the spoils of true honour would share,
All that's noxious to hunt to the toils in life's chase,
   All that's harmless and useful to spare.
So the blessings of thousands shall make up their lot,
And each sporting-box vie with Humanity's Cot.

THE WATCHMAN.

A watchman I am, and I knows all the round,
  The housekeepers, the strays, and the lodgers,
Where low devils, rich dons, and high rips, may be
      found,
  Odd dickies, queer kids, and rum codgers.
Of money and of property I'm he that takes the care,
And cries when I see rogues go by, Hey! what are you
  doing there?

" Only a little business in that house! You understand me?" " Understand you! Well, I believe you
are an honest man. Do you hear,—Bring me an odd
silver candlestick."

          Then to my box I creep,
          And then fall fast asleep.

          Saint Paul's strikes ONE!
          Thus, after all the mischief's done,
      I goes and gives them warning,
          And loudly bawls,
          As strikes St. Paul's,
      Past one o'clock, and a cloudy morning.

Then, round as the hour I merrily cries,
  Another fine mess I discover,—
For a curious rope-ladder I straightway espies,
  And Miss Forward expecting her lover.
Then to each other's arms they fly—
  My life—my soul! Ah, ah!
Fine work, Miss Hot-upon't! cries I;
  I'll knock up your papa.

"No, no, you won't." "I shall! worthy old soul!—
to be treated in this manner." "Here, here, take this."
"Oh, you villain! want to bribe an honest watchman!
and with such a trifle too!" "Well, well, here is
more!" "More! You seem to be a spirited lad. Now
do make her a good husband. I am glad you tricked
the old hunks. Good night. I wish you safe at Gretna
Green!"

> Then to my box I creep,
> And then fall fast asleep.
>
> Saint Paul's strikes TWO ;
> The lovers off, what does I do,—
> I gives the father warning,
> And loudly bawls,
> As strikes St. Paul's,
> Past two o'clock, and a cloudy morning.

Then towards the square from my box as I looks,
　I hears such a ranting and tearing:
'Tis Pharaoh's whole host, and the pigeons and rooks
　Are laughing, and singing, and swearing.
Then such a hubbub and a din,
　How they blaspheme and curse !
That thief has stole my diamond pin,—
　Watch, watch,—I've lost my purse !

"Watch, here; I charge you." "And I charges you."
"'Tis a marvellous thing that honest people can't go
home without being robbed. Which is the thief?"
"That's the thief that tricked me out of two hundred
pounds this evening." "Ah! that, you know, is all in
the way of business. But which is the thief that stole
the gentleman's purse?" "That's him." "What!

Sam Snatch? Give it to me, Sam. He has not got your purse,—you are mistaken in your man. Go home peaceably, and don't oblige me to take you to the watch-house."

> Then to my box I creep,
> And then fall fast asleep.
> St. Paul's strikes THREE—
> Thus from all roguery I gets free,
> By giving people warning,
> And loudly balls,
> As strikes St. Paul's,
> Past three o'clock, and a cloudy morning.

BACHELOR'S HALL.

To Bachelor's Hall we good fellows invite,
To partake of the chase that makes up our delight.
We have spirits like fire and of health such a stock,
That our pulse strikes the seconds as true as a clock.
Did you see us, you'd swear, as we mount with a grace,
That Diana had dubb'd some new gods of the chase.
Hark, away! hark, away! all nature looks gay,
And Aurora with smiles ushers in the bright day.

Dick Thickset came mounted upon a fine black,
A better fleet gelding ne'er hunter did back;
Tom Trigg rode a bay, full of mettle and bone;
And gaily Bob Buxom rode on a proud roan;
But the horse of all horses that rivall'd the day
Was the Squire's Neck-or-Nothing, and that was a grey.
  Hark, away! &c.

Then for hounds, there was Nimble, so well that climb'd
    rocks ;
And Cock-nose, a good one at scenting a fox ;
Little Plunge, like a mole, who will ferret and search ;
And beetle-brow'd Hawk's-eye, so dead at a lurch ;
Young Sly-looks, who scents the strong breeze from the
    south,
And musical Echo-well, with his deep mouth.
      Hark, away ! &c.

Our horses thus all of the very best blood,
'Tis not likely you'll easily find such a stud ;
And for hounds, our opinions with thousands we'd back
That all England throughout can't produce such a pack.
Thus, having described you dogs, horses, and crew,
Away we set off, for the fox is in view.
      Hark, away ! &c.

Sly Reynard 's brought home, while the hounds sound a
    call,
And now you're all welcome to Bachelor's Hall.
The savoury sirloin grateful smokes on the board,
And Bacchus pours wine from his favourite hoard.
Come on, then, do honour to this jovial place,
And enjoy the sweet pleasures that spring from the chase ;
Hark, away ! hark, away ! while our spirits are gay,
Let us drink to the joys of the next coming day.

FATHER AND MOTHER AND SUKE.

Says my father, says he, one day, to I,
　　Thou knowest by false friends we are undone,
Should my law-suit be lost, then thy good fortune try
　　Amongst our relations in London.
Here's Sukey, the poor orphan child of friend Grist,
　　Who once kept thy father from starving;
When thy fortune thou'st made, thou shalt take by the
　　　　fist,
　　For a wife,—for she's good and deserving.
But mind thee in heart this one maxim, our Jack,
　　As thou'st read thy good fate in a book,
Make honour thy guide, or else never come back
　　To father and mother and Suke.

So I buss'd Suke and mother, and greatly concern'd,
　　Off I set, with my father's kind blessing,
To our cousin the wine-merchant, where I soon learn'd
　　About mixing, and brewing, and pressing:
But the sloe-juice, and ratsbane, and all that fine joke,
　　Was soon in my stomach arising;
Why dom it, cried I, would you kill the poor folk?
　　I thought you sold wine, and not poison.
Your place, my dear cousin, won't do, for you lack
　　To make your broth, another guess cook;
Besides, without honour, I cannot go back
　　To father and mother and Suke.

To my uncle, the doctor, I next went my ways;
   He teach'd me the mystery quickly,
Of those that were dying to shorten their days,
   And they in good health to make sickly.
Oh, the music of groans! cried my uncle, dear boy,
   Vapours set all my spirits a flowing;
A fit of the gout makes me dancing for joy;
   At an ague I'm all in a glowing!
Why then, my dear uncle, cries I, you're a quack,
   For another assistant go look;
For, you see, without honour, I munna go back
   To father and mother and Suke.

From my cousin, the parson, I soon comed away,
   Without either waiting or warning,
For he preach'd upon soberness three times one day,
   And then comed home drunk the next morning.
My relation, the author, stole other folks' thoughts,
   My cousin, the bookseller, sold them;
My pious old aunt found in innocence faults,
   And made virtue blush as she told them!
So the prospect around me quite dismal and black,
   Scarcely knowing on which side to look,
I just saved my honour, and then I comed back
   To father and mother and Suke.

I found them as great as a king on his throne,—
   The law-suit had banish'd all sorrow.
I'm come, said I, father, my honour's my own.
   Then thou shalt have Sukey to-morrow.
But how about London? 'Twon't do for a clown;
   There vice rides with folly behind it;
Not, you see, that I says there's no honour in town,—
   I only says I could not find it.

If you sent me to starve, you found out the right track;
   If to live, the wrong method you took;
For I poor went to London, and poor I comed back
   To father and mother and Suke.

THE FLOWING BOWL.

Of all heav'n gave to comfort man,
   And cheer his drooping soul,
Show me a blessing, he who can,
   To top the flowing bowl:
When amorous Strephon, dying swain,
   Whose heart his Daphne stole,
Is jilted, to relieve his pain
   He seeks the flowing bowl.

When husbands hear, in hopeless grief,
   The knell begin to toll,
They mourn awhile, then, for relief,
   They seek the flowing bowl.
The tar, while swelling waves deform
   Old Ocean as they roll,
In spite of danger and the storm,
   Puts round the flowing bowl.

The miner, who his devious way
   Works like the purblind mole,
Still comfort for the loss of day
   Finds in the flowing bowl.
It gives to poets lyric wit,
   To jesters to be droll,
Anacreon's self had never writ
   But for the flowing bowl.

Moisten your clay, then, sons of earth,
   To Bacchus, in a shoal,
Come on, the volunteers of mirth;
   And by the flowing bowl
Become immortal, be adored,
   'Mongst gods your names enroll,—
Olympus be the festive board,
   Nectar the flowing bowl.

THE MARGATE HOY.

STANDING one summer's day on the Tower Slip,
   Careless how I my time should employ,
It popp'd in my head that I'd take a trip
   Aboard of a Margate Hoy.
I took a few slops, such as shirts and a coat,
   For of prog I knew well they'd be stored;
Then I hail'd a pair of oars, shoved off my boat,
   And away I dashed aboard.

"Ah, my dear Commodore! who thought of seeing you? What, Mrs. Garbage! How is the Alderman?" "There is my husband, sir." "'Pon my word and dicky, I declare." "Give me leave, Commodore, to introduce you to my friends: Mr. Shadrack, Commodore Kelson—Commodore Kelson, Mr. Shadrack." "Very much at your sharvice, sir." "Miss Minnikin, Commodore Kelson—Commodore Kelson, Miss Minnikin." "Very happy to have the pleasure of knowing you,

sir." " Dr. Quibus, Commodore Kelson—Commodore
Kelson, Dr. Quibus; Captain Squash, Commodore Kel-
son—Commodore Kelson, Captain Squash; Sir Phelim
O'Drogheda, Commodore Kelson—Commodore Kelson,
Sir Phelim O'Drogheda."—Hollo, there! Cast off the
painter. Sit still, ladies and gentlemen.

> So off we went with a flowing jib,
>   Full of merriment and joy;
> The alderman munching and prattling his rib.
>   Sing who so blythe as we,
>   Who take a voyage to sea,
> Aboard of a Margate Hoy.

Then such glee and good humour, our joy to prolong,
    Pervaded us fore and aft;
Some were telling a story, some whistling a song,
    As we turn'd in and out 'mongst the craft.
Then we'd talk of our danger, and then we were gay;
    Then how we'd astonish the folks
When at Margate arrived: then cut out of our way,
    To laugh at the watermen's jokes.

" Ho! the ship, ahoy!" " Ay, ay!" " Pray, have you
one Wiseman aboard?" " No, no." " Then you are
all fools, heh?" " Ha, ha, ha!" went Miss Minnikin.
" Dat is very coot chokes," said the Jew. " Why, I
say, Moses," said the man that was affronted, " are you
a bull or bear? Damme, I think you look more like a
monkey. And you, Miss Dolly Drylips, take a reef in
your perriwig, and clap a stopper on your muzzle, clue
up the plaits in your jaw-bags, and give your tongue
leave of absence. About ship—helm's alee—here she
comes."

So we made t'other tack, and lay gunnel to,
   Which soon gave a damp to our joy,—
Miss Minnikin squall'd.   Mine Cot! cried the Jew.
      Sing who so blythe as we,
      Who take a voyage to sea
On board of a Margate Hoy.

The company's merriment now out of joint, .
   And their tattlers not moving so quick,
Scarce right a-head did we twig Cuckold's Point,
   But the alderman 'gan to be sick.
Then we'd like to fall foul of an oyster-smack,
   The wind freshing towards the Nore;
Then, stretching too far on the larboard tack,
   By and by we came bump on shore.

"Ah, we shall all be cast away! My poor dear pattern-cap!" "Cash'd away! What shall I do to be shaved?" "Why, faith!" said I, "I fancy we shall have a touch of the salt water before we get to Margate." "Yes, sir," said the doctor, "not that I have any quarrel with death, but I am afraid we shall take in too large a dose." "How do you do, Sir Phelim?" "Arrah! I should be well enough if I was not so cursedly sick." She rights, she rights!

Next a gale coming on we did preciously kick,
   Which finish'd completely our joy;
'Twas, Madam, how do you do? Oh! I am monstrously sick.
      Sing who so blythe as we,
      Who take a voyage to sea
Aboard of a Margate Hoy.

And now 'twould have made a philosopher grin
    To have seen such a concourse of muns;
Sick as death, wet as muck, from the heel to the chin,
    For it came on to blow great guns.
Spoil'd clothes and provisions now clogg'd up the way,
    In a dreary and boisterous night!
While apparently dead every passenger lay
    With the sickness, but more with the fright.

    " Oh, oh! I wish I was at home in my bed !" " Oh,
that I was a hundred miles off!" " Mashy upon my
shins!" " Oh, oh! will nobody throw me overboard !"
" Avast, there!"   " Ah, my poor dear pattern-cap's
blown into the pond !" " Oh, my soul! what a devil of
a sickness!" " Arrah, stop the ship! let me out! Sir,
would you be so kind as to be after handing me a caudle-
cup?" Land, land, upon the starboard bow!

At last after turning on two or three tacks,
    Margate lights soon restored all our joy;
The men found their stomachs, the women their clacks.
        Sing who so blythe as we,
        Who take a voyage to sea
    Aboard of a Margate Hoy.

NONGTONGPAW.

JOHN BULL for pastime took a prance,
Some time ago to peep at France ;
To talk of sciences and arts,
And knowledge gain'd in foreign parts.

Monsieur, obsequious, heard him speak,
And answer'd John in heathen Greek:
To all he ask'd, 'bout all he saw,
'Twas *Monsieur, Je vous n'entends pas.*

John to the Palais-Royal come,
Its splendour almost struck him dumb.
I say, Whose house is that there here?
Hosse ! Je vous n'entends pas, Monsieur.
What, Nongtongpaw again! cries John;
.This fellow is some mighty Don:
No doubt he's plenty for the maw,
I'll breakfast with this Nongtongpaw.

John saw Versailles from Marli's height,
And cried, astonish'd at the sight,
Whose fine estate is that there here?
Stat! Je vous n'entends pas, Monsieur.
His? what, the land and houses too?
The fellow's richer than a Jew:
On everything he lays his claw;
I should like to dine with Nongtongpaw.

Next, tripping, came a courtly fair,
John cried, enchanted with her air,
What lovely wench is that there here?
Ventch! Je vous n'entends pas, Monsieur.
What, he again? Upon my life!
A palace, lands, and then a wife
Sir Joshua might delight to draw :
I should like to sup with Nongtongpaw.

But hold! whose funeral's that? cries John.
Je vous n'entends pas :—What, is he gone?
Wealth, fame, and beauty could not save
Poor Nongtongpaw then from the grave!
His race is run, his game is up,
I'd with him breakfast, dine and sup;
But since he chooses to withdraw,
Good night t'ye, Mounseer Nongtongpaw!

THE LABOURER'S WELCOME HOME.

THE ploughman whistles o'er the furrow,
The hedger joins the vacant strain,
The woodman sings the woodland thorough,
The shepherd's pipe delights the plain :
Where'er the anxious eye can roam,
Or ear receive the jocund pleasure,
Myriads of beings thronging flock
Of nature's song to join the measure,
Till to keep time the village clock
Sounds, sweet, the labourer's welcome home.

The hearth swept clean, his partner smiling,
Upon the shining table smokes
The frugal meal; while, time beguiling,
The ale the harmless jest provokes.
Ye inmates of the lofty dome
Admire his lot: his children playing,
To share his smiles, around him flock;
And faithful Tray, since morn that straying,
Trudg'd with him, till the village clock
Proclaim'd the labourer's welcome home.

The cheering faggot burnt to embers,
While lares round their vigils keep,
That Power the poor and rich remembers,
Each thanks and then retires to sleep.
And now the lark climbs heav'n's high dome,
Fresh from repose, toil's kind reliever ;
And furnish'd with his daily stock,
His dog, his staff, his keg, his beaver,
He travels, till the village clock
Sounds, sweet, the labourer's welcome home.

CAPTAIN WATTLE AND MISS ROE.

DID you ever hear of Captain Wattle,
He was all for love and a little for the bottle.
We know not, though pains we have taken to inquire,
If gunpowder he invented, or the Thames set on fire ;
If to him was the centre of gravity known,
The longitude, or the philosopher's stone ;
Or whether he studied from Bacon or Boyle,
Copernicus, Locke, Katerfelto, or Hoyle :
But this we have learnt, with great labour and pain,
That he loved Miss Roe and she loved him again.

Than sweet Miss Roe none e'er look'd fiercer,
She had but one eye, but that was a piercer.
We know not, for certainty, her education,
If she wrote, mended stockings, or settled the nation ;
At cards if she liked whist and swabbers or voles,
Or at dinner loved pig, or a steak on the coals ;

P

Whether most of the Sappho she was or Thalestris,
Or if dancing was taught her by Hopkins or Vestris :
But, for your satisfaction, this good news we obtain,
That she loved Captain Wattle and he loved her again.

When wedded he became lord and master, depend on't;
He had but one leg, but he'd a foot at the end on't,
Which, of government when she would fain hold the
      bridle,
He took special caution should never lie idle :
So, like most married folks, 'twas my plague and my
      chicken,
And sometimes a kissing, and sometimes a kicking :
Then for comfort a cordial she'd now and then try,
Alternately bunging or piping her eye :
And these facts of this couple the history contain,
For when he kick'd Miss Roe she kick'd him again.

THE COUNTRY CLUB.

Now we're all met here together,
In spite of wind and weather,
   To moisten well our clay ;
Before we think of jogging,
Let's take a cheerful noggin.
   Where's the waiter ?   Ring away.
Bring the glees and the catches,
The tobacco-pipes and matches,
   And plenty of brown stout.

Get the glasses, e'er we start 'em,
Let's proceed *secundem artem,*
   Let the clerk all the names read out.

" Gentlemen of the Quizzical Society, please to answer to your names. Farmer Scroggins?" "Why I be here." — " Dr. Horseleach ?" " Here." — " Parson Paunch ?" " Here."—" Tailor Tit?" " Here."—So he goes on for about twenty. At last, " You here! are you all assembled ?" " All, all, all, all, all."

Then here's to you, mister Wiggins ;
Here's to you, master Figgins ;
   So put the beer about.

Come tell us what the news is,
Who wins and who loses,
   Of the times what do people say ?
Hard, hard, the landlord racks us ;
Then we've such a load of taxes.
   Indeed ! Well, and how goes hay ?
Why now there's master Wiseman,
He told the exciseman
   That the cause of this pother and rout—
Order, order, and sobriety ;
The rules of this society—
   Let the secretary read 'em out.

" Every member of this society that spills his liquor in his neighbour's pocket shall forfeit two-pence. Every member of this society that singes his neighbour's wig with his pipe shall forfeit two-pence. Every member of this society that refuses to laugh at a good joke shall forfeit two-pence. Every member of this society who

reproaches his neighbour with coming to distress by un-
avoidable misfortunes shall forfeit two-pence."—" Mr.
President, I move that this forfeit be a shilling." "And
I second the motion."—" Are you all agreed?" "I am,
unanimously." " A noble resolution." " D'ye think
so?"

> Why, then, here's to you, Mr. Figgins—
> Here's to you, Mr. Higgins;
> So put the beer about.

> And now the potent liquor
> Not even spares the vicar,
> But in all their noddles mounts;
> While among this set of queerers,
> All talkers and no hearers,
> Each his favourite tale recounts:
> The soldier talks of battle,
> The grazier sells his cattle,
> Conversation to provoke;
> Till the juice of the barrel
> Begets some curious quarrel,
> While the company's lost in smoke.

" Upon my soul, neighbour, I had no hand in the
death of your wife: it was all in the way of business."
" Nay, but Doctor, 'twere a cursed unneighbourly thing
of you: not that the woman were any sitch great things,
but to put a body to sitch an expense."—" Why, you
don't tell me so! killed fifteen with your own hand!"
" Fifteen, by my laurels!"—" D'ye hear that, butcher?"
" Hear it, yes; but I'll lay an what he dares he has not
killed so many as I by hundreds." "Powder my whiskers!" " Come, come, gentlemen," says the bellows-

maker, " no breezes!" " Let me exhort you to temperance," says the parson. "Amen!" says the clerk. " That's right," says the undertaker, " let us bury all animosity." " Now that's what I like," says the fidler, " I like to see harmony restored." D'ye, though? You like to see harmony restored ? Why then

> Here's to you, Mr. Higgins—
> Here's to you, Mr. Wiggins—
> So put the beer about.

JACKEY AND THE COW.

THERE were Farmer Thrasher, and he had a cow,
　And gammer were very fond on un ;
And they'd a son Jackey, that made a fine bow,
　So they sent un a prentice to London.

Jackey's master a barber and hair-dresser were,
　Than some squires 'cod he thought unself bigger,
In the day through the town he would cut and dress
　　　hair,
　And dressed out at night—cut a figure.

To ape Jackey's master were all his delight,
　The soap-suds and razor both scorning,
He's been took't by the nose by the same fop at night
　That he took by the nose in the morning.

Now to see the cow moan would have made a cat laugh!
　　Her milk were his food late and early ;
And even if Jackey had been her own calf,
　　She could not ha loved un more dearly.

She moan'd and she moan'd, nor knew what she did ail,
　　To heart so she took this disaster ;
At last roaming about, some rogues cut off her tail,
　　And then sent her back to her master.

Here's the kiaw come home, Gammer, come bring out
　　　　the pail,
　　Poor creature, I'ze glad we have found her.
Cried dame, ten't our cow, she's got never a tail ;
　　Here, Roger, goo take her and pound her.

'Tis our kiaw, but you zee she's been maimed by some
　　　　brute ;
　　Why, dame, thou'rt a vool !　Give me patience !
So to squabbling they went : when, to end the dispute,
　　Came home Jackey to see his relations.

His spencer he sported, his hat round he twirl'd,
　　As whistling a tune he came bolt in ;
All bedock'd and belopp'd, wounds ! he look'd all the
　　　　world
　　Like trimmed bantums, or magpies a-moulting.

Oh, dear ! 'tis our Jackey ; come, bring out the ale :
　　So Gammer fell skipping around him.
Our Jackey, why, dam't, he's got never a tail !
　　Here, Roger, go take un and pound him.

'Tis the kick, I say, old one, so I brought it down,
   Wore by Jemmies so neat and so spunky.
Ah, Jackey! thou went'st up a puppy to town,
   And now thou be'st come back a monkey.

Gammer storm'd, Gaffer swore, Jackey whistled, and
     now
   'Twas agreed, without any more passion,
To take Jackey in favour as well as the cow,
   Because they were both in the fashion.

THE LADY'S DIARY.

Lectured by Pa and Ma o'er night;
Monday, at ten, quite vexed and jealous;
Resolv'd, in future, to be right,
And never listen to the fellows:
Stitch'd half a wristband, read the text,
Receiv'd a note from Mrs. Racket:
I hate that woman,—she sat next,
All church-time, to sweet Captain Clackit.

Tuesday, got scolded, did not care;
The toast was cold, 'twas past eleven;
I dreamt the Captain through the air
On Cupid's wings bore me to heaven.
Pouted and dined, dressed, looked divine,
Made an excuse, got Ma to back it;
Went to the play,—what joy was mine;
Talked loud, and laughed with Captain Clackit.

Wednesday, came down, no lark so gay;
The girl's quite altered, said my mother;
Cried Dad, I recollect the day
When, dearee, thou wert such another.
Danced, drew a landscape, skimmed a play;
In the paper read that widow Flackit
To Gretna Green had run away,
The forward minx, with Captain Clackit.

Thursday, fell sick;—poor soul, she'll die!
Five doctors came, with lengthened faces;
Each felt my pulse; Ah, me! cried I,
Are these my promised loves and graces?
Friday, grew worse; cried Ma, in pain,
Our day was fair; heaven do not black it:
Where's your complaint, love? In my brain.
What shall I give you? Captain Clackit.

Early next morn a nostrum came,
Worth all their cordials, balms, and spices.
A letter; I had been to blame;
The Captain's truth brought on a crisis.
Sunday, for fear of more delays,
Of a few clothes I made a packet,
And, Monday morn, stept in a chaise,
And ran away with Captain Clackit.

MARY, MARRY JOHN.

OLD Mary, her poor husband dead,
  And buried but a week,
Tired of her fate, with hobbling gait,
  The parson went to seek.
I'll tell you, sir, says she, the truth,
  My poor man's dead and gone;
Our servant John's a comely youth,
  Ought I to marry John?
The parson cried, who quickly knew
  She'd not his counsel hear,
The proverb tells you what to do
  This knotty point to clear.
      " As the fool thinks,
        So the bell tinks;"
So, when the bell shall ring anon,
  Take care you don't mistake the sound,
  They'll tell you, as the peal goes round,
If you should marry John.

Now, Mary listens to each bell,
  " Hey, that's a knell that tolled;
'Tis not for me, thank heaven! well, well,
  I'm not yet quite so old.
But of a burying should you think,
  They say a wedding's near;
I hope the bells will sweetly tink
  That I should wed my dear."

At length the ringers rouse her hopes,
    And all her senses charm,
And as they singly pull the ropes,
    Her aged blood gets warm :
        " But, as the fool thinks
        So the bell tinks ;"
And now the sprightly peal comes on,
    While Mary, as they tug away,
    Cries, Lovely bells ; how plain they say,
Do, Mary, marry John.

Now, at both ends the candle's burned ;
    She's beggared to a souse ;
Each thing is topsy-turvy turned,
    Out of the window goes the house.
" I cannot this distress survive ;
    What scandal and disgrace !
Would my first husband were alive,
    Or I were in his place !
A curse upon the fatal day
    I listened to the bells,
That took my reason quite away,
    Just like so many spells ;
        ' But, as the fool thinks
        So the bell tinks ;'
Why, what must I be thinking on,
    To fancy, as they rang away,
The bells so stupid were, to say
    That I should marry John ?"

Straight to the parson Mary goes,
    And soundly lays it on :
You are the cause of all my woes,
    You married me to John.

THE LAST SHILLING.

" Nay, nay, to lay the blame on me,
　　Good Mary, is unkind ;
I never yet advised the sea,
　　A woman, or the wind.
Hark, hark, the bells are ringing now !
　　They sound with might and main ;
I what they say can hear.　Canst thou ?"
　　" I hear 'em, sir, too plain.
　　　　' But, as the fool thinks
　　　　So the bell tinks :'
But folly 'twas set me on,　　　　－
　　Intent upon my foolish freak,
　　They cry, as plain as they can speak,
Don't, Mary, marry John."

THE LAST SHILLING.

As pensive, one night, in my garret I sate,
　　My last shilling produced on the table ;
That advent'rer, cried I, might a histr'y relate,
　　If to think and to speak it were able.
Whether fancy or magic 'twas play'd me the freak,
　　The face seem'd with life to be filling,
And cried, instantly speaking, or seeming to speak,
　　Pay attention to me thy last shilling.

I was once the last coin of the law a sad limb,
　　Who in cheating was ne'er known to faulter ;
'Till at length, brought to justice, the law cheated him,
　　And he paid me to buy him a halter :

A Jack Tar, all his rhino but me at an end,
   With a pleasure so hearty and willing,
Though hungry himself, to a poor distress'd friend,
   Wish'd it hundreds, and gave his last shilling.

'Twas the wife of his messmate, whose glistening eye
   With pleasure ran o'er as she view'd me;
She chang'd me for bread, as her child she heard cry,
   And at parting, with tears she bedew'd me;
But I've other scenes known, riot leading the way,
   Pale want their poor families chilling;
Where rakes, in their revels the piper to pay,
   Have spurn'd me, their best friend and last shilling.

Thou thyself hast been thoughtless, for profligates bail,
   But to-morrow all care shalt thou bury
When my little history thou offerest for sale;
   In the interim, spend me and be merry!
Never, never, cried I, thou'rt my Mentor, my muse,
   And grateful thy dictates fulfilling,
I'll hoard thee in my heart; thus men counsel refuse,
   'Till the lecture comes from the last shilling.

RATIONAL VANITY.

Man, poor forked animal, why art thou vain?
   Of thy form that so matchless the deity owns,
Where beauty, proportion, and symmetry reign,
   Adding grace to distinction, and splendour to thrones?

While, by folly and fashion, this form so divine
· Is abused 'till all figures fantastic it wears,
Till worn by diseases and bloated by wine,
   Men the Deity's image turn monkies and bears.
A mass of remorse, of reflection, of pain,
Man, poor forked animal, why art thou vain?

Art vain of thy mind? still, the deity there;
   Where virtues angelic their natures impress,
Pale anguish to chase, smooth the brow of despair,
   And with charity's hand, dry the tear of distress.
While this generous mind, on beneficence bent,
   Fair gratitude's height shall in vain strive to climb,
And those lavish'd riches, so liberally meant,
   'Stead of virtue rewarding shall sanctify crime.
While philanthropy gives disappointment to gain,
Man, poor restless animal, why art thou vain?

Take the rational mean. If thou'rt proud of thy form,
   Let health given by temperance glow in thy face;
Let simplicity's hand, as it decks every charm,
   To decorum add neatness, to decency grace.
Then to temper thy mind neither tower nor stoop,
   Nor with sordidness grovel nor arrogance ride;
Be not niggard nor lavish, a churl nor a dupe,
   But let prudence the hand of benevolence guide.
Thus in form and in heart shall the deity reign;
Thus reason shall teach, and thus man shall be vain.

ANOTHER CUP, AND THEN.

MAT MUDGE, the sexton of our town,
 Though oft a little heady,
The drink not so his wits could drown
 But some excuse was ready.
Mat said the parson loved a sup,
 And eke also the clerk;
And then it kept his spirits up
 'Mongst spirits in the dark:
Swore 'twas his predecessor's fault,
 A cursed drunken fellow,
The very bells to ring he taught,
 As if they all were mellow:
Hark! hark! cried he, in tipsy peal,
Like roaring topers as they reel;
Hark! what a drunken pother:
Another cup, and then—What then?—Another.

For good news Mat got drunk for joy,
 If he could beg or borrow;
Did anything his mind annoy
 He drank to drown his sorrow:
Thus he'd rejoice, or he'd condole,
 Cried Mat, be't joy or grief,
As the song says, the flowing bowl
 Still gives the mind relief.
'Twas all my predecessor's fault, &c.

Were peace the theme and all its charms,
　　Mat fill'd the sparkling noggin :
If war, he drank—May British arms
　　Still give the foe a flogging.
The parson once took Mat to task,
　·Bid him beware the bowl ;
Your pardon I most humbly ask,
　'Cried he, but 'pon my soul
　　　'Twas all my predecessor's fault, &c.

And then, no liquor came amiss,
　　Wherever he could forage :
That gave him spirits, wisdom this,
　　And t'other gave him courage.
Thus was he merry and jocose,
　　If fortune smiled or frown'd ;
And when he fairly got his dose,
　　And all the things turn'd round,
　　　Swore 'twas his predecessor's fault, &c.

A LITTLE.

Wid my Lor Anglois I come over un valet,
From my own country to 'scape the galley :
By'm by, grow rich, I teach the ballet,
All while I play mine fittle.
A little I earn, a little I sheat,
A little sometime I lodge in the Fleet,
A little I roll in my shariot the street,
And I ogle the girls a little.

I go de governess de school
I want to teach, you know de rule ;
I find de governess no fool,
She say, Vell, pring your fittle.
A little I go and I teach de dance,
A little they jompe, a little they prance ;
By and by, when I took a little entrance,
The governess touch a little.

To they dinner the ask this man such merit,
I stuff the turtle, the beef, and the carrot ;
And with the ale, the punch, and the claret,
I figure away the first fittle.
A little give toast, 'bout politic bawl,
A little they sing, tol, lol, de rol, lol ;
So my ticket I sell while I sing small,
And pocket de ginnay a little.

By'm by he come grand benefice,
Where the aunt, and the mother, the daughter, the
       niece ;
Everybody good nature. so come to be fleece,
While I scrape away de fittle.
A little they jompe, a little they jig,
A little de lady some time lose his wig ;
While their head grow empty my purse he grow big,
And I take in the flat a little.

So den, at last, my scholar he flock,
That I get my banker, and puy de stock ;
And their head for good sense in vain they may knock,
I drive it all out with my fittle.

A little I flash at the opera, de play,
In my shariot a little I figure away;
And keep, like myself, un damn'd rogue de valet,
To laugh at the English a little.

FATHER AND I.

MOTHER were dead, and sister were married,
And nobody at home but Father and I;
So I thought, before I longer tarried,
To get a good wife my fortune I'd try:
But I swore she the moral should be of my mother,
For ne'er was a better wife under the sky;
So we mounted our nags to find out such another,
And we set out a courting, Father and I.

Farmer Chaff have a datur that's famous for breeding,
She do daunce, and do play, and do sing, and do write:
But she never would talk, she were always a reading
'Bout ravishments, devils, and ghostes in white.
Woons! says I, at that fun you won't find me a good
        one;
To be mine, girl, far other guess fish thou must fry;
The wife for my money must make a good pudding,
So we'll wish you good morning, Father and I.

As to Lunnun, to manage like other folks scorning,
They sat down to breakfast when we went to sup;
At midnight they dined, and they supp'd in the morning,
And went to bed just at the time we got up:

Q

Then so poor, but that I had no heart to make fun on,
They could not afford any covering to buy;
So shivering with cold we the girls left in Lunnun,
And came back to the country, Father and I.

But, Lord! farmers' girls be as bad as their betters,
Poor prudence and decency left in the lurch:
They paints pictures and faces, writes stories and letters,
And dresses like sheets standing up in a church.
'Stead of sitting at home shirts and table-cloths darning,
Or pickling of cabbage, or making a pie,
All the clodpoles are standing astound at their larning,
Sad wives for the likes of Father and I!

So just as we did not know what to be atur,
" Odds wouns!" cried our father, " a neighbour of mine
Died a twelvemonth ago, left a sister and datur,
And they both can milk cows and make gooseberry-
    wine."
On to see 'em we went—this fell out on a Monday—
Neither stood shilly-shally, looked foolish or shy:
The licence were bought, and the very next Sunday
They were both of them married to Father and I.

THE LAMPLIGHTER.

I'M jolly Dick, the lamplighter,
  They say the Sun's my dad;
And truly I believe it, sir,
  For I'm a pretty lad.

Father and I the world do light,
   And make it look so gay,
The difference is, I lights by night,
   And Father lights by day.

But Father's not the likes of I
   For knowing life and fun,
For I queer tricks and fancies spy,
   Folks never show the sun.
Rogues, owls, and bats, can't bear the light,
   I've heard your wise ones say;
And so, d'ye mind, I sees at night
   Things never seen by day.

At night men lay aside all art
   As quite a useless task,
And many a face and many a heart
   Will then pull off the mask:
Each formal prude and holy wight
   Will throw disguise away,
And sin it openly all night
   Who sainted it all day.

His darling hoard the miser views,
   Misses from friends decamp,
And many a statesman mischief brews
   To his country o'er his lamp.
So Father and I, d'ye take me right,
   Are just on the same lay;
I barefaced sinners light by night,
   And he false saints by day.

THE HIGH METTLED RACER.

SEE, the course throng'd with gazers, the sports are be-
 gun!
The confusion but hear!—I'll bet you, sir!—Done,
 done!
Ten thousand strange murmurs resound far and near,
Lords, hawkers, and jockies assail the tired ear.
While with neck like a rainbow, erecting his crest,
Pamper'd, prancing, and pleas'd, his head touching his
 breast,
Scarcely snuffing the air, he's so proud and elate,
The high-mettled racer first starts for the plate.

Now Reynard's turn'd out, and o'er hedge and ditch
 rush
Hounds, horses, and huntsmen, all hard at his brush:
They run him at length, and they have him at bay,
And by scent and by view cheat a long tedious way:
While, alike born for sports of the field and the course,
Always sure to come thorough a staunch and fleet horse,
When fairly run down the Fox yields up his breath,
The high-mettled racer is in at the death.

Grown aged, used up, and turn'd out of the stud,
Lame, spavin'd, and windgall'd, but yet with some blood;
While knowing postilions his pedigree trace,
Tell his dam won that sweepstakes, his sire gain'd that
 race;

And what matches he won to the ostlers count o'er,
As they loiter their time at some hedge alehouse-door,
While the harness sore galls, and the spurs his sides
    goad,
The high-mettled racer's a hack on the road.

Till at last, having labour'd, drudg'd early and late,
Bow'd down by degrees, he bends on to his fate;
Blind, old, lean, and feeble, he tugs round a mill,
Or draws sand, till the sand of his hour-glass stands
    still.
And now, cold and lifeless, exposed to the view
In the very same cart which he yesterday drew;
While a pitying crowd his sad relics surrounds,
The high-mettled racer is sold for the hounds!

EVERY MAN'S FRIEND.

Come, all jolly topers! the toast as ye pass,
    Who have sworn to keep Bacchus's laws,
The conditions repeat, lay your hands on the glass,
    And vindicate wine and its cause.
So long as the power of generous wine
    Shall the practice of honour inspire,
Our affections and passions to rule and refine,
    As gold issues pure from the fire:
So long o'er the mind may its empire extend,
And the generous bottle be every man's friend.

While in brisk circulation it genially glows
　Through each sluice of the heart in full speed,
Turning sourness to milk in the veins as it flows,
　The children of sorrow to feed :
While its lib'ral influence to honour so dear,
　With such pity the heart shall impress,
As with Charity's hand to wipe off the sad tear
　That glistens to mark out distress :
So long o'er the mind may its empire extend,
And the generous bottle be every man's friend.

But when in the glass the fiend Envy shall lurk,
　Her foul train waiting near at her call,
On the credulous mind to achieve her fell work,
　And the milk of the heart turn to gall :
Then may wine change to poison, and each cankerous
　　elf,
　Detected, ashamed, and alone,
Despised by the world, and despised by himself,
　By death for his errors atone :
So shall wine to the last serve humanity's end,
And the generous bottle be every man's friend.

COME ALL YE GEM'MEN VOLUNTEERS.

Come all ye gem'men volunteers,
　Of glory who would share,
And leaving with your wives your fears,
　To the drum-head repair ;

Or to the noble Sergeant Pike
  Come, come, without delay,
  You'll enter into present pay,
My lads, the bargain strike.
A golden guinea and a crown,
Besides the Lord knows what renown,
  Her Majesty the donor;
    And if you die,
    Why then you lie
  Stretch'd on the bed of honour.

Does any 'prentice work too hard?
  Fine clothes would any wear?
Would any one his wife discard?
  To the drum-head repair.
    Or to the, &c.

Is your estate put out to nurse?
  Are you a cast-off heir?
Have you no money in your purse?
  To the drum-head repair.
    Or to the, &c.

THE NEGRO AND HIS BANJA.

One negro, wi my banjer,
  Me from Jenny come,
    Wid cunning yiei
    Me savez spy
  De buckra world one hum,
As troo a street a stranger
  Me my banjer strum.

My missy for one black dog about the house me kick,
Him say, my nassy tawny face enough to make him sick;
But when my massa he go out, she then no longer rail,
For first me let the captain in, and then me tell no tale.

So aunt Quashy say,
Do tabby, brown, or black, or white,
You see um in one night,
Every sort of cat be gray.
One negro, &c.

To fetch a lilly money back, you go to law they call,
The court and all the tie-wig soon strip you shirt and all.

The courtier call him friend him foe,
And fifty story tell;
To-day say yes, to-morrow no,
And lie like any hell:
And so though negro black for true,
He black in buckra-country too.
One negro, &c.

THE BOATSWAIN CALLS.

My name d'ye see's Tom Tough, I've seen a little ser-
vice,
Where mighty billows roll and loud tempests blow;
I've sail'd with gallant Howe, I've sail'd with noble
Jervis,
And in valiant Duncan's fleet I've sung out yo heave
ho!

Yet more ye shall be knowing,
I was coxon to Boscawen,
And even with brave Hawke have I nobly faced the foe.
· Then put round the grog,
So we've that and our prog,
We'll laugh in Care's face, and sing yo heave ho!

· When from my love to part I first weigh'd anchor,
And she was sniv'ling seed on the beach below,
I'd like to cotch'd my eyes sniv'ling too, d'ye see, to
thank her,
But I brought my sorrows up with a yo heave ho!
For sailors, though they have their jokes,
And love and feel like other folks,
Their duty to neglect must not come for to go;
So I seized the capstern bar,
Like a true honest tar,
And, in spite of tears and sighs, sung out yo heave ho!

But the worst on't was that time when the little ones were
sickly,
And if they'd live or die the doctor did not know;
The word was gov'd to weigh so sudden, and so quickly,
I thought my heart would break as I sung yo heave
ho!
For Poll's so like her mother,
And as for Jack, her brother,
The boy when he grows up will nobly face the foe;
But in Providence I trust,
For you see what must be must,
So my sighs I gave the winds and sung out yo heave ho!

And now at last laid up in a decentish condition,
　For I've only lost an eye and got a timber toe;
But old ships must expect in time to be out of com-
　　　mission,
　Nor again the anchor weigh with yo heave ho!
　　　　So I smoke my pipe and sing old songs,
　　　　My boys shall well revenge my wrongs,
And my girls shall breed young sailors nobly for to face
　　the foe;
　　　　Then to country and king,
　　　　Fate can no danger bring,
While the Tars of old England sing out yo heave ho!

THE ANCHORSMITHS.

LIKE Ætna's dread volcano see the ample forge
Large heaps upon large heaps of jetty fuel gorge,
While salamander-like, the pond'rous anchor lies
Glutted with vivid fire thro' all its pores that flies;
The dingy anchorsmiths, to renovate their strength,
Stretch'd out in death-like sleep are snoring at their
　　length,
Waiting the master's signal when the tackle's force
Shall, like split rocks, the anchor from the fire divorce;
While, as old Vulcan's cyclops did the anvil bang,
In deafening concert shall their pond'rous hammers
　　clang,
And into symmetry the mass incongruous beat,
To save from adverse winds and waves the gallant Bri-
　　tish fleet.

Now, as more vivid and intense each splinter flies,
The temper of the fire the skilful master tries;
And, as the dingy hue assumes a brilliant red,
The heated anchor feeds that fire on which it fed.
The huge sledge-hammers round in order they arrange,
And waking anchorsmiths await the look'd-for change,
Longing with all their force the ardent mass to smite,
When issuing from the fire array'd in dazzling white;
And, as old Vulcan's cyclops did the anvil bang,
To make in concert rude their pond'rous hammers
    clang,
So the misshapen lump to symmetry they beat,
To save from adverse winds and waves the gallant Bri-
    tish fleet.

The preparations thicken ; with forks the fire they goad,
And now twelve anchorsmiths the heaving bellows load ;
While, arm'd from every danger, and in grim array,
Anxious as howling demons waiting for their prey.
The forge the anchor yields from out its fiery maw,
Which, on the anvil prone, the cavern shouts hurraw!
And now the scorch'd beholders want the power to
    gaze,
Faint with its heat, and dazzled with its powerful rays :
While, as old Vulcan's cyclops did the anvil bang
To forge Jove's thunderbolts, their pond'rous hammers
    clang ;
And, till its fire's extinct, the monstrous mass they beat.
To save from adverse winds and waves the gallant Bri-
    tish fleet.

THE GIRL WHO'D CHOOSE A SAILOR.

THAT girl who fain would choose a mate
　　Should ne'er in fondness fail her,
May thank her lucky stars if Fate
　　Should splice her to a sailor:
He braves the storm, the battle's heat,
　　The yellow boys to nail her;
Diamonds, if diamonds she could eat,
　　Would seek her honest sailor.

If she'd be constant, still his heart
　　She's sure will never fail her,
For though a thousand leagues apart
　　Still faithful is her sailor.
If she be false, still he is kind,
　　And, absent, does bewail her:
Her trusting, as he trusts the wind,
　　Still faithless to the sailor.

A butcher can provide her prog,
　　Three threads to drink, a tailor;
What's that to biscuit and to grog,
　　Procured her by her sailor?
She who would such a mate refuse,
　　The devil sure must ail her;
Search round, and if you 're wise, you'd choose
　　To wed an honest sailor.

ADDENDA.

SONGS

SELECTED FROM THE WORKS

OF

·T. DIBDIN,

AUTHOR OF THE ENGLISH FLEET—MOUTH OF THE NILE—NAVAL PILLAR—
NELSON'S GLORY—THE CABINET, &c &c.

THE HEART OF A TRUE BRITISH SAILOR.

[Gratefully inscribed to the Hon. EDMUND BYNG.]

WOULD you know the ingredients that make up a tar?
    Take of courage and truth *quantum suff.*
A soul, unsubdued by toil, tempest, and war;
    And a body of durable stuff;
A temper quite easy—yet firm in a squall—
    When Boreas, that blustering railer!
Blows great guns, that shivers stays, braces, and all,—
    Save the heart of a true British sailor!

Would you know what that heart is composed of? Just
    take
    All that friendship and love know of feeling;
For sweetheart, or mate in distress, for whose sake
    He'd stand firm, were the universe reeling!

Too proud to complain, be his lot e'er so low;
   Show him want!—with his best he'll regale her;
Oppress him! and Jack's but a word and a blow,
   From the heart of a true British sailor!

About sympathy! Jack he knows nothing at all,
   Though he practises all its sweet duty;
Of purse-proud assurance whilst taking the wall,
   He yields it to age, worth, and beauty!
His ship is his glory! His captain a king!
   Whose fiat ne'er finds him a failer!
Call ye that degradation? 'tis no such thing
   In the heart of a true British sailor!

Then mingle whate'er ye deem manly or mild,
   Tough, tender, keen,—yet unsuspicious;
The nerve of a hero! the sigh of a child;
   All that nature esteems most delicious;
Fire the cauldron of fancy! and put in all these,
   Envy's malice shall nothing avail her,
When she finds all on earth, that can warm, charm, and
      please,
   In the heart of a true British sailor!

[The Music of the above Song, which is copyright, may be had
of the Composer, Mr. Williams, 2, Trafalgar Square, Charing
Cross.]

MY ANCHOR AND COMPASS.

O LIFE is an ocean, where tempests from far
   Endanger our peace and repose;
And care fires his broadsides, to keep up the war
   With the passions, our natural foes.

What tack shall we try, then? for safety where run?
    How fly from the breakers of fate?
What harbour from sorrow?   I know but of one—
    My anchor and compass is Kate.

False friendship oft changes a calm to a storm;
    Love's frowns may give birth to a squall;
Dissension the sweet calm of peace may deform;
    To be poor, is worse weather than all!
Then how to find shelter; what course shall we steer?
    Good sense be my master and mate;
True love be my pilot, then what need I fear,
    When my anchor and compass is Kate.

Of your purse-strings the doctor may haul in a reef,
    The lawyer steer close to the mark;
But, for all their fine tricks, 'tis my honest belief
    One's a grampus, the other a shark.
Then keep your helm steady, boys, thus, and go clear
    A-midways, though danger be great;
Neither rocks, shoals, nor quicksands, nor breezes, I'll
        fear,
    While my anchor and compass is Kate.

Should prosperity fill ye an o'erswelling sail,
    Haul down a top-gallant or two;
Should adversity blow, and you'd weather the gale,
    Work at industry's pumps till all's blue.
Should your crew be increased by dad Hymen, what
        then?
    Let such blessings come early or late,
To me all are welcome, though eight, nine, or ten,
    While my anchor and compass is Kate.

HOME & VICTORY; OR, THE COMRADES.

[Composed by Mr. Williams.]

CAPTAIN.

Say, gallant soldier, do I see
   The comrade who on Egypt's sands
Dash'd forward side by side with me
   And charged thro' Gallia's fiercest bands?
When Abercrombie at our head
Resistless led, and when he bled!
In victory resign'd his sword
To death! and dying gave the word!
     "Albion adored! we fight for thee!
     Our watchword,—Home and Victory!"

LIEUTENANT.

Say, brother soldier, was it you
   Fought near me on that glorious day,
When Wellington at Waterloo
   The Gallic eagle bore away?
When, ere the awful fight began,
One feeling ran from man to man!
And as each phalanx drew the sword,
From rank to rank thus pass'd the word!
     "Albion adored! we fight for thee!
     Our watchword,—Home and Victory!"

TOGETHER.

Yes! brother soldier, we have seen
   Together sanguine wars imbue,
With purple tide, the laurels green
   Of conqu'ror and of conquer'd too!
     "Albion adored! we fought for thee!
     Our watchword,—Home and Victory!"

THE DEATH OF WOLFE.

[Composed by Mr. Williams.]

RECIT.

SHADES of Britannia's sons, who sleep
In hallow'd earth!—or in the deep!
Spirits of patriots dead—who fell—
Inspire me!—while a hero's fate I tell.

AIR.

The martial strife is heard once more,
　　Again the din of war now reigns,
On that far-famed Columbian shore
　　Where blood o'erflowed Canadian plains.
Wolfe! dauntless Wolfe! who boldly led
　　Of gallant chiefs a patriot band,
And in the arms of vict'ry bled—
　　For "Freedom and his Native Land!"
The foe did thrice his force display;
Yet thrice was conquer'd on that day!

No father e'er his children loved,
　　No children more revered a sire,
Beyond what Briton's hero proved
　　'Mid Gallia's fierce, unceasing fire!
His shatter'd wrist he calmly binds,
　　While cheerly "Onward!" was his cry—
A second shot his heart now finds;
　　And victory mourns that Wolfe must die!
Then, raise to him the patriot lay,
In Victory's arms who fell that day!

R

THE SNUG LITTLE ISLAND.

DADDY Neptune one day to Freedom did say,
  If ever I lived upon dry land.
The spot I should hit on would be little Britain!
  Says Freedom, " Why that's my own island!"
    O, it's a snug little island!
    A right little, tight little island,
    Search the globe round, none can be found
    So happy as this little island.

Julius Cæsar the Roman, who yielded to no man,
  Came by water,—he couldn't come *by* land;
And Dane, Pict, and Saxon, their homes turn'd their
      backs on,
  And all for the sake of our island;
    O, what a snug little island!
    They'd all have a touch at the island!
    Some were shot dead, some of them fled,
    And some staid to live on the island.

Then a very great war-man, called Billy the Norman,
  Cried D—n it, I never liked my land;
It would be much more handy to leave this Nor*man*dy,
  And live on yon beautiful island.
    Says he, 'tis a snug little island:
    Sha'n't us go visit the island?
    Hop, skip, and jump, there he was plump,
    And he kick'd up a dust in the island.

But party-deceit help'd the Normans to beat;
  Of traitors they managed to buy land;
By Dane, Saxon, or Pict, Britons ne'er had been lick'd,
  Had they stuck to the King of their island.

Poor Harold, the king of the island!
He lost both his life and his island.
That's very true; what more could he do?
Like a Briton he died for his island!

The Spanish Armada set out to inyade-a,
  Quite sure, if they ever come nigh land,
They couldn't do less than tuck up Queen Bess,
  And take their full swing in the island.
    Oh, the poor Queen of the island!
    The Dons came to plunder the island;
    But, snug in the hive, the Queen was alive,
    And buz was the word in the island.

These proud puff'd-up cakes thought to make ducks and
    drakes
  Of our wealth; but they hardly could spy land,
When our Drake had the luck to make their piide duck
  And stoop to the lads of the island.
    Huzza for the lads of the island!
    The good wooden walls of the island;
    Devil or don, let 'em come on;
    But how would they come *off* at the island?

Since Freedom and Neptune have hitherto kept time,
  In each saying, "This shall be my land;"
Should the "Army of England," or all they could bring,
    land,
  We'd show 'em some play for the island.
    We'll fight for our right to the island;
    We'll give them enough of the island;
    Invaders should just—bite at the dust,
    But not a bit more of the island!

THE LAND IN THE OCEAN.

[Air—" Meg of Wapping."]

In the midst of the sea, like a tough man of war,
    Pull away, pull away, yo ho there!
Stands an island surpassing all islands by far,
    If you doubt it, you've only to go there.
By Neptune 'twas built upon Freedom's firm base,
    And for ever 'twill last, I've a notion ;
All the world I defy to produce such a place :
    Pull away, pull away, pull away, pull, I say!
As the neat bit of land in the ocean.

From the opposite shore, puff'd with arrogant pride,
    Pull away, pull away so clever!
They've oft swore as how they would come alongside,
    And destroy the poor island for ever.
But Britannia is made of such durable stuff,
    And so tightly she's rigg'd, I've a notion,
She'd soon give the saucy invaders enough ;
    Pull away, pull away, pull away, pull, I say!
If they touch at the land in the ocean.

There was Howe, ever bold in the glorious cause,
    Pull away, pull away, so stout, boys!
Who gain'd on the first day of June such applause,
    And put every foe to the rout, boys.
The next was St. Vincent, who kick'd up a dust,
    As the Spaniards can tell, I've a notion ;
For they swore not to strike ; says he, " Damme but you
        must ;"
    Pull away, pull away, pull away, pull, I say!
To the lads of the land in the ocean.

Adam Duncan came next; 'twas in autumn, you know,
  Pull away, pull away, so jolly.
That he made big Mynheer strike his flag to a foe,
  Against whom all resistance was folly:
And they sent, as you know, if you're not quite a dunce,
  But a sad story home, I've a notion;
So Duncan he beat a whole Winter at once,
  Pull away, pull away, pull away, pull, I say!
What d'ye think of the land in the ocean?

Next the Frenchmen again they came in for their share,
  Pull away, pull away, so hearty!
For Nelson he set all the world in a stare,
  And land-lock'd the great Bonaparte.
Then he beat them again, when with Spain they com-
      bined,
  Till they all were done up, I've a notion;
When victory's sword did the olive entwine;
  Pull away, pull away, pull away, pull, I say!
And peace crown'd the land in the ocean!

THE HEART OF A SAILOR.

[Composed by John Braham.]

'Tisn't the jacket or trousers blue,
  The song, or the grog so cheerly,
That show us the heart of a seaman true,
  Or tell us his manners sincerely.
'Tis the hour of strife, when venturing life,
  Where the spirits of prudence might fail her,
In battle he'll sing for Britannia and king,
  And this shows the heart of a sailor!

'Tisn't his merriment kindled ashore,
　　By the cash oft too quickly expended;
'Tisn't his going to sea for more,
　　When the store in the locker is ended.
'Tis the hour of distress, when misfortunes oppress,
　　And virtue finds sorrow assail her;
'Tis the bosom of grief made glad by relief,
　　That pictures the heart of a sailor!

ON CHARLES DIBDIN'S MONUMENT
AT GREENWICH.

STOP! shipmate, stop! He can't be dead,
　　His lay yet lives to memory dear;
His spirit, merely shot a-head,
　　Will yet command Jack's smile and tear!
Still in my ear the songs resound,
　　That stemm'd the torrent at the Nore!
Avast! each hope of mirth's aground,
　　Should Charley be indeed no more!

The evening watch, the sounding lead,
　　Will sadly miss old Charley's line.
Saturday Night may go to bed,
　　His sun is set no more to shine!
"Sweethearts and wives," though we may sing,
　　And toast, at sea, the girls on shore;
Yet now 'tis quite another thing,
　　Since Charley spins the yarn no more!

Jack Rattlin's story now who'll tell?
   Or chronicle each boatswain brave?
The sailor's kind historian fell
   With him who sung the soldier's grave!
Poor Jack! Ben Backstay! but, belay!
   Starboard and larboard, aft and fore,
Each from his brow may swab the spray,
   Since tuneful Charley is no more!

The capstan, compass, and the log,
   Will oft his Muse to memory bring;
And when all hands wheel round the grog,
   They'll drink and blubber as they sing.
For grog was often Charley's theme,
   A double spirit then it bore;
It sometimes seems to me a dream,
   That such a spirit is no more.

It smooth'd the tempest, cheer'd the calm,
   Made each a hero at his gun;
It even proved for foes a balm,
   Soon as the angry fight was done.
Then, shipmate, check that rising sigh;
   He's only gone a-head before;
For even foremast men must die,
   As well as Charley, now no more!

THE ORIGIN OF NAVAL ARTILLERY.

[Music by John Davy.]

When Vulcan forged the bolts of Jove
    In Etna's roaring glow,
Neptune petition'd he might prove
    Their use and power below;
But finding in the boundless deep
Their thunders did but idly sleep,
He with them arm'd Britannia's hand,
To guard from foes her native land.

Long may she own the glorious right,
    And when through circling flame
She darts her thunder in the fight,
    May justice guide her aim!
And when opposed in future wars,
Her soldiers brave and gallant tars
Shall launch her fires from every hand
On every foe to Britain's land.

PETER PULLHAUL'S MEDLEY.

Near Kew one morn was Peter born,
    At Limehouse educated;
I learnt to pull of Simon Skull,
    And a tightish lad was rated.

For coat and badge I'd often try,
And when first oars, 'twas who but I ;
While the pretty girls would archly cry,
"O did'nt you hear of a jolly young waterman
  Who at Blackfriars Bridge used for to ply ?
He feather'd his oars with such skill and dexterity,
  Winning each heart, and delighting each eye."

When grown a man I soon began
  To quit each boyish notion ;
With old Benbow I swore to go,
  And tempt the roaring ocean.
Ten years I sarved with him or nigh,
And saw the gallant hero die ;
Yet 'scaped each shot myself, for why,—
  "There's a sweet little cherub that sits up aloft,
    To keep watch for the life of poor Jack !"

To Italy a great grandee
  Brought me through fortune's steerage,
By chance of war a British tar
  May meet Italian peerage.
Now hither sent by friends unkind,
And in this island close confined,
I sigh for that I've left behind,
Because its a nice little island.
"A right little, tight little island :
  May its commerce increase,
  And the blessings of peace
Long glad every heart in the island !"

THE DEATH OF ABERCROMBIE.

[Composed by Braham.]

RECITATIVE.

'Twas on the spot in ancient lore oft named
　Where Isis and Osiris once held sway
　　O'er kings who sleep in pyramidic pride:
But, now for British valour far more famed,
　Since Nelson's band achieved a glorious day,
　　And graced by conquest Abercrombie died!

AIR.

Her orient colours the dawn had not spread
O'er a field that stern slaughter had tinted too red ;
All was dark, save one flash at the cannon's harsh
　　sound,
When the brave ABERCROMBIE received his death-wound !
His comrades with grief unaffected deplore,
Though to Albion's renown he gave one laurel more.

With a mind unsubdued still the foe he defied,
On the steed which the hero of Acre supplied ;
'Till feeling he soon to Fate's summons must yield,
He gave Sidney the sword he no longer could wield.
His comrades with grief unaffected deplore,
Tho' to Briton's renown he gave one laurel more.

The standard of Briton, by victory crown'd,
Waved over his head while he sunk on the ground.
"Take me hence, my brave friends !" he exclaimed with
　　a sigh:
" My duty's complete, and contented I die !"

POLL OF WAPPING STAIRS.

[Music by Reeve.]

Your London girls with all their airs
Must strike to Poll of Wapping Stairs;
   No tighter lass is going,
From Iron Gate to Limehouse Hole
You'll never meet a kinder soul,
   No while the Thames is flowing.
              And sing Pull away, &c.

Her father he's a hearty dog,
Poll makes his flip and sarves his grog,
   And never stints his measure;
She minds full well the house affairs,
She seldom drinks, and never swears;
   And is'nt that a pleasure?
              Pull away, &c.

And when we wed, that happy time,
The bells of Wapping all shall chime;
   And, ere we go to Davy,
The girls like her shall work and sing,
The boys like me shall sarve the king,
   On board Old England's Navy!
             And sing Pull away, &c.

ALL'S WELL.

[Composed by Braham.]

DESERTED by the waning moon,
When skies proclaim night's cheerless noon,
On tower, fort, or tented ground,
The sentry walks his lonely round ;
And should some footstep haply stray
Where caution marks the guarded way:
" Who goes there? Stranger, quickly tell ! "—
" A Friend ! "—" The word ? "—" Good-night ! All's
    well ! "

Or sailing on the midnight deep,
When weary messmates soundly sleep,
The careful watch patrols the deck,
To guard the ship from foes or wreck ;
And while his thoughts oft homeward veer,
Some well-known voice salutes his ear:
" Who goes there? Brother, quickly tell ! "
" Above ! Below ! "—" Good-night ! All's well ! "

THE CABIN BOY.

[The Music of this Song may be had of Messrs. Purday, Holborn.]

THE sea was rough, the clouds were dark,
    Far distant every joy,
When forc'd by fortune to embark,
    I went a Cabin Boy.

My purse soon fill'd with Frenchmen's gold,
    I hasten'd back with joy,
When, wreck'd in sight of port, behold
    The hapless Cabin Boy !

LOVE AND GLORY.

[Music by Braham.]

Young Henry was as brave a youth
　As ever graced a martial story;
And Jane was fair as lovely truth,
　She sighed for Love, and he for Glory!

With her his faith he meant to plight,
　And told her many a gallant story;
Till war, their coming joys to blight,
　Call'd him away from Love to Glory.

Young Henry met the foe with pride;
　Jane followed, fought! ah, hapless story!
In man's attire, by Henry's side,
　She died for Love, and he for Glory!

SIR SIDNEY SMITH.

Gentlefolks, in my time, I've made many a rhyme,
　But the song I now trouble you with
Lays some claim to applause, and you'll grant it, be-
　　cause
　The subject's Sir Sidney Smith.　It is,
　The subject's Sir Sidney Smith.

We all know Sir Sidney, a man of such kidney,
　He'd fight every foe he could meet;
Give him one ship or two, and without more ado,
　He'd engage, if he met, a whole fleet.　He would,
　He'd engage, &c.

Thus he took, every day, all that came in his way,
　　Till Fortune, that changeable elf,
Order'd accidents so, that, while taking the foe,
　　Sir Sidney got taken himself.　He did,
　　Sir Sidney got, &c.

His captors, right glad of the prize they now had,
　　Rejected each offer we bid,
And swore he should stay, lock'd up till Doomsday,
　　But he swore he'd be d—d if he did.　He did,
　　He swore he'd be, &c.

So Sir Sid got away, and his gaoler next day
　　Cried " Sacre diable morbleu!
Mon prisonnier 'scape, I av got in von scrape,
　　And I fear I must run away too.　I must,
　　I fear," &c.

If Sir Sidney was wrong, why then blackball my song,
　　E'en his foes he would scorn to deceive:
His escape was but just, and confess it you must,
　　For it was only taking French leave.　You know,
　　It was only, &c.

NAVAL PROMOTION.

The Cabin Boy's over the sea,
For his sisters and mother weeps he;
Till good conduct prevails, and homeward he sails,
To land his full pockets with glee.

The Middy's away o'er the wave,
'Tis his fortune in action to save
His officer's life, in the heat of the strife,
And he lands at home happy and brave.

The Officer's over the main,
Fresh laurels on ocean to gain,
Till, commanding a prize, his friends see him rise,
And a Captain's commission obtain.

The Captain adventures once more,
Returning a bold Commodore;
And, his wishes to crown, he comes up to town
With an Admiral's flag at the fore.

TOBACCO, GROG, AND FLIP.

WHATE'ER the pleasures known on shore,
    They've little charms for me;
Be mine the sea—I ask no more,
    'Tis Jack's variety.
Give me tobacco, grog, and flip,
An easy sail, a tight-built ship;
In ev'ry port a pretty lass,
And round, for me, the globe may pass.

When tired of land, our pockets low,
    With will alert we steer
O'er hostile seas, attack the foe,
    For sailors know no fear.
Our prize in tow, we're all agog
For fresh tobacco, flip, and grog:
In port each seeks his fav'rite lass,
And bids the world unheeded pass.

BRITISH SAILORS.

[Music by Reeve.]

BRITISH sailors have a knack,
    Haul away, yo ho, boys!
Of pulling down a foeman's jack,
    'Gainst all the world, you know, boys!
Come any odds, right sure am I,
If we can't beat 'em, yet we'll try
To make our country's colours fly,
    Haul away, yo ho, boys!

British sailors, when at sea,
    Haul away, yo ho, boys!
Pipe all hands with glorious glee,
    While up aloft they go, boys!
And when with pretty girls on shore
Their cash is gone, and not before,
They wisely go to sea for more.
    Haul away, yo ho, boys!

British sailors love their king,
    Haul away, yo ho, boys!
And round the bowl delight to sing,
    And drink his health, you know, boys!
Then while his standard owns a rag,
The world combined shall never brag
It made us strike our country's flag,
    Haul away, yo ho, boys!

THE BARD OF POOR JACK.

*This song was written by the son of the Bard for the
meeting which proposed the erection of a monument
to his Father's memory.*]

ONE sigh for the bard by philanthropy fired,
 Who ne'er wrote but some truth to impart,
Whose Muse, while pourtraying what Nature inspired,
 Brought ev'ry touch home to the heart ;
On his plain honest lay fools would censure intrude,
 Forgetting the theme of his song
Was the " Heart of a Tar," or the " Billows so rude,"
 Which bore his trim vessel along ;
But grumblers can seldom achieve ought beyond
 The false taste which directs their attack,
And till pedants can rail Nature's " seal from his
   bond,"
 They'll ne'er injure the bard of " Poor Jack !"

Ye fair ones, who love the bold sons of true blue,
 Your hearts will be ever allied
To him who ne'er yet breath'd a verse but which you
 Might approve, and this fact was his pride :
His harp's speaking melody ne'er own'd a strain
 Which could poison convey to the ear,
Make semblance of pleasure a passport to pain,
 Or " cause ruin'd beauty a tear !"
If mirth, with sound moral commingled, may claim
 Recollection, his Muse ne'er will lack
The wreath of true genius which justly-earn'd fame
 Entwines for the bard of " Poor Jack !"

s

Ye tars of our island, what " Saturday Night,"
   Tho' waves roll, and weather blow hard,
Shall call you to toast her in whom you delight,
   Without some grateful thought of the bard?
While the can circles gaily, give one manly sigh
   To him who recorded your worth;
And who, tho' " gone aloft," will with you never die,
   But in each seaman's heart find a berth;
And you, Brother Britons, met nobly to-day,
   With applause his past merits to back,
With delight will oft think of each patriot lay,
   Which " poor Charles " sung to solace " Poor Jack."

SAM SPLICEM.

SAM SPLICEM, d'ye mind me? is one of those boys
   Who from dangers and duty ne'er flinches,
He as well can sail through the world's bustle and noise
   As any tight lad of his inches:
For Sam had a sweetheart, and meant to be wed,
   Till a trifling accident knock'd up his plan—
He found she had married another instead;
   But his courage he boldly pluck'd up like a man:
" Let her go, if she will, 'tis but folly to sorrow,
If a storm comes to-day why a calm comes to-morrow."

Sam sail'd to the Indies, and safely came back,
   After braving hard knocks and foul weather,
Of rupees in his chest he had more than a lac,
   And his heart was as light as a feather;

While himself and his treasure were hoisting on shore
    A press-gang prevented his reaching the land,
And his chest of rupees he set eyes on no more,
    For the rogues knew the value of what they'd in hand :
Yet it cost honest Sam little more than a sigh,
" For," says he, " all this here will rub out when it's dry."

Sam once more return'd with his pockets well lined,
    Yet his cloth was too shabby for wearing,
So determined no more it should shake in the wind,
    From a bum-boat he purchased repairing.
Then when Sam was new-rigg'd, his old trousers · de-
    spised,
    He threw into the sea—when a thought struck his
    nob,
And sure no poor devil was e'er so surprised,
    When he found all his cash had been left in the fob !
Some folks would have died, but our Sam had more
    sense, ·
" For," says he, " 'twill be all one a hundred years
    hence."

Sam was going again for fresh rhino to work,
    When his uncle, a lucky wind falling,
Left Sam all his wealth, for the terrible Turk
    With Old Davy for cash had no calling.
Then Sam, having gold, didn't long want a wife,
    And, what's better, his lass to her sailor proves true.
With his girl and his grog he floats easy thro' life,
    And laughs at the troubles he formerly knew :
" For," says Sam, " on this maxim you'll safely depend,
When things come to the worst they'll be sartain to
    mend."

WHO'LL SERVE THE QUEEN?

" Who'll serve the Queen?" cried the sergeant aloud,
  Roll went the drum, and the fife play'd sweetly.
" Here, master sergeant!" said I, from the crowd,
  " Is a lad who will answer your purpose completely."
My father was a corporal, and well he knew his trade;
Of women, wine, and gunpowder, he never was afraid.
      He'd march, fight, left! right!
      Front flank! centre rank!
      Storm the trenches, court the wenches,
      Loved the rattle of a battle;
      Died in glory, lives in story!
And, like him, I found a soldier's life, if taken smooth
      and rough,
A very merry, hey-down derry, sort of life enough.

" Hold up your head!" cried the sergeant at drill,
  Roll went the drum, and the fife play'd loudly.
" Turn out your toes, Sir!"—Says I, " Sir, I will;"
  For a nimble-wristed round rattan the sergeant
      flourish'd proudly.
My father died when corporal, but I ne'er turn'd my back,
Till promoted to a halbert, I was sergeant in a crack.
      In sword and sash cut a dash;
      Spurr'd and booted, next recruited,
      Hob and Clod, awkward squad,
      Then began my rattan!
      When boys unwilling came to drilling.
Till made the colonel's orderly, then who but I so bluff!
Led a very merry, hey-down derry, sort of life enough.

" Homewards, my lads !" cried the general, " huzza !"
  Roll went the drum, and the fife play'd cheerly.
To quick time we footed, and sung all the way,
  " Hey, for the pretty girls we all love dearly !"
My father liv'd with jolly boys in bustle, jars, and strife,
And, like him, being fond of noise, I mean to take a
      wife.
        Soon as miss blushes y-i-s,
        Rings, gloves, dears, loves,
        Bells ringing, comrades singing,
        Honeymoon finish'd soon ;
        Scolding, sighing, children crying !
Yet still a wedded life may prove, if taken smooth and
      rough,
A very merry, hey-down derry, sort of life enough.

THE COLOUR OF THE OCEAN.

When the world first began, and some folks say be-
    fore,
As old Neptune was quaffing his grog at the Nore,
He cried out in his cups, " As my land is the sea,
'Tis high time to consult what its colour shall be."

Amphitrite had been to drink tea at Sheerness,
And had seen at the barracks a captain's spruce dress,
To her husband she cried, as she flirted her fan,
''Let its colour be red, do now, that's a dear man."

Neptune shook his rough locks, at his wife gave a frown,
When his tailor call'd in with some patterns from town ;
He still was perplex'd, till he cast up his eye,
And resolved that the ocean should match the bright sky.

Thus the sea, as philosophers know to be true,
As it wash'd our white cliffs bore a fine azure hue,
Till the laurel of Britain victorious was seen
To reflect on its surface, and change it to green.

You may guess our opponents were sad at the sight,
As the sea grew more green our pale foes grew more
         white,
And never beheld it, but, vex'd at the view,
They scolded old Neptune, and cried out " Mor-bleu !"

May its colour remain, and good luck to the boys
Who o'er its salt surface through danger and noise,
With Howe, Duncan, and Jarvis, and Nelson maintain,
That the tight little island will govern the main.

THE LASS FOR A SAILOR.

THE lass for a sailor is lively and free,
   Meaning yes, she would scorn to say no ;
Such a girl as would dangers encounter with me,
   When over the billows we go.

One on deck, when bright moonbeams bespangle the
    deep,
  Who would sing while the plummet we throw;
Or, while loud blows the wind, would unconsciously
    sleep,
  While over the billows we go.

Oh, had I for life such a free-hearted lass,
  I'd envy no mortal below!
On shipboard or shore time would merrily pass,
  As over life's billows we go.

WATERLOO.

  The lofty hall with trophies proud,
    And dazzling panoply of gold,
  Was graced, and trumpets long and loud
    Of Britain's former glories told;
  Of laurels won on that famed field,
    Where warriors, to Old England true,
  In phalanx fix'd to die ere yield,
    Together fought at Waterloo.

  The " royal feast for Persia won,"
    Less splendid victory proclaim'd,
  Nor were the deeds of " Philip's son "
    Than British gallantry more famed.
  The hero who those squadrons led,
    Earth's greatest captain to subdue,
  Now sat triumphant at the head
    Of chiefs who fought at Waterloo.

Each canopy some standard bore,
  Or eagled ensign in the fray,
By England won ; each bosom bore
  Some proud memorial of that day !
And splendid symbols pending round
  Recall'd to all, with mem'ry true,
Some action on that hard-fought ground,
  By each achiev'd at Waterloo.

In every warlike dazzling hue
  Of martial pomp each chief was dress'd
Beyond all pencil ever drew,
  Or Fancy's boldest tints express'd ;
And, sovereign of our happy land,
  Sate William, that famed scene to view,
Enthroned among the gallant band
  Of those who fought at Waterloo.

With honest pride the cup he took,
  To grace the leader of that day,
When, casting round an anxious look,—
  " And why," he ask'd, "are those away,
Whose proud insignia caught my eye
  On ent'ring here—an humble two,
Who in the ranks might haply vie
  With all who fought at Waterloo ?"

Think how their lovers, friends, and wives,
  With beating hearts, from year to year,
That humble two, throughout their lives,
  Describing that glad day will hear ;

In William's presence call'd to drain
  The cup, " To every warrior true,
And him who led the victor-train
  To conquer peace at Waterloo."

KING WILLIAM'S MEMORIAL.

[*Written on the proposal to erect a monument at
Greenwich in honour of our late beloved Sovereign,
William IV., and dutifully dedicated to Her Ma-
jesty Queen* ADELAIDE.]

WHEN pyramids, form'd by the fiat of pow'r,
  The mem'ry of monarchs preserv'd,
Who strutted and fretted on earth their short hour,
  Amid plaudits not always deserved:
Of those massy memorials, how many proclaim
  That oblivion of pride is the lot,
And their ruins alone remain sacred to fame,
  While for whom they were form'd is forgot?
The lesson this teaches we can't read too oft,
  Object to its moral who can?
Truth longest preserves in Time's annals aloft,
  Not the rank, but the worth of a man!

So thought Albion's William, when born to a crown,
  The splendour of courts he resign'd,
For the seaman's rude cot changed his cradle of down,
  And soft airs for the rude roaring wind;

Royal birthdays and balls to gay courtiers he left,
    No berth but his cabin he knows;
Save his sword, of each dazzling distinction bereft,
    While he only gave balls to our foes.
His station unenvied by folly, though oft
    Noble hearts warmly share in his plan,
Of ascending to honour's maintopmast aloft,
    Not by rank, but the merit of man!

Able seaman, smart middy, lieutenant, and post,
    By experience he gain'd every grade,
And no sovereign but ours of a son e'er could boast
    Such a tar as our William was made.
When commodore, admiral—ranks bravely won,
    For through each by desert did he pass—
From the hour when he only stood last at his gun,
    To the day he rose first of his class.
With Digby, Keate, Rodney, and Hardy, how oft
    Up the shrouds of true honour he ran;
While Britain, exulting, beheld him aloft
    By his worth, not the rank of the man!

When regal succession encircled his brow
    With that crown he oft sail'd to defend,
Once obedient to others, commanding them now,
    Of our tars he's the father and friend;
Brave hearts, who, as he did, knew how to obey,
    With distinction to hail he delights;
And age, worn by service, old Greenwich can say,
    He protects in their comforts and rights;

While gratitude renders the toughest heart soft,
  When to recompense worth is the plan
Of our blue-jacket King, in our hearts throned aloft,
  Not for rank, but desert as a man!

Then where is the subject with nobler claim
  Than our King to the tribute we'd pay,
In adding one shaft to the columns of fame
  Which his worth shall in story convey?
And when the full canvass shall homeward impel
  Gallant tars, as they gratefully view
William's tow'ring memorial, their hearts too will swell,
  As their lips give our Sovereign his due!
Whose sailors and soldiers, and country so oft
  Proved that honour alone was the plan
That taught Britain to place her loved Sov'reign aloft
  Less from rank than desert as a man!

SONGS

FROM THE WORKS

OF

C. DIBDIN, Jun.

AUTHOR OF "THE FARMER'S WIFE," "MY SPOUSE AND I," &c., &c.

ALL IN HIS GLORY.

JACK JUNK was a tar who could tether his tack,
 Of his merits who never was talking ;
If his friend was in limbo, he ne'er hung aback,
 And his courage, it ne'er wanted caulking :
Then Jack was, moreover, a comical dog,
 And, if rightly I stick to my story,
He would now and then get so aboard of the grog !
 Then, d'ye see, he was all in his glory.

In battle one day, with a jorum of flip,
 Jack, while crossing the deck, began reeling,
And fell, for his leg was shot off at the hip,
 But the liquor he just saved from spilling.
" Don't you see," cried his captain, "your leg's off,
    you dog !"
 Jack answer'd, if right is my story,
" Never mind it, for splice me, I've sav'd all the grog,"
 So, d'ye see, he was all in his glory.

Discharg'd on a pension, he'd not live forlorn,
   But wedlock's wide ocean would weather;
There he made Cuckold's Point, and he doubled Cape
      Horn,
   And his course and command lost together;
For his wife slipt her cable with some pirate dog,
   And Jack, just to wind up the story,
Sprung the leak of despair, and so swigg'd at the grog,
   That to Davy he went in his glory!

BEN BOWSPRIT OF WAPPING.

Ben Bowsprit I am, and a true bonny boy,
   Pull away! pull away! so funny;
And was always the first to pipe hands a-hoy,
   When the signal was out to be sunny;
I can weather all seas like a good jolly dog,
   With the best he that ever went hopping;
But the ocean for me is the ocean of grog,
   Pull away! pull away! Pull! I say.
What d'ye think of Ben Bowsprit of Wapping?

My grandfather bulg'd with a freighting of flip,
   Pull away! pull away! so frisky;
Old Davy contrived my dad's cable to slip,
   One day when o'erladen with whisky;
My wife's christian name it was Brandy-fac'd Nan,
   The native to Nick sent her hopping;
So, the family cause I'll support while I can;
   Pull away, pull away! Pull! I say.
      What d'ye think, &c.

Avast! don't suppose I have launch'd out a lie,
  Pull away! pull away! so groggy;
Don't you see, in the service I've bung'd up one eye?
  And t'other, I own, 's rather foggy;
Then, to stand on I've scarcely a leg left, d'ye mind,
  And, should death t'other daylight be stopping,
The worst you can say is, I've drunk till I'm blind;
  Pull away! pull away! Pull, I say.
        What d'ye think, &c.

While one leg I've left, I'll stand to my gun,
  Pull away! pull away! beauty!
One's enough for to stand on, and as for to run,
  Why, that's not set down in our duty;
For England's good King, and our dear native shore,
  Should the foe in our Channel be chopping,
I'll show 'em, d'ye see, what I've shown 'em before,
  Pull away! pull away! Pull! I say.
What d'ye think of Ben Bowsprit of Wapping?

BRITANNIA.

Britannia is a noble ship,
  Her colours are true blue,
Her hull is royal heart of oak,
  And heart of oak her crew;
Her rigging's tight for every tack,
  Her planks without a starter;
The gallant union is a' her jack,
  Her sheathing Magna Charta.

How gallantly she bears her port,
　The ocean's pride and dread ;
The envied cap of liberty
　Adorns her glorious head :
Her pride is commerce to increase,
　In war she is no starter ;
But may she anchor soon in peace,
　Secur'd by Magna Charta.

MARINER'S COMPASS.

WHEN a sailor goes to sea,
　Merrily, cheerily, yo! yo! yo!
A weather the helm, or a lee,
　He sings aloft, or below,
　　Rifol, derol, &c.
　　　When a foe appears,
　　　The deck he clears,
And, d—e, he comes it so,
　　　(*Putting himself in attitude of defence.*)
　　　Bold and bluff,
　　　Till his man has enough,
And then it's yo! heave ho!
　　　Fol, lol, &c.

When a sailor comes ashore,
　Merrily, &c.
Stor'd with gold galore,
　He's but an odd fish we know,
　　Rifol, &c.

But on shore as at sea,
    If a foe there be,
D—e, he comes it so.

> (*Drawing his cutlass.*)

Bold, &c.

When a sailor's spent his chink,
    Merrily, &c.
As he can't stay ashore to think,
    To sea again he must go,
        Rifol, &c.
            For his country's right,
            Like the devil will fight,
And, d—e, he comes it so.

> (*Fires a pistol.*)

Bold, &c.

SAILOR'S LOG ASHORE.

I UNSHIPP'D from aboard the Sky Rocket,
    At seven, P.M., and half-past,
An odd guinea burnt in my pocket,
    And, d—e, why that was my last;
To spend it at eight, and get groggy,
    I swore; at half-past eight thought as how
I wouldn't, because when I'm foggy
    I'm sartain to kick up a row.
        Fol, &c.

At nine, Betty Sly overhaul'd me;
　The guinea, says I, get you sha'n't,
For tho' your true blue boy you call me,
　The yellow boy, hussey, you want:
At ten, a Jew wanted to bone it;
　Says I, Smouchee, I won't buy your stuff,
And, d'ye mind, tho' pork you disown it,
　You like guinea-pigs well enough.
　　　Fol, &c.

At eleven, I pip'd like a ninny,
　To see an old tar in distress;
So I took and I gave him the guinea;
　And, splice me! how could I do less?
At twelve, sail'd to old Mother Crocket,
　At whose house I'd thrown hundreds about,
But I hadn't a kick in my pocket,
　So she soon enough kick'd me out.
　　　Fol, &c.

The rain was most preciously pouring;
　In a watch-box I look'd for a bed,
But the old woman in it was snoring,
　So I kept the watch in his stead:
To me watching wa'nt a new notion;
　Thro' many a terrible squall,
For Old England, I've watch'd on the ocean,
　And her watch-word is " Liberty Hall!"
　　　Fol, &c.

GOOD SHIP BRITANNIA.

OLD England's a ship of the line, do you mind,
   The Britannia ;—no force can withstand her ;
Her old wooden walls defy quicksands and winds,
   And the king,—Heaven bless him ! commander :
Lieutenants, you know, are your lords, and them there ;
   Then midshipmen, many a grace on,
Are your big-wigs and justices ; then, my lord-mayor,
   Why, d—e, he must be the boatswain.
       Then pull away, yeo ! yea !
       Merry push the can about,
Drink success to the good ship Britannia.

Chaplains, stewards, and cooks, you may very soon name,
   And the mess just as easy be filling ;
Of doctors and gunners, for they're all the same,
   As they're both of them dabsters at killing :
But for lawyers one can't find a station so pat,
   For their likes on board never caught are,
Except cat-and-nine-tails, and if they a'nt that,
   They must be sharks in the water.
       Then pull, &c.

Prime min'ster is purser ; and when the bag's full,
   He empties it, state cares to soften ;
And then, as ship-owner, his honour, John Bull,
   Must fill it, and that pretty often ;
But his honour, John Bull, is as rich as a Jew,
   And swears, to the length of his cable,
He'll stick to Britannia,—and pray, wou'dn't you ?
   Ay, d—e, as long as you're able.
       Pull away, &c.

MODES OF INVASION.

We're told that the French to invade us intend,
And no wonder if Buonaparte's madness thus end;
For the man is most likely, it must be allow'd,
In the air to build castles who lives at St. *Cloud.*
  Tol de rol.

They'll come, we are told, or fame makes a faux pas,
In balloons, to be fill'd with the smoke of burnt straw,
And it's quite a-pro-pos that a plan without joke,
Which is founded in vapour should finish in smoke.
  Tol de rol.

Then some say they'll come here in flat-bottom'd boats,
To reap a good harvest, and sow their wild oats;
But the harvest they fancy to reap will be smash'd,
And their oats and themselves get confoundedly thrash'd.
  Tol de rol.

But how to get here the French needn't take pains,
To project this or that way; or puzzle their brains;
Let them once put to sea, and they'll soon find escorts,
For our sailors will pilot them into our ports.
  Tol de rol.

As a proof that they'll come, the French ev'ry day toast,
" That Frenchman who first sets his foot on our coast;"
But he'll not keep his footing, I'll wager a crown,
So let us toast "The Briton, that first knocks him
  down!"
  Tol de rol, &c.

A TAR'S DUTY.

BORN at sea, and my cradle a frigate,
   The boatswain he nurs'd me true blue;
I soon learn'd to fight, drink, and jig it,
   And quiz every soul of the crew.
So merrily push round the glasses,
   And strike up the fiddles, huzza!
And foot it away with the lasses,
   Tol de rol, heave a head, pull away!

A tar, tho' his hopes should be lopp'd off,
   His courage should ever hold fast;
So, Tom Tough, when the colours were popp'd off,
   His red jacket nail'd to the mast.
     So merrily, &c.

To love and to fight's a tar's duty,
   And either delight to him bring,
To live with his fav'rite beauty,
   Or die for his country and king.
     So merrily, &c.

BEN THE BOATSWAIN.

BEN BACKSTAY was our boatswain, a very merry boy,
For no one half so merrily could pipe all hands a-hoy;
And when it chanc'd his summons we didn't well attend,
No lad, than he, more merrily could handle a rope's
     end.
   With a chip, chow, fol.

While sailing once, our captain, who was a jolly dog,
One day he gave to ev'ry mess a double share of grog;
Ben Backstay he got tipsy, all to his heart's content,
And, being half-seas over, why overboard he went.
    With a chip, &c.

A shark was on the starboard—sharks don't for manners
    stand—
But grapple all that they come near, just like your sharks
    on land;
We threw out Ben some tackling, of saving him in hopes,
But the shark had bit his head off, so he could not see
    the rope.
    With a chip, &c.

Without a head his ghost appear'd, all on the briny lake;
He pip'd all hands a-hoy, and cried, " Lads, warning
    by me take!
By drinking grog I lost my life! so, lest my fate you
    meet,
Why, never mix your liquor, lads, but always drink it
    neat."
    With a chip, &c.

LET 'EM COME.

The foe on one string always strumming, boys,
Declare to attack us they're coming, boys,
But I fancy they're only humming, boys.
    What say you? (*To Soldier.*)

SOLDIER.

Let 'em come, if resolv'd to attack,
The best way to come, they their brains needn't rack;
They'd much better study the way to get back!
 What say you? (*To Sailor.*)

SAILOR.

I say so too.

SOLDIER.

And so do I.

BOTH.

Let 'em come, let 'em come; we their force defy!
Then strike hands, (*join hands*) for together we'll
   conquer or die.
   Tol de rol, de rol liddle lol, &c.
   Cheery, my hearts, yo! yo!

SOLDIER.

If to make us pay shot they require, boys,
We'll give them their heart's desire, boys;
With, make ready! present, and fire, boys!
 What say you? (*To Sailor.*)

SAILOR.

Helm-a-port, helm-a-lee, or aloft or below,
Wind foully, or fairly, we'll soon make the foe,
When once half-seas-over, quite how come you so.
 What say you? (*To Soldier.*)

SOLDIER.

I say so too, &c.

SONS OF ALBION.

Sons of Albion, sound to arms!
　　The hour of glory's near;
And, if the name of Briton charms,
　　Or freedom's sweets are dear,
Fly, fly to prove your charter'd claim
To those blest sweets, that envied name.
And when, in freedom's cause, you go
To meet a proud insulting foe,
Oh, emulate your race of yore,
" Return victorious, or return no more ! "

TOM TACK.

Tom Tack was the shipmate for duty,
　　Till Fortune she gave him a twitch ;
For Tom fell in love with a beauty ;
　　He'd better have fall'n in a ditch :
With his fair he could get no promotion,
　　So Tom, like a desperate dog,
He drown'd all his cares in the ocean—
　　But then, 'twas the ocean of grog.

True love, when it's slighted, will canker,
　　So, Tom, when the bo'swa'n wa'nt by,
Minded less about heaving the anchor
　　Than he did about heaving a sigh.

Then, for the last time to be jolly,
    He invited each soul in the ship;
With a shot, then, he finished his folly,—
    But 'twas the shot paid for the flip.

In folly, thus, faster and faster,
    Tom went on, in search of relief;
Till one day a shocking disaster
    Without a joke finish'd his grief:
If his fair one's heart he couldn't mellow,
    He'd hang himself, often, he said;
So, his neck in a noose put, poor fellow!—
    In plain English,—one day he got wed.

NAVAL WORTHIES.

Your grave politicians may kick up a rout,
    Of invasions, and such sort of stuff,
With as how, and as what, all the French are about,
    Why, lord, they're about sick enough;
Their armies, in Egypt, might conquer bashaws,
    And deck with their tails each brow,
But their navies can ne'er hope to conquer, because
    They've forgot—no; they can't forget Howe!
      While British cannons their thunder boast,
        And every sailor's a Mars,
      Secure from all squalls,
        Be this our toast,
    God bless the king! Long life to our tars!
      And success to our old wooden walls.

The Mounseers, your worships can never forget,
    Just when they were lather'd by Howe,
Because that's the don shouldn't die in our debt,
    How Jarvis kick'd up such a row.
Then how Duncan he pepper'd our flat-bottom'd foes,
    They'll think of a pretty long while;
And if they forget all this here, I suppose
    They'll remember the mouth of the Nile.
       While, &c.

Their army of England was once a great gun;
    But we've taught 'em ecod! to sing small;
And for navy, if things go on as they've begun
    I think they'll soon have none at all;
Their tri-colour'd flag's very pretty belike,
    But, spite of their humming, 'twon't do,
For you and I know that all colours must strike
    To king George, and Old England's true blue.
       While, &c.

POLL OF HORSLEYDOWN.

YE landsmen and ye seamen, be you a-head or stern,
Come listen unto me, and a story you shall learn;
It's of one Captain Oakum that you shall quickly hear,
Who was the bold commander of the Peggy privateer:
And he his colours never struck, so great was his renown,
To never no one soul on earth, but Poll of Horsley-
    down.

Miss Polly was a first-rate, trick'd out in flashy gear,
And Captain Oakum met her, as to Wapping he did
      steer :
And as he stood a viewing her, and thinking of no hurt,
A porter passing with a load, capsized him in the dirt;
Then taking out his 'bacco-box, that cost him half-
      a-crown,
He took a quid, and heav'd a sigh to Poll of Horsley-
      down.

He soon found out Poll's father, and dress'd in rich
      array,
He got permission for to court, and so got under-weigh :
Miss Polly she received him, all for a lover true,
And quite inamorated of her he quickly grew :
He squir'd and convey'd her all over London town,
Until the day was fix'd to wed with Poll of Horsley-
      down.

But Poll, she was a knowing one, as you shall quickly
      find,
And this here Captain Oakum,—why, love had made him
      blind !
One morning, in her chamber, he found a cockney lout,
So, captain shov'd the window up, and chuck'd my
      gem'man out ;
Then cock'd his arms a kimbo, and looking with a frown,
He took a quid, and bid good-bye to Poll of Horsley-
      down.

JACK GUNNEL, THE OBSTINATE DOG.

Jack Gunnel, an odd fish as ever hove anchor
  Or clew'd up a top-sail, lov'd Poll of Spithead;
But Poll was a Tartar, a terrible canker;
  For, tho' a tight vessel, false colours she spread;
Jack, oftens he told me, he lov'd her more better
    Than deep sounding, smooth sailing, good biscuit, or
      grog;
But I thought he was wrong, so his senses to fetter,
  And reason'd, d'ye mind, with the obstinate dog;
    For it's always my way when a shipmate I sees
  Deceived in his reck'ning or hanging astarn,
    To take him in tow, if I drives with the breeze,
  Or point out those shallows he cannot dissarn.

Her false arms she lash'd round his neck when they
    parted,
  That time when the Dreadnought she sail'd from the
    Nore,
A leak in her eye for to queer him she started,
  And shamm'd for to faint, when the boat put off shore.
How oft of her constancy Jack would be talking!
  And toasted her still when we push'd round the grog;
But I told him her constancy oft would want calking,
  And a scowl lour'd the eye of the obstinate dog:
    But it's always my way, &c.

Each prize that we took gave Jack's spirits fresh canvass,
  And the compass of Hope seem'd to point to Port
    Joy;
But I knew in my mind how mistaken the man was,
  And tried still his senses to pipe hands-a-hoy!

For which, in the presence of every mess-brother,
    He struck me one night while we push'd round the
        grog—
So, I trounc'd him, d'ye see, and how could I do other?
    And I left to himself, then, the obstinate dog.
        Yet it's always, &c.

When to port we return'd, Jack soon heard that his Polly
    Did'nt single long after his sailing remain;
The latitude then he first found of his folly,
    And wanted the timbers to start of his brain;
But I captur'd his pistols, and bid him weigh anchor,
    And leave Port Despair for the Ocean of Grog;
He took my advice, overboard threw his rancour,
    And never more turn'd out an obstinate dog.
        And it's always, &c.

PRO ARIS ET FOCIS.

I'M a true honest-hearted gay fellow,
    And scorn to be hanging aback,
Who fear neither bullet nor billow,
    And this has been always my Jack:
In defence of my system to pledge heart and hand,
And to fight for my King and my dear native land.

    Some people about Whig and Tory,
        And such sort of trash, and to do,
    Will tell you all day a tough story,
        And, perhaps, all they say may be true;
But such outlandish lingo I don't understand;
So I fight for, &c.

Both parties they quarrel most rarely;
   I'm puzzled with which side to strike—
For both find sound argument fairly,
   To prove they're all patriots alike;
Yet I side with no maxims I don't understand,
But I fight for, &c.

LIEUTENANT YEO.

Off Cape Finisterre lay the king's ship La Loire,
When a privateer foe Captain Maitland he saw;
So a boat's crew he sent, with the Spaniards to cope,
Who was call'd L'Esperance—in plain English, The
      Hope;
Tho' but a forlorn Hope she prov'd to the foe,
Made a prize by the boat's crew and Lieutenant Yeo!
     Yeo! Yeo! for ever.

" 'Tis the birth of our King, boys!" the captain he cried,
"To crown it with victory then be your pride;
Yes, the birth of your Sov'reign distinguish, in short,
By planting his flag on that proud Spanish fort:"
So the gallant boat's crew volunteer'd all to go,
To conquer or die with brave Lieutenant Yeo!
     Yeo, &c.

Then Lieutenant Yeo, to his lasting renown,
The fort he knock'd up, and the governor down;
The Dons' captur'd ensign wav'd over his head,
And planted the flag of King George in its stead!
Let the trumpet of fame then thro' all the world blow
To the glory of Britons and Lieutenant Yeo.
     Yeo, &c.

NATIONAL SONGS,

FROM POPULAR AUTHORS,

INSERTRD BY SPECIAL DESIRE.

OLD ENGLAND'S A LION.

[Written by John O'Keeffe.   Music by Shield.]

OLD ENGLAND's a lion, stretch'd out at his ease,
A sailor his keeper, his couch the green seas;
Should a monkey dare to chatter, or a tiger claw,
They tremble at his roar as he lifts his paw.
I loved a neighbour's friendship, but he turn'd foe,
Prepare to receive him with blow for blow.

THE LAND, BOYS, WE LIVE IN.

SINCE our foes to invade us have long been preparing,
'Tis clear they consider we've something worth sharing,
    And for that mean to visit our shore,
It behoves us, however, with spirit to meet 'em,
And though 'twill be nothing uncommon to beat 'em,
    We must try how they'll take it once more.
So fill, fill your glasses, be this the toast given—
Here's England for ever, the land, boys, we live in!
So fill, fill your glasses, be this the toast given—
Here's England for ever, huzza!

Here's a health to our tars on the wild ocean ranging,
Perhaps even now some broadsides are exchanging,
    We'll on shipboard and join in the fight;
And when with the foe we are firmly engaging,
Till the fire of our guns lulls the sea in its raging,
    On our country we'll think with delight.
  So fill, fill your glasses, &c.

On that throne where once Alfred in glory was seated,
Long, long may our king by his people be greeted;
    Oh! to guard him we'll be of one mind.
May religion, law, order, be strictly defended,
And continue the blessings they first were intended,
    In union the nation to bind.
  So fill, fill your glasses, &c.

BLACK EYED SUSAN.

[By John Gay.]

All in the Downs the fleet was moor'd,
    The streamers waving in the wind,
When black-eyed Susan came on board—
    Oh! where shall I my true love find?
Tell me, ye jovial sailors, tell me true,
If my sweet William sails among your crew.

William, who high upon the yard,
    Rock'd with the billows to and fro,
Soon as her well-known voice he heard,
    He sigh'd, and cast his eyes below:
The cord glides swiftly thro' his glowing hands,
And quick as lightning on the deck he stands.

So the sweet lark, high pois'd in air,
 Shuts close his pinions to his breast,
If chance his mate's shrill call he hear,
 And drops at once into her nest.
The noblest captain in the British fleet
Might envy William's lips those kisses sweet.

O Susan, Susan, lovely dear!
 My vows shall ever true remain;
Let me kiss off that falling tear,
 We only part to meet again.
Change as ye list, ye winds, my heart shall be
The faithful compass that still points to thee!

Believe not what the landmen say,
 Who tempt with doubts thy constant mind;
They'll tell thee sailors, when away,
 In every port a mistress find:
Yes, yes, believe them, when they tell thee so,
For thou art present wheresoe'er I go!

If to far India's coast we sail,
 Thy eyes are seen in diamonds bright;
Thy breath is Afric's spicy gale,
 Thy skin is ivory so white:
Thus every beauteous object that I view
Wakes in my soul some charm of lovely Sue.

Though battle calls me from thy arms,
 Let not my pretty Susan mourn;
Though cannons roar, yet, safe from harms,
 William shall to his dear return:
Love turns aside the balls that round me fly,
Lest precious tears should drop from Susan's eye.

The boatswain gave the dreadful word,
  The sails their swelling bosom spread,
No longer must she stay on board:
  They kiss'd, she sigh'd, he hung his head.
The less'ning boat unwilling rows to land;
Adieu! she cried, and waved her lily hand.

THE STORM.

[By G. A. Stevens. Music by Leveridge.]
CEASE, rude Boreas, blust'ring railer!
  List, ye landsmen all, to me;
Messmates, hear a brother sailor
  Sing the dangers of the sea.
From bounding billows first in motion,
  When the distant whirlwinds rise,
To the tempest-troubled ocean,
  Where the seas contend with skies.

Hark! the boatswain hoarsely bawling,
  By topsail-sheets and haulyards stand,
Down top-gallants, quick, be hawling,
  Down your stay-sails, hand, boys, hand!
Now it freshens, set the braces,
  Now the top-sail sheets let go;
Luff, boys, luff! don't make wry faces,
  Up your top-sails nimbly clew.

Now all you, on down-beds sporting,
  Fondly lock'd in beauty's arms;
Fresh enjoyments, wanton courting,
  Safe from all but love's alarms;

U

Round us roars the tempest louder,
   Think what fears our minds enthral ;
Harder yet, it yet blows harder ;
   Hark ! again the boatswains call !

The top-sail yards point to the wind, boys,
   See all clear to reef each course ;
Let the foresheet go, don't mind, boys,
   Though the weather should prove worse ;
Fore and aft the spritsail yard get,
   Reef the mizen, see all clear,
Hands up, each preventer-brace set,
   Man the foreyard.   Cheer, lads, cheer !

Now the dreadful thunder rolling,
   Peal on peal, contending, clash ;
On our heads fierce rain falls pouring,
   In our eyes blue lightnings flash :
One wide water all around us,
   All above us one black sky,
Different deaths at once surround us.—
   Hark ! What means that dreadful cry ?

The foremast's gone ! cries every tongue out,
   O'er the lee, twelve feet 'bove deck ;
A leak beneath the chest-tree's sprung out,
   Call all hands to clear the wreck.
Quick ! the lanyards cut to pieces ;
   Come, my hearts, be stout and bold !
Plumb the well, the leak increases,
   Four feet water in the hold !

While o'er the ship wild waves are beating,
   We for wives or children mourn ;
Alas! from hence there's no retreating ;
   Alas! from hence there's no return.
Still the leak is gaining on us,
   Both chain-pumps are choak'd below ;
Heav'n have mercy here upon us !
   For only that can save us now.

O'er the lee-beam is the land, boys !
   Let the guns o'er board be thrown ;
To the pump come every hand, boys !
   See, our mizen-mast is gone !
The leak we've found, it cannot pour fast ;
   We've lighten'd her a foot or more ;
Up and rig a jury foremast.
   She rights! she rights, boys ! we're off shore.

Now once more on joys we're thinking,
   Since kind Fortune saved our lives ;
Come, the can, boys ! let's be drinking
   To our sweethearts and our wives :
Fill it up, about ship wheel it,
   Close to the lips a brimmer join.
Where's the tempest now ? who feels it ?
   None ! Our danger's drown'd in wine.

MINDEN'S PLAINS OF GLORY.

[The Rev. Sir H. Dudley Bate.   Music by Shield.]

FROM Minden's Plains of glory
I date my warlike story,
When conquest never yet outdone,
By British arms was nobly won.
See old Kingley's lads present,
    Revenge desiring,
    Incessant firing,
On fame and Britain's glory bent.
All our powder and ball expended,
The Monsieurs thought the battle ended,
Till, with bayonets advancing,
We quickly set their columns prancing;
And, to make our victory good,
Follow'd through a crimson flood.
From Minden's Plains of glory
I date my warlike story,
When conquest never yet outdone,
By British arms was nobly won.

RUSSELL'S TRIUMPH.

THURSDAY in the morn, the nineteenth of May,
  Recorded be for ever the famous Ninety-two,
Brave Russell did discern, by break of day,
  The lofty sails of France advancing too.

All hands aloft! they cry, let English courage shine,
Let fly a culverine, the signal of the line;
   Let every man supply his gun,
      Follow me,
      You shall see,
That the battle it will soon be won.

Tourville on the main triumphant roll'd
   To meet the gallant Russell in combat o'er the deep:
He led his noble troops of heroes bold
   To sink the English admiral and his fleet.
Now ev'ry gallant mind to victory does aspire:
The bloody fight's begun—the sea is all on fire;
   And mighty Fate stood looking on,
      Whilst the flood
      All with blood
Fill the scuppers of the Rising Sun.

Sulphur, smoke, and fire, disturbing the air,
   With thunder and wonder, affright the Gallic shore;
Their regulated bands stood trembling near,
   To see their lofty streamers now no more.
At six o'clock the Red the smiling victors led
To give the second blow—the total overthrow.
   Now Death and Horror equal reign;
      Now they cry,
      Run or die—
British colours ride the vanquish'd main.

See, they fly amazed o'er rocks and sands!
   One danger they grasp to shun a greater fate:
In vain they cried for aid to weeping lands,
   The nymphs and sea-gods mourn their lost estate.

For ever more adieu, thou ever dazzling Sun!
From thy untimely end thy master's fate begun.
   Enough, thou mighty God of War!
       Now we sing,
       Bless the King!
Let us drink to ev'ry English tar.

THE SPANISH ARMADA.

[John O'Keeffe. Music by Dr. Arnold.]

In May fifteen hundred and eighty and eight,
  Cries Philip, the English I'll humble;
I've taken it into my majesty's pate,
  And their lion, oh! down he shall tumble.
They lords of the sea, then his sceptre he shook,
  I'll prove it an arrant bravado.
By Neptune! I'll sweep 'em all into a nook,
  With th' invincible Spanish Armada!

This fleet then sail'd out, and the winds they did blow,
  Their guns made a terrible clatter;
Our noble Queen Bess 'cause she wanted to know,
  Quill'd her ruff and cried, " Pray what's the matter?"
" They say, my good Queen," replied Howard so stout,
  " The Spaniard has drawn his toledo;
Cock sure that he'll thump us, and kick us about,
  With th' invincible Spanish Armada."

The Lord Mayor of London, a very wise man,
  What to do in this case vastly wonder'd:
Says the Queen, " Send in fifty good ships, if you can."
  Says my Lord, " Ma'am, I'll send in an hundred."

Our fire-ships they soon struck their cannons all dumb,
   For the Dons run to ave and credo.
Great Medina roars out, " Sure the Devil is come
   For th' invincible Spanish Armada."

On Effingham's squadron, though all in a breast,
   Like open-mouth curs they came bowling;
His sugar-plums finding they could not digest,
   Away home they ran yelping and howling.
Whene'er Britain's foes shall, with envy agog,
   In our Channel make such a bravado—
Huzza, my brave boys! we're still able to flog
   An invincible Spanish Armada!
      Huzza, my brave boys! &c.

THE BRITISH SEAMAN'S PRAISE.

[Words and music by Mr. Smart.]

I SING the British seaman's praise,
   A theme renown'd in story:
It well deserves more polish'd lays,
   Oh, 'tis your boast and glory!
When mad-brain'd War spreads death around
   By them you are protected,
But when in peace the nation's found
   These bulwarks are neglected.
Then, oh! protect the hardy tar,
   Be mindful of his merit,
And when again we're plung'd in war,
   He'll show his daring spirit.

When thickest darkness covers all
 Far on the trackless ocean,
When lightnings dart, when thunders roll,
 And all in wild commotion ;
When o'er the bark the white-topp'd waves
 With boist'rous sweep are rolling—
Yet coolly still the whole he braves,
 Serene amidst the howling.
  Then oh! protect, &c.

When deep immersed in sulph'rous smoke
 He feels a glowing pleasure ;
He loads his gun, right heart of oak,
 Elated beyond measure.
Though fore and aft the blood-stain'd deck
 Should lifeless trunks appear,
Or should the vessel float a wreck,
 The sailor knows no fear.
  Then, oh! protect, &c.

When long becalm'd on southern brine,
 Where scorching beams assail him,
When all the canvass hangs supine,
 And food and water fail him—
Then oft he dreams of Britain's shore,
 Where plenty still is reigning.
They call the watch. His rapture's o'er—
 He sighs—forbears complaining.
  Then, oh! protect, &c.

Or burning on that noxious coast,
 Where death so oft befriends him ;
Or pinch'd by hoary Greenland's frost,
 True courage still attends him.

No clime can this eradicate—
   He's calm amidst annoyance—
He fearless braves the storms of fate,
   On heav'n is his reliance.
      Then, oh! protect, &c.

Why should the man, who knows no fear,
   In peace be then neglected?
Behold him move along the pier,
   Pale, meagre, and dejected!
Behold him begging for employ!
   Behold him disregarded!
Then view the anguish in his eye,
   And say, are tars rewarded?
      Then, oh! protect, &c.

To them your dearest rights you owe;
   In peace, then, would you starve them?
What say ye, Britain's sons? Oh, no!
   Protect them and preserve them.
Shield them from poverty and pain—
   'Tis policy to do it;
Or when grim War shall come again,
   Oh, Britons! ye may rue it.
      Then, oh! protect, &c.

OUR COUNTRY IS OUR SHIP.

[Written by James Cobb, Esq.   Music by Storace.]

OUR country is our ship, d'ye see,
  A gallant vessel, too;
And of his fortune proud is he,
  Who's of the Albion's crew.
Each man, whate'er his station be,
  When duty's call commands,
    Should take his stand,
    And lend a hand,
  As the common cause demands.

And when our haughty enemies
  Our noble ship assail,
Then all true-hearted lads despise
  What peril may prevail;
But shrinking from the cause we prize,
  If lubbers skulk below,
    To the sharks
    Heave such sparks,
  They assist the common foe.

Among ourselves, in peace, 'tis true,
  We quarrel, make a rout;
And, having nothing else to do,
  We fairly scold it out:
But once the enemy in view,
  Shake hands, we soon are friends;
    On the deck,
    Till a wreck,*
  Each the common cause defends.

NEPTUNE'S RESIGNATION.

[Written by Mr. Wagnell. Music by Worgan.]

THE wat'ry god, great Neptune, lay
In dalliance soft and amorous play
   On Amphitrite's breast,
When Uproar rear'd its horrid head,
The tritons shrunk, the nereids fled,
   And all their fear confess'd.

Loud thunder shook the vast domain,
The liquid world was wrapt in flame;
   The god, amazed, spoke—
" Ye Winds, go forth and make it known
Who dares to shake my coral throne,
   And fill my realms with smoke."

The Winds, obsequious, at his word
Sprung strongly up t' obey their lord,
   And saw two fleets a-weigh—
One, victorious Hawke, was thine,
The other, Conflans' wretched line—
   In terror and dismay.

Appall'd, they view Britannia's sons
Deal death and slaughter from their guns,
   And strike the dreadful blow,
Which caused ill-fated Gallic slaves
To find a tomb in briny waves,
   And sink to shades below.

With speed they fly and tell their chief
That France was ruin'd past relief,
   And Hawke triumphant rode.
" Hawke !" cried the Fair ; " Pray who is he
That dare usurp this power at sea,
   And thus insult a god ?"

The Winds reply—" In distant lands
There reigns a king whom Hawke commands,
   He scorns all foreign force ;
And when his floating castles roll
From sea to sea, from pole to pole,
   Great Hawke directs their course.

" Or when his winged bullets fly
To punish fraud or perfidy,
   Or scourge a guilty land ;
Then gallant Hawke, serenely great,
Though death and horror round him wait,
   Performs his dread command."

Neptune, with wonder, heard the story
Of George's sway and Britain's glory,
   Which time shall ne'er subdue ;
Boscawen's deeds, and Saunders' fame,
Join'd with brave Wolfe's immortal name,
   Then cried—" Can this be true ?

" A king ! he sure must be a god,
Who has such heroes at his nod
   To govern earth and sea :
I yield my trident and my crown
A tribute due to such renown,
   Great George shall rule for me."

HEARTS OF OAK.

[Written by Mr. Garrick.   Composed by Dr. Boyce.]

COME cheer up, my lads! 'tis to glory we steer,
To add something more to this wonderful year :
To honour we call you, not press you like slaves;
For who are so free as we sons of the waves?
    Heart of oak are our ships,
    Heart of oak are our men,
      We always are ready ;
      Steady, boys, steady!
We'll fight and we'll conquer again, and again.

We ne'er see our foes but we wish them to stay,
They never see us but they wish us away ;
If they run, why we follow, or run them ashore ;
For if they won't fight us we cannot do more.
    Heart of oak, &c.

They swear they'll invade us, these terrible foes!
They frighten our women, our children, and beaux ;
But should their flat bottoms in darkness get o'er,
Still Britons they'll find to receive them on shore.
    Heart of oak, &c.

Britannia triumphant, her ships sweep the sea ;
Her standard is Justice—her watch-word, "Be free."
Then cheer up, my lads! with one heart let us sing,
" Our soldiers, our sailors, our statesmen, and king."
    Heart of oak, &c.

THE ARETHUSA.

[Written by P. Hoare, Esq. Composed by Shield.]

COME, all ye jolly sailors bold,
Whose hearts are cast in honour's mould,
While English glory I unfold—
    Huzza! to the Arethusa!
She is a frigate tight and brave
As ever stemm'd the dashing wave:
      Her men are stanch
      To their fav'rite launch,
And when the foe shall meet our fire,
Sooner than strike, we'll all expire,
    On board of the Arethusa.

'Twas with the Spring-fleet she went out,
The English Channel to cruise about,
When four French sail, in show so stout,
    Bore down on the Arethusa.
The famed Belle Poule straight a-head did lie,
The Arethusa seem'd to fly;
      Not a sheet, or a tack,
      Or a brace did she slack;
Though the Frenchmen laugh'd, and thought it stuff;
But they knew not the handful of men, how tough,
    On board of the Arethusa.

On deck five hundred men did dance,
The stoutest they could find in France;
We with two hundred did advance,
    On board of the Arethusa.

Our captain hail'd the Frenchman, " Ho !"
The Frenchman then cried out, " Hallo !"
 " Bear down, d'ye see,
 To our admiral's lee."
" No, no," says the Frenchman, " that can't be."
" Then I must lug you along with me,"
 Says the saucy Arethusa.

The fight was off the Frenchman's land,
We forced them back upon the strand ;
For we fought till not a stick would stand
 Of the gallant Arethusa.
And now we've driv'n the foe a-shore,
Never to fight with Britons more,
 Let each fill a glass
 To his favorite lass ;
A health to the captain and officers true,
And all that belong to the jovial crew
 On board of the Arethusa.

WHAT SHOULD SAILORS DO ON SHORE?

[Written by O'Keeffe. Composed by Dr. Arnold.]
WHAT should sailors do on shore?
 Kiss the girls and toss the can !
When the cannons cease to roar,
 Sweet the voice of smiling Nan.
Bring me first a spacious bowl,
 Deeper than a plummet sound ;
Give me next a gen'rous soul,
 That in loving knows no bound.

Flowing ever let it be,
  If the tide good liquor prove ;
Thus, my hearts, let's keep the sea,
  Sailing with the girl we love.
    What should sailors, &c.

Nancy be my true love's name,
  And to compliment my dear,
Bonny ship, secure thy fame,
  Thou the darling title bear.
To guard and bless my fav'rite realm,
  Smiling thus, old Neptune spoke ;
I place my William at the helm ;
  Royal Will is heart of oak.
Whether moor'd or on a cruise,
  Sailor still, in peace or war :
Poise the linstock, brim the booze,
  Sing long live the royal tar.
    What should sailors, &c.

SLING THE FLOWING BOWL.

[Written by Mrs. Linley.   Composed by Mr. Linley.]
COME, come, my jolly lads, the wind's abaft,
  Brisk gales our sails shall crowd ;
Come, bustle, bustle, bustle, boys, haul the boat,
  The boatswain pipes aloud :
The ship's unmoor'd ; all hands on board,
The rising gale fills ev'ry sail,
  The ship's well mann'd and stor'd :

Then sling the flowing bowl!
Fond hopes arise, the girls we prize
   Shall bless each jovial soul;
The can, boys, bring, we'll drink and sing,
   While foaming billows roll.
      Then sling, &c.

Tho' to the Spanish coast we're bound to steer,
   We'll still our rights maintain;
Then bear a hand, be steady, boys, soon we'll see
   Old England once again:
From shore to shore, while cannons roar,
Our tars shall show the haughty foe,
   Britannia rules the main.
    Then sling the flowing bowl!
Fond hopes arise, the girls we prize
   Shall bless each jovial soul;
The can boys bring, we'll drink and sing,
   While foaming billows roll.
      Then sling, &c.

THE TOPSAILS SHIVER IN THE WIND.

[Michael Arne.]

THE topsails shiver in the wind,
   The ship she casts to sea;
But yet my soul, my heart, my mind,
   Are, Mary, moor'd with thee.
For tho' thy sailor's bound afar,
Still, love shall be his leading star.

x

Should landmen flatter when we've sail'd,
   O doubt their artful tales ;
No gallant sailor ever fail'd,
   If Love breath'd constant gales :
Thou art the compass of my soul
Which steers my heart from pole to pole.

Sirens in every port we meet,
   More fell than rocks or waves;
But such as grace the British fleet
   Are lovers, and not slaves :
No foes our courage shall subdue,
Altho' we've left our hearts with you.

These are our cares ; but if you're kind
   We'll scorn the dashing main,
The rocks, the billows, and the wind,
   The power of France and Spain :
Now England's glory rests with you ;
Our sails are full, sweet girls, adieu !

THE HARDY SAILOR.

[Dr. Arnold.]

THE hardy sailor braves the ocean,
   Fearless of the roaring wind ;
Yet his heart, with soft emotion,
   Throbs to leave his love behind.

To dread of foreign foes a stranger,
   Tho' the youth may dauntless roam,
Alarming fears paint ev'ry danger
   In a rival left at home.
     The hardy sailor, &c.

THE WANDERING SAILOR.

[Written by M. P. Andrews, Esq. Music by Dr. Arnold.

THE wand'ring sailor ploughs the main
A competence in life to gain;
Undaunted braves the stormy seas
To find, at last, content and ease:
In hopes, when toil and danger's o'er,
To anchor on his native shore.

When winds blow hard, and mountains roll,
And thunders shake from pole to pole;
Tho' dreadful waves surrounding foam,
Still flatt'ring fancy wafts him home;
    In hopes, &c.

When round the bowl the jovial crew
The early scenes of youth renew,
Tho' each his fav'rite fair will boast,
This is the universal toast:—
" May we, when toil and danger's o'er,
Cast anchor on our native shore."

THE MIDWATCH.

[The Rt. Hon. Richard Brinsley Sheridan. Music by Linley.]

WHEN 'tis night, and the midwatch is come,
And chilling mists hang o'er the darken'd main,
Then sailors think of their far distant home,
And of those friends they ne'er may see again.

But when the fight's begun,
Each serving at his gun,
Should any thought of them come o'er our mind,
We think, should but the day be won,
How 'twill cheer
Their hearts to hear
That their old companion he was one!

Or, my lad, if you a mistress kind
Have left on shore, some pretty girl, and true;
Who many a night doth listen to the wind,
And sighs to think how it may fare with you:
O when the fight's begun,
Each serving at his gun,
Should any thought of her come o'er your mind,
Think, only should the day be won,
How 'twill cheer
Her heart to hear
That her own true sailor he was one!

BLOW, BOREAS, BLOW.

[R. Bradley (1700).]

Blow, Boreas, blow, and let thy surly winds
Make the billows foam and roar.
Thou canst no terror breed in valiant minds,
But, spite of thee, we'll live and find a shore!
Then cheer, my hearts, and be not aw'd,
But keep the gun-room clear;
Tho' hell's broke loose, and the devils roar abroad,
Whilst we have sea-room here, boys, never fear! —

Hey! how she tosses up, how far;
The mounting topmast touch'd a star!
The meteors blaz'd as thro' the clouds we came,
And, salamander-like, we live in flame!—
But now we sink! now, now we go
Down to the deepest shades below.
Alas! where are we now? who, who can tell?
Sure 'tis the lowest room of hell!
Or where the sea gods dwell!—
With them we'll live; with them we'll live and reign,
With them we'll laugh and sing, and drink amain :—
But see, we mount! see, see, we rise again!

Tho' flashes of light'ning, and tempests of rain,
Do fiercely contend who shall conquer the main;
Tho' the captain does swear, instead of a pray'r,
And the sea is all fired by the demons of the air!—
We'll drink, and defy
The mad spirits that fly
From the deep to the sky,
   And sing whilst the thunder does bellow;
For Fate will still have a kind fate for the brave,
And ne'er make his grave of a salt water wave,
   To drown,—no, never to drown a good fellow.

YE GENTLEMEN OF ENGLAND.

[Music by Calcott.]

Ye gentlemen of England,
   Who live at home at ease,
Ah! little do you think upon
   The dangers of the seas;

While pleasure does surround you,
　Our cares you cannot know,
Or the pain, on the main,
　When the stormy winds do blow.

The sailor must have courage,
　No danger he must shun;
In every kind of weather
　His course he still must run :
Now mounted on the topmast,—
　How dreadful 'tis below !
Then we ride, as the tide,
　When the stormy winds do blow.

Proud France, again insulting,
　Does British valour dare ;
Our flag we must support now,
　And thunder in the war :
To humble them, come on, lads,
　And lay their lilies low ;
Clear the way for the fray,
　Tho' the stormy winds do blow.

Old Neptune shakes his trident,
　The billows mount on high ;
Their shells the Tritons sounding,
　The flashing light'nings fly.
The wat'ry grave now opens,
　All dreadful from below ;
When the waves move the seas,
　And the stormy winds do blow.

But when the danger's over,
  And safe we come on shore;
The horrors of the tempest,
  We think of them no more.
The flowing bowl invites us,
  And joyfully we go;
All the day drink away,
  Tho' the stormy winds do blow.

LITTLE DO THE LANDSMEN KNOW.

How little do the landsmen know
  Of what we sailors feel,
When waves do mount, and winds do blow,
  But we have hearts of steel:
No danger can affright us;
  No enemy shall flout;
We'll make the Monsieurs right us,
  So, toss the can about.

Stick stout to orders, messmates;
  We'll plunder, burn, and sink!
Then, France, have at your first-rates,
  For Britons never shrink:
We'll rummage all we fancy;
  We'll bring them in by scores;
And Moll, and Kate, and Nancy,
  Shall roll in Louis d'ors.

While here at Deal we're lying,
 With our noble commodore,
We'll spend our wages freely, boys,
 And then to sea for more.
In peace we'll drink and sing, boys,
 In war we'll never fly!
Here's a health to George our King, boys,
 And the royal family.

NOW AWAY, MY BRAVE BOYS.

Now away, my brave boys, hoist the flag, beat the drum,
 Let the streamers wave over the main;
When Old England she calls us, we merrily come,
 She can't call a sailor in vain.
Already we seem an armada to chase,
 Already behold the galleons;
Undaunted, unconquer'd, look death in the face,
 And return with a load of doubloons.

Then, farewell for a time, lovely sweethearts, dear wives;
 Nancy, fear not the fate of true blue;
Tho' we leave you and merrily venture our lives,
 To our girls we will ever be true.
With spirit we go, an armada to chase,
 With rapture behold the galleons;
Undaunted, unconquer'd, look death in the face,
 And return with a load of doubloons.

HARK! THE BOATSWAIN'S WHISTLE.

[Dr. Green.]

LIFE is chequer'd!—toil and pleasure
Fill up all the various measure.
See the crew, in flannel jerkins,
Drinking, toping flip by firkins;
    And as they raise the tip
    To their happy lip,
On the deck is heard no other sound,
    But prithee, Jack, prithee, Dick,
    Prithee, Sam, prithee, Tom,
Let the can go round.
Then, hark to the boatswain's whistle!
    Bustle, bustle, bustle, my boy;
    Let us stir, let us toil,
    But let us drink all the while,
For labour's the price of our joy.

Life is chequer'd!—toil and pleasure
Fill up all the various measure.
Hark! the crew, in sun-burnt faces,
Chanting black-ey'd Susan's graces!
    And as they raise their notes
    Thro' their rusty throats,
On the deck is heard no other sound,
    But prithee, Jack, prithee, Dick,
    Prithee, Sam, prithee, Tom,
Let the can go round.
    Then hark, &c.

Life is chequer'd!—toil and pleasure
Fill up all the various measure.
Hark! the crew, their cares discarding,
With hustle-cap, or with chuck-farthing;
    Still in a merry pin,
    Let 'em lose or win,
On the deck is heard no other sound,
    But prithee, Jack, prithee, Dick,
    Prithee, Sam, prithee, Tom,
Let the can go round.
    Then hark, &c.

ALOFT THE SAILOR LOOKS AROUND.

[By J. Cobb, Esq. Music by Storace.]

FROM aloft the sailor looks around,
And hears below the murm'ring billows sound.
Far off from home he counts another day,
Wide o'er the seas the vessel bears away!
    His courage wants no whet,
    But he springs the sail to set,
With a heart as fresh as rising breeze of May;
    And caring nought,
    He turns his thought
To his lovely Sue or his charming Bet.

Now to heav'n the lofty topmast soars,
The stormy blast like dreadful thunder roars:

Now oceans deepest gulfs appear below,
The curling surges foam, and down we go!
    When skies and seas are met,
    They his courage serve to whet;
With a heart as fresh as rising breeze of May;
    And dreading nought, &c.

LOOSE EVERY SAIL TO THE BREEZE.

[Michael Arne.]

Loose ev'ry sail to the breeze,
    The course of my vessel improve;
I've done with the toils of the seas,
    Ye sailors, I'm bound to my love.

Since Emma is true as she's fair,
    My griefs I fling all to the wind;
'Tis a pleasing return to my care,
    My mistress is constant and kind.

My sails are all fill'd to my dear;
    What Tropic bird swifter can move?
Who cruel shall hold his career,
    That returns to the nest of his love?

Hoist ev'ry sail to the breeze;
    Come, shipmates, and join in the song:
Let's drink, while the ship cuts the seas,
    To the gale that may drive her along.

COME, BUSTLE, BUSTLE.

[Words Anonymous. Music by Dibdin.]

COME, bustle, bustle, drink about,
  And let us merry be;
Our can is full, we'll see it out,
  And then all hands to sea.
    And a sailing we will go.

Fine Miss, at dancing school, is taught
  The minuet to tread;
But we go better when we've brought
  The fore-tack to cat-head.
    And a sailing, &c.

The Jockeys call to horse, to horse!
  And swiftly rides the race;
But swifter far we shape our course,
  When we are giving chase.
    And a sailing, &c.

When horns and shouts the forest rend,
  His pack the huntsman cheers;
As loud we hollow when we send
  A broadside to Monsieur.
    And a sailing, &c.

The What's-their-names at uproars squall,
  With music fine and soft;
But better sounds our boatswain's call,
  All hands, all hands aloft.
    And a sailing, &c.

With gold and silver streamers fine
  The ladies rigging show;
But English ships more grander shine,
  When prizes home we tow.
      And a sailing, &c.

What's got at sea we spend on shore,
  With sweethearts or with wives;
And then, my boys, hoist sail for more:—
  Thus passes sailors' lives.
      And a sailing, &c.

A HEALTH TO GEORGE OUR KING.

[Old Ballad.]

COME, let's drink a health to George our King,
  And his brave commanders;
Another glass let us toss off,
  To the valiant Salamander;
Who fought so bravely for their King, sir,
For their country, and their crown,
To put the Mounsieurs' courage down,
By the brave Salamander.

When we cruised on the raging main,
  Our guns they roar'd like thunder;
Along the coast of France and Spain,
  Brave boys, we search for plunder!

We'll make the French and Spaniards quake,
Our English merchant-ships retake,
For the glory of Old England's sake,
By the valiant Salamander.

One night we fought, in a mistake,
  With a Bristol privateer, sir;
With one broadside we made them shake,
  And laid them on the careen, sir.
They swore no mortals we could be,
But devils, sure, that liv'd at sea;
But to their joy they soon did see
'Twas the valiant Salamander.

Who can pretend for to withstand
  A creature bred by fire?
When man can live by sea or land,
  What fool would e'er come nigh her?
With hand-grenades and musket-shot,
Their cannon-ball, altho' red hot,
We neither fear nor value not,
On board the Salamander.

And when that we do come on shore,
  We'll all fill up our glasses;
We'll drink and make the taverns roar,
  Along with our English lasses:
We'll dance and sing and roam about,
And spend our money, and then go out
Another cruize, and search about
For more French and Spanish plunder.

HOW BLEST ARE WE SEAMEN.

[Anonymous.]

How blest are we seamen! how jovial and gay!
Together we fight, or together we play;
Our hearts are true sterling,—their worth shall be seen;
We'll fight for our country, and die for our Queen!
For plenty, for freedom, we'll range the wide flood,
And for England, Old England, we'll shed our last
    blood!

By land, other nations their forces may boast;
'Tis we, only we, can protect Britain's coast!
Our strong floating castles, our loud English guns,
Shall convince the proud Spaniards we're Neptune's true
    sons.
  For plenty, &c.

Our Admirals lead, and our flag is let fly;
Our cross, like a comet, appears in the sky;
Portending destruction! our sea-lion roars;
And his voice, like loud thunder, breaks full on the
    shores.
  For plenty, &c.

Come, bustle, my boys! let us form the good line;
Come, cheer up, Old England,—the day shall be thine!
Huzza for our country! huzza for our king!
We'll raise its renown, and ennoble his reign.
  For plenty, &c.

HOW HAPPY ARE WE NOW THE WIND IS ABAFT.

[Aldrich.]

How happy are we now the wind is abaft,
And the boatswain he pipes, haul both our sheets aft.
Steady, says the master, it blows a fresh gale;
We'll soon reach our port, boys, if the wind doth not fail.
Then drink about, Tom, altho' the ship roll,
We'll save our rich liquor by slinging the bowl.

WHEN IN WAR ON THE OCEAN.

[By the Composer of Admiral Benbow.]

WHEN in war on the ocean we meet the proud foe,
Tho' with ardour for conquest our bosoms may glow,
Let us see on their vessels Old England's flag wave,
They shall find British sailors but conquer to save.

See their tri-coloured ensigns we view from afar,
With three cheers they are welcomed by each British
     tar;
Whilst the genius of Britain still bids us advance,
And our guns hurl in thunder defiance to France.

But mark our last broadside,—she sinks—down she goes!
Quickly man all your boats, boys—they no longer are
     foes,
To snatch a brave fellow from a wat'ry grave
Is worthy of Britons who conquer to save.

MAY OUR NAVY FOR EVER OLD ENGLAND PROTECT.

[Composed by Shield.]

Tho' hurricanes rattle—tho' tempests appear,
　　We sailors have pleasure in store,
For the pride of our hearts is to hand, reef, and steer,
　　Weigh anchor, and bear off from shore.
If contention of winds raise the waves mountains high,
　　O'er our quarters a heavy sea break,
Or the reef tackle fall we undauntedly ply;
　　Nor from danger e'er lubber-like sneak.
But the storm gone astern, and the mainmasts erect,
　　Then with messmates we cheerily sing,
May our navy for ever Old England protect,
　　Our laws, constitution, and king.

Why lately we spied 'fore the jib right ahead
　　A three decker, trim, gallant and gay,
And thwart of her poop a French ensign was spread,
　　That the tri-coloured stripes did display.
Then by skill of our helmsman the weather-gage got,
　　And soon as alongside her we lay,
We so pepper'd her hull, and her masts away shot,
　　That to strike she was forced to obey.
So we took her in tow, and to Plymouth direct,
　　Where our crew did all manfully sing,
Thus our navy shall ever Old England protect,
　　Our laws, constitution, and king.

Y

STAND TO YOUR GUNS.

[Composed by C. Carter.]

STAND to your guns, my hearts of oak,
Let not a word on board be spoke;
Victory is ours, 'mid fire and smoke;
  Be silent and be ready.
Ram home the guns and sponge them well;
Let us be sure the balls will tell;
The cannon's roar shall sound their knell;
  Be steady, boys, be steady,
· Not yet, nor yet, nor yet;
Reserve your fire, I do desire.

Now the elements do rattle;
The gods amazed behold the battle.
  A broadside, my boys.
See the blood in purple tide
Trickle down her batter'd side.
Wing'd with fate the bullets fly;
Conquer, boys, or bravely die.
  She sinks, she sinks, she sinks, huzza!
To the bottom down she goes!

BRITAIN'S BEST BULWARKS.

[Written and composed by Dr. Arne.]

WHEN Britain on her sea-girt shore
  Her ancient Druids erst address'd,
What aid, she cried, shall I implore?
  What best defence by numbers press'd?

The hostile nations round thee rise,
　　The mystic oracles replied,—
And view thine isle with envious eyes,
　　Their threats defy, their rage deride,
Nor fear invasion from those adverse Gauls:
Britain's best bulwarks are her wooden walls.

Thine oaks descending to the main,
　　With floating forts shall stem the tide,
Asserting Britain's liquid reign,
　　Where'er her thund'ring navy rides.
Nor less to peaceful arts inclined,
　　Where commerce opens all her stores,
In social bands shall league mankind,
　　And join the sea-divided shores.
Spread thy white sails where naval glory calls:
Britain's best bulwarks are her wooden walls.

Hail, happy isle! What tho' thy vales
　　No vine-impurpled tribute yield,
Nor fann'd with odour-breathing gales,
　　Nor crops spontaneous glad the field.
Yet liberty rewards the toil
　　Of industry to labour prone,
Who jocund ploughs the grateful soil,
　　And reaps the harvest she has sown;
While other realms tyrannic sway enthrals,
Britain's best bulwarks are her wooden walls.

Six " Songs of The Mid Watch," written by Captain Willes
Johnson, R.N.   Composed by Klitz.

No. 1.—THE SAILOR'S BEQUEST.

[The Music of this and the following five Songs may be had of
Messrs. Purday, 45, High Holborn.]

THE fight was o'er, and strew'd around
   Lay many a seaman brave,
And those who nobly died had found
   A deep unfathom'd grave.
One ling'ring lived, who vainly strove
   The manly tear to hide;
A pray'r he breath'd to Heav'n above
   For her, his promised bride.

'Twas poor Tom Ratline wounded lay,
   His life-blood ebbing fast;
On her he loved, far, far away,
   He felt he 'd look'd his last.
" Shipmate," said he, " it is not dread
   Of death which fills my eye;
'Tis Mem'ry's dream of joys, though fled,
   Which makes it sad to die.

" If our good prize should pay us well,
   Which I 've no doubt she 'll do,
Take all my share, and, hark' ye! tell
   The rhino out to Sue.
Dry her sweet eyes—salt tears they 'll pour
   At poor Tom's fate," he cried;
" Say my last thought "—he could no more,
   But, whisp'ring " Susan! " died.

No. 2.—THE MARINER'S INVOCATION.

BRIGHT Moon! fair Moon! the mariner's friend,
　When wintry storms prevail,
Deign from thy throne of state to bend
　And list a lover's tale.
She I adore is far away,
　And I may roam the main
For years ere comes the happy day
　When we can meet again.
Then, beauteous Moon, fair Queen of Night!
　Still more thy friendship prove;
Reflect, as in a mirror bright,
　The face of her I love.

I 'd forfeit all thy cheerful light,
　When danger 's lurking round,
The dread lee-shore, and craggy height,
　The boldest hearts astound;
I 'd brave the wreck, nor seek thy aid,
　If sometimes to my view
Thou'd'st bring the form of that sweet maid,
　So tender and so true.
Then, beauteous Moon, fair Queen of Night!
　My fondest wish approve,
And show me in thy mirror bright
　The face of her I love.

No. 3.—THE HEART KNOWS ONLY ONE.

THE landsmen tell you those who roam
  O'er Ocean's boundless tide,
On ev'ry shore can find a home,
  In ev'ry port a bride.
Heed not, sweet maid, their idle prate,
  They ne'er such feelings knew
As warm the heart of thy sailor-mate,
  Which beats alone for you.

What though when storms our bark assail,
  The needle trembling veers,
When night adds horror to the gale,
  And not a star appears:
True to the Pole as I to thee,
  It faithful still will prove,
An emblem, dear, of constancy,
  And of a sailor's love.

Then turn from what the landsmen say,
  Who would thy faith beguile;
They seize the time when we 're away
  To practise every wile;
O'er beauty bright our looks may rove,
  We ne'er its influence shun,
But though the eye has many a love,
  The heart knows only one.

No. 4.—HURRAH FOR THE SEA!

Your poets may sing of the pleasures of home,
　Of the land and a bright sunny sky;
Give me the rough ocean, with bosom of foam,
　And a bark, when in chase, that will fly:
Tho' aloft to the clouds on the billow we soar,
　And then sink to the valley below,
We danger defy 'mid the hurricane's roar,
　And reck not how hard it may blow!
Then, hurrah for the sea, boys! Hurrah for the sea!
The mariner's life is the life for me.

The dear ones we love, when our pockets are lined,
　Help to spend all our rhino on shore,
And when empty, "Up Anchor!" we're sure soon to
　　　find
　A prize that will furnish them more.
All friends we avoid as we roam on the wave;
　The sail which we welcome's a foe;
And should Death heave us to, there's a ready-made
　　　grave;
　And down to the bottom we go!
Then, hurrah for the sea, boys! Hurrah for the sea!
A mariner's life is the life for me.

No. 5.—THE LIGHTHOUSE.

Our sea-born chimes eight bells have told
   Far o'er the wat'ry waste ;
To distant ships their sound has roll'd ;
The canvass drips with night-dew cold ;
   The mid'-hour watch is placed.
Look out! look out, my trusty crew!
   Strain ev'ry anxious eye ;
Tho' spray and mist obscure the view
   We know the land is nigh!

And spare ye not the plunging lead,
   As carefully we steer ;
What star shines o'er the lee cathead,
Which now gleams forth with lustre red,
   Now seems to disappear?
It is no star! I see it now!
   It is the lighthouse beam,
Which, from yon tall cliff's beething brow,
   Sheds forth its changeful gleam.

A sailor's thanks to those who tend
   Its true, tho' fitful light,
Who, like our guardian angels, lend
Their ceaseless vigils to befriend
   The wand'ring vessel's flight.
No strangers, now, the deep we roam!
   Shake out, shake out the reefs ; make sail ;
That lighthouse is the light of home,
   And hope breathes in the gale.

As still we coast the rugged steep,
  The lighthouse sheds its ray;
But there 's a love which does not sleep,
And hearts which watch as constant keep,
  When we are far away.
What transport in each breast will glow,
  When with to-morrow's sun,
Our well known signal flags shall show
  The destined port we 've won.

No. 6.—THE SAILOR'S FUNERAL.

OUR ship had struck soundings, and blithe were our tars,
  As up Channel, for England, we joyfully bore;
Tho' shatter'd her hull, we were proud of her scars,
  And the riddled blue flag in the battle she wore.
Each heart was elate; e'en the wounded forgot
  All their pangs, as the land of their home they drew
      near;
And the late sunken eye lighted up as the spot
  (Tho' distant) was seen which we 'd left with a tear.

But where is the gallant, the brave, and the gay,
  Whom we hoped to have saved from the fate of the
      slain?
Alas! he survived but to watch the last ray
  Of the sun's setting beams on the queen of the main!

His war-broken frame had with hope been sustain'd
That the land he had bled for again he might see;
"Farewell, my lov'd country!" he faintly exclaim'd,
Then bow'd with submission to Heaven's decree.

No ashes were strew'd o'er his wat'ry grave!
We sounded no knell save the cannon's deep boom;
But his bier was bedew'd with the tears of the brave,
Ere we launch'd him below to his dark ocean
tomb:—
Rest, rest! gallant spirit! tho' lonely thy bed,
Thy virtues in fondest remembrance we'll guard;
And when the sea's summon'd to render its dead
Aloft thou wilt rise, to receive thy reward.

THE BAY OF BISCAY O!

[Written by Andrew Cherry.—Old Air.]

Loud roar'd the dreadful thunder,
The rain a deluge show'rs;
The clouds were rent asunder
By lightnings' vivid powers!
The night both drear and dark,
Our poor deluded bark!
Till next day,
There she lay,
In the Bay of Biscay O!

Now, dash'd upon the billow,
  Her op'ning timbers creak:
Each fears a wat'ry pillow!
  None stop the dreadful leak!—
To cling to slipp'ry shrouds,
Each breathless seaman crowds,
    As she lay,
    Till the day,
  In the Bay of Biscay O!

At length, the wish'd for morrow
  Broke thro' the hazy sky;
Absorb'd in silent sorrow,
  Each heav'd a bitter sigh!—
The dismal wreck to view
Struck horror to the crew,
    As she lay,
    On that day,
  In the Bay of Biscay O!

Her yielding timbers sever;
  Her pitchy seams are rent!
When Heav'n (all bounteous ever)
  Its boundless mercy sent!
A sail in sight appears!
We hail her with three cheers!
    Now we sail
    With the gale
  From the Bay of Biscay O!

THE OLD COMMODORE.

[Written by Mark Lonsdale.   Music by W. Reeve.]

'Blood! what a time for a seaman to sculk
  Under gingerbread hatches a-shore!
What a d—d bad job that this batter'd old hulk
  Can't be rigg'd out to sea once more.
     The puppies, as they pass,
     Cocking up a squinting-glass,
    Thus run down the Old Commodore:—
    " That 's the rum Old Commodore,
    The tough Old Commodore,
   The fighting Old Commodore, he!
     But the bullets and the gout
     Have so knock'd his hull about,
  That he 'll never more be fit for sea."

Here am I in distress, like a ship water-logg'd,
  Not a tow-rope at hand, nor an oar;
I am left by my crew, and, may I be flogg'd,
  But the doctor 's a son of a wh—e!
     While I 'm swallowing his slops,
     How nimble are his chops
    To run down the Old Commodore:—
    " Can't say, Commodore;
    Mustn't flatter, Commodore;
  Though a brave Old Commodore you be,
     Yet the bullets and the gout
     Have so knock'd your hull about,
  That you 'll never more be fit for sea."

What, no more be afloat! Blood and fury, they lie!
  I 'm a seaman, and only threescore;
And if, as they tell me, I 'm likely to die,
  Oh, pray, let me not die a-shore!
     As for death, 't is all a joke!
     Sailors live on fire and smoke,
    At least so says an Old Commodore,
     The rum Old Commodore,
     The tough Old Commodore,
   The fighting Old Commodore, he!
     Whom the devil, nor the gout,
     Nor the French lads to boot,
Shall kill, till they grapple him at sea.
Shall kill, till they grapple him at sea.

OUR COUNTRY; OR, BRITISH HEROES.

[Written by R. Oldfield. Composed by T. Williams.]

  Our Country is the land we love;
    Nought with it can compare,
  For statesmen wise, and heroes brave,
    For commerce and the fair!
     'Tis Britain's pride,
     No land beside
   Such influence can maintain;
     Go where you will,
     Our Country still,—
  You 'll never find its like again!

For ages past our admirals brave
    Pre-eminent have stood;
And, spite of all the world, have held
    The mast'ry of the flood.
        Howe, Duncan, Hood,
        And Collingwood,
    Long triumph'd o'er the main;
        While Nelson's name,
        So dear to Fame!—
    We may never see their like again!

Brave heroes in the field we 've had;
    Remember Marlboro's name,
With Abercrombie, Wolfe, and Moore,
    Who died to live in Fame!
        Anglesea still,
        With gallant Hill
    And Wellington, remain;
        Each to the end
        His Country's friend;—
    We may never see their like again!

[Concluding Verse by T. Dibdin.]
Her people, soldiers, tars, adore
    Their Queen; and for her crown,
Should danger threaten, as of yore,
    Their lives would all lay down!
        She 's Albion's boast,
        Whose cliff-robed coast
    Her sceptre will maintain;
        While Truth shall own
        On Britain's throne
    We ne'er may see her like again.

RULE BRITANNIA.

[Written by James Thomson. Composed by Purcell.]

When Britain first at Heaven's command,
  Arose from out the azure main,
This was the charter of the land,
  And guardian angels sung this strain,—
Rule, Britannia, Britannia rule the waves;
Britons never shall be slaves.

The nations not so blest as thee
  Must in their turn to tyrants fall;
While thou shalt flourish great and free,
  The dread and envy of them all.
Rule, Britannia, &c.

Still more majestic shalt thou rise,
  More dreadful from each foreign stroke;
As the loud blast that tears the skies
  Serves but to root thy native oak.
Rule, Britannia, &c.

Thee haughty tyrants ne'er shall tame;
  All their attempts to bend thee down
Will but arouse thy generous flame,
  And work their woe and thy renown.
Rule, Britannia, &c.

To thee belongs the rural reign;
   Thy cities shall with commerce shine;
All thine shall be the subject main,
   And every shore it circles thine.
Rule, Britannia, &c.

The Muses, still with freedom found,
   Shall to thy happy coast repair;
Blest isle! with matchless beauty crown'd,
   And manly hearts to guard the fair.
Rule, Britannia, Britannia rule the waves:
   BRITONS NEVER SHALL BE SLAVES!

FINIS.

London: Printed by WILLIAM CLOWES and SONS, Stamford Street.

ee UK Ltd.
UK
8210223
K00007B/260